American Influence in Greece
1917–1929

American Influence
in Greece
1917–1929

Louis P. Cassimatis

THE KENT STATE UNIVERSITY PRESS
Kent, Ohio, and London, England

© 1988 by The Kent State University Press, Kent, Ohio 44242
All rights reserved
Library of Congress Catalog Card Number 88-3021
ISBN 0-87338-357-5
Manufactured in the United States of America

The paper in this book meets the guidelines for permanence and durability of the Committee on Production Guidelines for Book Longevity of the Council on Library Resources.

Library of Congress Cataloging-in-Publication Data

Cassimatis, Louis P.
    American Influence in Greece, 1917–1929.

    Bibliography: p.
    Includes index.
    1. Greece—Relations—United States. 2. United
States—Relations—Greece. 3. Greece—History—
1917–1944. 4. United States—History—1919–1933.
I. Title.
DF787.U5C37 1988   303.4′8273′0495   88-3012
ISBN 0-87338-357-5 (alk. paper)

British Library Cataloging-in-Publication data are available.

For Antoinette, Nicholas, and Peter

Contents

Preface

Sixty years ago Brainerd P. Salmon, president of the American Chamber of Commerce in Greece, wrote: "American interests in Greece are commercial, financial, educational, and at times philanthropic, but never political."[1] This estimate of Greek-American relations between the two World Wars is essentially correct, but it is also simplistic, for it tends to reinforce the prevailing perception that the significance of those relations is minimal. To be sure, before 1940 the dominant foreign influences in Greece emanated from Europe, while the United States remained very much on the periphery of the political arena in which the Greek government had to operate. Moreover, to the extent that one government's influence over another government's political and military affairs constitutes direct involvement or intervention, the period after 1947 represents a radical point of departure for Greek-American political relations. But the course of history is not determined by military and political events alone. Social, cultural, and economic forces are integral parts of a nation's existence. Any foreign influence that helps to shape these forces must be considered an important factor in that nation's destiny.

Contrary to much that has been written on American foreign policy after the First World War, the United States did not become isolationist, but took an active interest in the affairs of Europe and the Near East. Diplomatically, the 1920s were far more complex than sweeping generalizations for that period often suggest. The American farmer became aware, as never before, of the interdependence inherent in a global economy. The American businessman became ever more aggressive in his efforts to obtain the support of his government in foreign enterprises. Public forums and the press advanced the idea that no nation can live unto itself. After the war, when the victorious Allies strove for the creation of new spheres of influence, for new markets, and for territorial realignments in the Near East, the United States was there to promote and protect its interests. Geographically and commercially, Greece remained on the periphery of the area in which the United States sought to expand its influence, so that Greek-American relations in the 1920s take the form of a microcosm that reflected the diplomatic setting and delineated the intense rivalries of the Great Powers (Great Britain, France, and Italy) in the Near East. Greece, therefore, came to occupy an important place in the Near-East policy of the State Department.

During the interwar years, the United States did not assume the role of a passive bystander, but was an active force in Greek life. After 1922, when the Greek people lay prostrate in the aftermath of a decade filled with foreign and domestic crises, it was American relief, technical know-how, and investment capital, as well as the cooperation of the United States government, which contributed in no small measure to the rehabilitation of the country. After allowing for the unique position of France and Great Britain in the political and military life of the country, it is clear that in the 1920s American influence in Greece increased more rapidly than that of any other power.

The role of America in Greece during those years represents a positive, though forgotten, chapter in the relations between the two countries. The pressures of international politics and the dominant political role that the United States has assumed there since the end of the Second World War have combined to diminish considerably the image of America as a benign and benevolent country. The purpose of this book is to analyze the major events that were largely responsible for that perception—a perception which, despite contemporary political realities, has been eroded, but not eradicated.

The question now arises as to the proper term to be used in describing the American presence in Greece in the interwar period. Perhaps the most appropriate is *influence* when used in its broadest sense. American influence in Greek affairs had modest beginnings, but with the profit of hindsight one can see that it played a vital role at a critical juncture in the history of the modern Greek State.*

The researcher who undertakes scholarly investigation in Greece is confronted with serious obstacles. Many of the diplomatic records have been lost, while much of the extant primary material has suffered the consequences of incompetence and neglect. It is only in recent years that serious efforts have been made by enlightened archivists to remedy the situation. Other primary sources remain closed to public scrutiny. The historian of the interwar period is thus forced to rely heavily on repositories outside Greece.

The research for this book was conducted initially in the United States at the National Archives, the Library of Congress, and the University of Cincinnati. A grant from the Graduate School of Kent State University enabled me to conduct additional research in Greece. In Athens, the Historical Archives of the Greek Foreign Ministry, the Li-

*The circumstances in which influence plays a role are difficult to isolate and to diagnose with precision because of the elusive quality of the term. Influence can be direct and open to public scrutiny or it can be indirect and tacit. In its overt form, "successful influence may be said to rest on a variety of bases which permit the influencer to change people's perceptions of contingencies or situations controlled by others." Such bases include prestige, "a debt or obligation on which the influencer can 'collect.' " David V. J. Bell, *Power, Influence and Authority: An Essay in Political Linguistics* (New York: Oxford Univ. Press, 1975), 26–28. Tacit influence "rests upon the capacity of human beings to imagine and thus anticipate the reactions of those who might spell disadvantage and even disaster for the actor who foresees the effect the action might have and alters it more or less in accordance with his foresight." Carl Joachim Friedrich, *Man and His Government: An Empirical Theory of Politics* (New York: McGraw-Hill, 1963), 201. Friedrich's detailed analysis of the "Rule of Anticipated Reactions" is found on 199–215. Perhaps the most authoritative summation of American influence in Greece during the interwar period was given in May 1944 by the American ambassador to the Greek government, Lincoln Mac-Veagh. The State Department suggested that he join the British ambassador, Reginald Leeper, in attending the Lebanon Conference that was convened to reconcile differences among Greek political factions and resistance organizations. MacVeagh replied: "But for us to be there too would seem certain to compromise our established policy which couples aloofness from internal politics with interest in the welfare of the whole nation.

"As the Department knows, strict observance of our traditional policy has hitherto maintained great American influence in Greece." U.S. Department of State, *Foreign Relations of the United States* (1944), 5:107.

brary of Parliament, the Gennadius Library, and the Benaki Museum yielded valuable primary and secondary material. The results of these investigations appeared in a Kent State University doctoral dissertation. Subsequently, I was able to undertake extensive revisions of the manuscript based on additional secondary sources and British archival material. One disappointing result of my efforts at the Benaki Museum was my failure to obtain any substantive information or gain any significant insights from the private papers of Eleutherios Venizelos. For this reason, this item has been omitted from the bibliography.

The critical reader will question, perhaps, the absence of a full treatment of Greek-American cultural and commercial relations and of the American role at the Paris Peace Conference vis-à-vis Greek territorial claims in Asia Minor and the Balkans. While these problems are not unrelated, they are sufficiently separate from the main course of events described in this book to justify independent treatment. I have chosen to concentrate on those issues which in the 1920s constituted unprecedented diplomatic initiatives and would be integral to the conduct of Greek-American diplomacy throughout the interwar period. It will be noted, further, that the treatment of Greek politics from 1925 to 1929 is less intensive. After 1924, Greek-American relations took on a more prosaic form and focused chiefly on issues that were contained within the geographical limits of Greece. The role of the State Department became essentially that of defender of American commercial and financial interests in the face of Western European competition. A sense of Greek internal affairs, as they relate to Greek-American diplomacy, can be obtained from a reading of chapter 10.

In the transliteration of names, I have adhered to the guidelines of the Library of Congress in a general way, though usage has often been the deciding factor. Thus, it is Prince Andrew and Andreas Papandreou; Constantine and not Konstantinos.

Unless otherwise indicated, all dates in this book correspond to the Gregorian calendar. Greece adopted the Gregorian calendar in 1923. Thus, 10 December 1837 is written as 10/22 December 1837.

It is not possible to list all the persons who assisted me in the preparation of this book, though I acknowledge their collective contribution for which I am grateful. Professor S. Victor Papacosma at Kent State University guided and encouraged me in all phases of my doctoral work. His readiness to render assistance went far beyond the call of duty. Subsequently, he continued his support by offering helpful suggestions as I prepared the manuscript for publication. The British Foreign Office records were loaned to me from his private collection. My debt to him is inestimable. Professors John O. Iatrides of Southern Connecticut State University, Theodore A. Couloumbis of the University of Thessaloniki, and Saul S. Friedman of Youngstown State University read the manuscript in its entirety and offered incisive analyses and commentaries. For the accuracy of my text and the validity of my conclusions I remain solely responsible.

In the initial stages of my research the late Professor Stephen G. Xydis provided illuminating suggestions relative to the delineation of my subject. Professor Peter Topping introduced me to the valuable Greek collection at the University of Cincinnati and facilitated the procurement of microfilmed documents from the University's library. I am indebted to Dr. Domna Dontas, Director of the Historical Archives in the Greek Foreign Ministry, who expedited my research under difficult circumstances. Mrs. Valentini Tselika of the Benaki Museum assisted me in the examination of Venizelos' private papers and the museum's photographic collection. Mrs. Hildegard Schnuttgen, Head Reference Librarian, and Mrs. Louise D. Karns, Assistant Reference Librarian, at Youngstown State University offered indispensable assistance in the procurement of documents and secondary sources, some of which were extremely difficult to locate. I am indebted to my son, Nicholas, whose wizardry with things technical enabled me to survive the quixotic propensities of my word processor.

It is to my wife, Antoinette, however, that I owe my greatest debt of gratitude. She typed several versions of the manuscript without complaint as she struggled to cope with my illegible script. Her selflessness, unswerving support, and seemingly inexhaustible forbearance are, in the final analysis, the factors that made this book possible.

Introduction

The American "discovery" of modern Greece dates back to the eighteenth century when Thomas Jefferson expressed his desire to see the Greek people free from Turkish domination and the establishment of a Greek national state with " 'the language of Homer becoming again a living language, as among possible events.' " Jefferson's concern was shared by many educated Americans whose familiarity with the history and literature of ancient Greece inspired strong philhellenic sentiments. During the Greek War of Independence (1821–30) thousands of American philhellenes gave their moral and material support to the Greek cause. Some even participated in the hostilities and distinguished themselves by their military service and dedication to the cause of freedom.[1]

In 1833 the United States recognized the new Greek government and on 10/22 December 1837 a commercial treaty was signed which regulated the trade between the two countries for the next eighty-two years. By 1900 American consulates were established in several locations on the mainland and the Aegean islands, though the development of Greek-American diplomatic and commercial relations progressed slowly throughout the nineteenth century.[2]

A notable exception was the interest taken by the United States government and by private American citizens in the Cretan revolt against Turkey (1866–69). This event gave promise of affecting the conduct of American commerce in the Eastern Mediterranean. The State Department and American private organizations received urgent appeals for assistance from the Greek government in an effort to involve the United States in the revolt. But since American interests were not in imminent jeopardy, the State Department assumed an official policy of watchful aloofness tinged with an obvious sympathy for the Cretan cause. To the American minister in Constantinople, Secretary of State William H. Seward wrote: "I see no impropriety in your consulting with representatives of the Christian powers at the Porte, with the view, through the use of your good offices, of ameliorating the unhappy condition of the inhabitants of Crete." Apparently, fruitful consultations were undertaken, because the newly appointed resident minister to Greece, Charles K. Tuckerman, became active in the efforts to help Cretan refugees and revolutionaries. He served as secretary on a relief committee formed for this purpose. For his humanitarian activities he was decorated by King George I.[3]

But if considerations of diplomacy constrained the United States government, there was little to inhibit the activities of American private citizens on behalf of the Cretan people. A leading figure in the relief effort was Samuel Gridley Howe, whose exploits in the Greek War of Independence had become legendary among Greeks. American philhellenes once again offered moral and material assistance, while a few participated directly in the hostilities. In Boston and New York, for example, "committees" (reminiscent of those established during the Greek War of Independence) were formed to expedite the relief effort on behalf of the refugees who flocked to the Greek mainland and the Aegean islands. In Athens an "American Relief Committee" was established by Americans living there. It is probably this committee of which Tuckerman was secretary. The reports of first-hand observers and American diplomatic officials stationed in Greece bear eloquent testimony to the success of this humanitarian undertaking.[4] This episode is significant because it anticipated the American relief effort of the 1920s and because it served to stimulate a greater awareness of Greece among American government officials and the American public.

During the nineteenth and early twentieth centuries, fewer Americans traveled to Greece than did Europeans. Nevertheless, American visitors comprised a fairly large group. Their ranks consisted of tourists, missionaries, naval personnel, commercial and consular agents, philhellenes, students, and scholars.[5] Most of them still revered the land of the ancient Greeks to the point of naiveté. Many Americans were prepared to agree with the Reverend Phillips Brooks who wrote to a friend in Boston in 1866: " 'Anybody who comes to Europe and not to Greece is a very much Donkey.' "[6] The role of American missionaries is especially significant.

Missionary work in Greece began shortly after 1800. Within a few years various American Protestant denominations succeeded in establishing congregations in Athens and in other parts of the country. Initially, they met with little success, for the Greeks proved to be unresponsive to Protestanism. This failure was due in part to the sectarian squabbles of the missionaries, who often spent more time in competition among themselves than in proselytizing. More important was the Greeks' tendency to identify religion with nationality because of the stabilizing influence of the Greek Orthodox Church during the four centuries of Ottoman domination. It was not until the end of the nineteenth century, when the missionaries shifted their efforts from proselytism to the areas of health and education, that their efforts were rewarded by a greater popular acceptance. An important by-product of these activities was a greater awareness of American civilization and culture on the part of the general Greek population.[7]

After the disastrous Greco-Turkish War of 1897 Greece looked once more to the United States for assistance. With the approval of the Greek government, the president of the Greek Supreme Court, C. N. Maniakes, addressed a florid and impassioned appeal to President William McKinley for American relief and financial aid.[8] There is no evidence that the American president responded, but the episode is significant because it points to the fact that even before 1900 the United States government was not an unknown factor in the thinking of Greek officials.

The most significant influence in the overall development of Greek-American relations after 1890 was the impact of Greek immigration to the United States. The Greek immigrant, and particularly that immigrant who returned to Greece to live, served as a cultural, economic, and spiritual bridge between the two countries. In reference to this phenomenon, Arnold J. Toynbee has written: "It is a strange experience to spend a night in some remote mountain village in Greece and see Americanism and Hellenism face to face. . . . [The repatriated Greek-American's] greatest gift to his country will be his American point of view." After 1924 the impact of immigration gradually came to play a lesser role, but by that time other factors would intervene to shape the course of Greek-American relations.[9]

In the spring of 1914, when relations between Greece and Turkey deteriorated and Turkey appeared to be preparing for war, the Greek government once again turned to the United States for help. President Woodrow Wilson proved to be a sympathetic listener who believed that Turkey's efforts to expand her naval presence in the Aegean were a direct threat to Greece's security and a detriment to the balance of power in the Balkans. After hectic negotiations, Wilson agreed to sell the battleships *Idaho* and *Mississippi* (rechristened the *Kilkis* and the *Lemnos*) for the sum of $12,535,276.58.[10]

On the eve of the First World War, Greek-American relations had reached a fair degree of maturity in the areas of commerce, education, and philanthropy. Diplomatically, the relations between the two countries remained in the formative stage. In 1914, however, the exigencies of war prompted the State Department to take an active interest in Greek internal affairs. After 1917 the United States would assume a greater role in the economic, social, cultural, and, to a limited extent, political life of Greece.

1
The Rise of American Influence in Greece

Intervention by one government in the internal affairs of another government is a constant reality in history. In the case of modern Greece this generalization is especially valid. Primarily for reasons of geography the Greek state never has been free of foreign interference; the intermediate location of the Greek peninsula is an open invitation to foreign intervention. Jutting southward into the eastern Mediterranean, Greece is simultaneously an integral part of Europe and the crossroads of three continents. For the Great Power this geographic extremity of Europe always has been of the greatest political concern, most particularly because of its accessibility and its strategic importance as a communications hub at the junction of Europe, Asia, and Africa. Thus, when the Greek state was created in 1830 under the aegis of France, Great Britain and Russia, their governments found no difficulty in concluding that the survival of the fledging Greek state as a constitutional monarchy depended on their "protection." From about 1825 until 1923 a variety of political and dynastic factors combined to create political instability in the country which enabled the three Protecting Powers to gain enormous control over the political, economic, and military affairs of Greece, ostensibly for the purpose of maintaining the fiscal integrity of the new nation. By 1914 the list of powers actively involved in the internal politics of Greece had been augmented by the exigencies of European diplomacy, especially as they related to the problem of the Eastern Question. On the eve of the First World War foreign intervention in Greek political and economic life was virtually complete. In these circumstances, there appeared to be no reason, and certainly no possibility, for the United States to take an active interest in Greek internal affairs. Many factors contributed to the rise of the American influence in Greece after 1917, but four developments emerge with particular significance: 1) American participation in the Tripartite Loan of 1918; 2) the shift of emphasis in the foreign policies of the major European powers during the 1920s; 3) a fundamental change in the attitudes of Greek statesmen after 1923; and 4) defeat of the Greek army in Asia Minor and the aftermath of that debacle.

On 10 February 1918 France, Great Britain, and the United States granted a three-part loan to Greece which totaled 750,000,000 francs ($150,000,000). In return, the Greek government agreed to put nine divisions at the disposal of the Allied Command for the purpose of buttressing the Balkan front. The loan, therefore, served as a catalyst in the evolution of Greek-American political relations.

The second development revolves around the foreign policies of the major European powers. The Treaty of Lausanne in 1923 brought about the resolution of the struggle for the Ottoman-Turkish succession in Europe, a problem that had plagued European statesmen for over one hundred years. With the signing of the treaty, the primary motive for interference was removed. After 1923 the thrust of the foreign policies of France and Great Britain shifted because their prestige and interests no longer centered on the internal conditions of Greece and Turkey. At the same time the newly established Soviet government was not in a position to provoke Turkey or to exert the historic Russian pressure on the Straits. Only Italy remained to serve as a gadfly in the Eastern Mediterranean, primarily because few opportunities for territorial expansion existed for her. These circumstances are significant—the relaxation of Great Power pressure was in itself an historical aberration.

The possibility of foreign intervention in Greek affairs also was diminished by the Lausanne treaty which brought to an end the centuries-old dream of a Greater Greece with its uncompromising irredentism. The influx of nearly one and a half million refugees from Asia Minor after 1922 forced the Greek government to concentrate its energies on domestic problems and to abandon any form of reckless diplomacy. After a decade of war and internal political strife Greece succeeded in gathering most of the Greek people within its borders, so that the security of the state rather than the liberation of "unredeemed" territories became the chief objective of Greek statesmen. The shift of emphasis from aggression and aggrandizement to defense and security offered hope of a more stable political environment, and encouraged the French and British governments to renounce their role as joint guarantors of the Greek monarchy.[1] Equally important was the realization that their legal hold over much of the machinery of the Greek government was an anachronism. The British especially were anxious to relieve themselves from an irksome obligation which, by 1923, was no longer viable. Indicative of this development was the inability of the British government to prevent the dethronement of Constantine in 1922, its failure to preserve the Greek constitution following the coup d'état of Colonels Plastiras and Gonatas, and its failure to save from execution the six ministers who were held responsible for the catastrophe in Asia Minor.[2]

American influence in Greece, however, received its greatest impetus in the aftermath of the Greek military defeat in Asia Minor. The expulsion from Turkey of nearly one and a half million people confronted the Greek government with a monumental refugee problem. The participation of the United States government, American relief agencies, and American private citizens in the search for the solution to that problem was, undoubtedly, the most important factor in the greater role that America came to play in Greek affairs during the interwar period. An analysis of that development must necessarily be viewed against the interests of the Great Powers.

Franco-British Rivalry in the Eastern Mediterranean and the Near East

In their attitudes toward the Near East (which, for the purposes of this book, will be defined to include the lands from western Greece to Mesopotamia), Great Britain and France fundamentally were opposed. In both countries, after the First World War, the idea of colonial development for the mutual benefit of the native populations in the underdeveloped lands of the world, on the one hand, and for the administering power, on the other, was practically an article of faith. However, it was at this point that agreement ceased, because the differing colonial traditions of the two powers led to different interpretations of the same principle.

France believed that the Europeans in Africa and the Near East held natural positions of leadership and that the native peoples' best hope for material and intellectual progress lay in wise guidance and education by Europeans. This attitude was reflected by intense religious, cultural, and economic activities in the Near East, whose origins can be traced to the sixteenth century, or even to the Crusades. In the generation before 1914 French religious orders established large complexes of schools, colleges, and hospices throughout the Near East. The role of France in that part of the world, then, rested on long cultural, educational, and religious traditions, as well as on strong emotional ties with the native populations. This historical reality lent the French presence a hue of doctrinaire emotionalism that was frequently a factor in the conduct of French diplomacy. It is not surprising, therefore, that the policy of France relative to Greece often was marred by vindictiveness and ruthless heavy handedness that contrasted with British diplomatic practice which tended to be somewhat more pragmatic and detached.

Altruistic considerations were but a corollary to the French concern for security of the Western Mediterranean, a security which could be safeguarded adequately only by the maintenance of a permanent position in North Africa in a line from Morocco to Syria. Any influence that might undermine that position, such as the encouragement of Arab nationalism or a change in the balance of power in Greece and Asia Minor, was to be resisted strenuously. From the French point of view, Great Britain posed the greatest threat. There was considerable anxiety in Paris lest the British exploit the emergence of autonomous Arab states, to the detriment of French military, cultural, and religious interests. France also retained some measure of her traditional interest in Egypt, despite the decline of her involvement in that country after 1880. The mere thought that French influence could reassert itself there or in the Suez Canal Zone, was anathema to British statesmen. Both countries, moreover, were interested in which government would rule the Straits. The result was a deep-seated imperial rivalry which was intensified after 1919 by the fundamental methods and aims of the two countries. Britain's policy was compatible with and was often influenced by the salient needs and aspirations of the native populations within her dominions and spheres of influence. French colonial policy, although not devoid of idealism, was not prepared to allow any significant concessions to the psychological needs and interests of her colonized peoples. Thus, both

France and Great Britain had strong, but conflicting, reasons for maintaining a firm position in the Near East. For reasons of geography, Greece and the Aegean also assumed an important place in the foreign policies of other nations with imperialistic and maritime aspirations.

The Role of Italy

Italy led the lesser powers in exerting its influence in Greek affairs after 1919. From the inception of the Italian state in 1861, successive regimes pursued a foreign policy which was characterized by a sense of sober realism. For intrinsic reasons, the fledgling Italian nation was compelled to take its stand first on one side and then on another. In general, this attitude meant closer ties with Great Britain. With the establishment of Benito Mussolini's fascist regime in 1922 this policy of moderation underwent a significant change. The Italian people found themselves serving a new master whose speeches erupted in defiance and praise of the old heroic (Roman) virtues. Mussolini put forward a variety of claims affecting lands around the Adriatic Sea and western Greece, the Dodecanese Islands, large sections of Asia Minor, and other parts of the Near East. But the fact remained that Italy was not strong militarily. The result was a conflict between the old doctrine of slow, patient negotiations toward modest goals and the new policy of pursuing ambitious and quick results. This conflict was the central problem in the formulation of Italian foreign policy during the first decade of fascist rule.

For Greece, the problem of Italian aggressiveness was very real for three primary reasons: 1) the geographic proximity of the two countries enhanced the chances for diplomatic confrontation; 2) the participation of Italy in the International Financial Commission[3] gave Rome considerable leverage in Greek financial and political affairs; and 3) the conflicting claims of the two countries in Asia Minor. The latter was the result of contradictory wartime and postwar treaties, as well as the by-product of the rivalries of France and Great Britain in the area. Consequently, when the United States began to expand its interests in Greece after 1917, it met with the opposition of not only the large western European powers, but of Italy as well.

Greek Foreign Policy

Greece emerged from the First World War under difficult circumstances. The disastrous campaign in Asia Minor left her economy strained, her finances ruined, her social structure shaken by the deluge

9

of approximately one and a half million refugees from Asia Minor, and her political life embittered and chaotic by political executions, coups d'état, and frequent changes of government. She also was engaged in intermittent and protracted disputes with her neighbors. The Corfu incident of 1923 brought national humiliation at the hands of Italy, while a series of border incidents on the Greek-Bulgarian frontier culminated in a military action in 1925 against Bulgaria, with equally embarrassing results. Nor were relations with Yugoslavia and Turkey better. With the former the issue concerned an outlet to the Aegean, while the latter problem revolved around the legal rights of the Partiarchate and the Greek minority in Constantinople. But despite these involvements in turbulent diplomatic episodes, Greece yearned for peace and domestic tranquility in order to put her house in order. Indicative of this desire was the resolution of her difficulties with Yugoslavia in 1929 and the rapprochement with Turkey in 1930.

American Expansionism

Even before the conclusion of the First World War the Greek Foreign Ministry had begun to search for the support of a nation that could act as a mitigating influence in the relations between Greece and the Allied Powers of Europe. The obvious candidate for that role seemed to be the United States of America. A case in point is the effort of the Royalists and Venizelists to embroil the United States government in the controversy that surrounded Greece's entrance into the war. In the opinion of Greek officials the time appeared favorable for a greater American role in Greece, since the entrance of the United States into the war (April 1917) prompted the State Department to take a closer look at the internal affairs of nations which hitherto had been under European spheres of influence. It also could be expected that the United States government would play an integral part in the formulation of peace agreements after the war in an effort to protect its interests in the Near East. The diplomatic correspondence of the period contains numerous allusions to this line of reasoning. However unrealistic these expectations might have been, they were not without some basis in fact.

Contrary to President Wilson's disclaimers at the Paris Peace Conference, there existed certain important and long-standing American commitments in Asia Minor. These included missionary activities, the establishment of philanthropic, educational, and cultural institutions, and the creation of relief agencies to render assistance to refugees driven from their homes by war. To cite but one example: From January 1915 to 31 December 1924 the Near East Relief agencies spent $90,337,830 for a wide variety of philanthropic and educational services.[4]

Despite this altruism and the absence of direct political involvement in the affairs of the Near East, pragmatic considerations were hardly absent. Efforts by the United States government to apply the Open Door policy in the area for the benefit of American oil companies, businessmen, and financiers were relentless. The Department of Commerce was especially aggressive, particularly in regard to drilling for oil. Its policy consisted of a coalition between government officials and oil companies which emphasized the necessity of controlling costs and employing new methods to discover, develop, and conserve oil and other strategic raw materials within the United States, while exploiting the same resources abroad under the banner of the Open Door. Throughout the 1920s this policy remained constant.

In order to understand the attitude of the United States, one must have an appreciation for the new and more aggressive economic role that America was prepared to play in world affairs. As one writer put it, America emerged from World War I with "two faces determinedly fixed in opposite directions. One, bearing a remarkable resemblance to Miss Liberty, gazed benignly on her own shores and righteously disclaimed foreign entanglements. The other, eagle-eyed, searched out opportunities abroad for economic penetration."[5] Inasmuch as the United States had not declared war on Turkey, and had played no active role in the vicious politics that attended Constantine's overthrow in 1917, its moral influence in that part of the world was greater than that of any European power. Despite the fact that America was protecting her own economic interests, this romantic image loomed very large. President Wilson was considered the champion of small and oppressed nations. The United States was hailed as the only nation which had entered the war for unselfish purposes. It became a veritable tradition to interpret every action of the European powers as an attempt to gain political domination over weak and undeveloped countries. America, on the other hand, was seen as the only nation which would replace political ambition with a sound and benign economic policy.

This view of America belied a more pragmatic set of circumstances which were the controlling factors in the Near East policy of the State Department. After the First World War the United States abandoned its traditional role as a debtor nation and became, instead, one of the chief creditors of the world. This fundamental transition was primarily the result of the immense public and private loans that America had granted to the Allies to finance their war effort. Important, too, was the expansion of American business. Before 1914 the United States was essentially self-sufficient in raw materials, while what few products it could not produce domestically were imported from abroad. The rapid expansion of American industry and commerce during the war introduced a new period in the economic history of the United States. Specialized materials such as rubber, nitrates, chrome, and petroleum came to represent a larger portion of the nation's import trade. American manufacturers became concerned lest the control of the sources of these commodities be lost to unfriendly governments. An inevitable consequence of this development was the simultaneous expansion of American exports. Articles manufactured in the United States were then competing in world markets which formerly were the exclusive sanctuaries of European nations. The result of these circumstances was the development of a greater interest in imperialism by the United States government.

After 1919 America began to reach out for what it considered its "fair share" of the earth's limited resources, for new markets, and for the opportunities for the profitable investment of capital. The State Department protested strenuously against what it considered to be the discriminatory treatment of American businessmen in the underdeveloped areas of the Near East. Its efforts were complemented by the Department of Commerce which, under the energetic leadership of its secretary, Herbert Hoover, was aggressive in its efforts to support the interests of American firms. The United States government was determined to protect American commercial interests abroad and was prepared to use coercive measures to accomplish this end.

The Navy Department was permitted to use destroyers for the transmission of commercial messages, for the transportation of American samples and business agents, and for the " 'moral effect' which the presence of an American warship frequently exerts in obtaining prompt shipment of goods."[6] When Jefferson Caffery was appointed chargé d'affaires ad interim to Greece in January 1922, one of his first acts was to convince the State Department to assign a destroyer to Piraeus in view of the uncertain conditions prevailing in the country. Under instructions from Washington a destroyer was assigned by the American high commissioner at Constantinople, Admiral Mark L. Bristol, and changed every week.[7] The British chargé in Athens, C. H. Bentinck, reported in 1924 that "America [had] shown her flag in Greek waters more than any country except Italy in Corfu; an American destroyer was almost always to be seen either at Phaleron Bay or Piraeus Harbour."[8] These circumstances gave rise to considerable friction among the governments of the United States, Great Britain, and France.

By the spring of 1921 the commercial and naval presence of the United States had become an important factor in the Eastern Mediterranean. American and British representatives began lengthy negotiations regarding the right of American capital to participate in the exploitation of the markets and natural resources in the Near East. The catalysts which helped to precipitate these negotiations were Standard Oil Company of New Jersey, the American Chamber of Commerce for the Levant, and the Guaranty Trust Company of New York, the second largest bank in the United States. The official history of the Standard Oil Company states frankly that the active support of the United States government in its policy of dollar diplomacy was crucial to the company's ability to compete in that part of the world. The most important American enterprise in Greece after the war was the Standard Oil Company.[9]

The American Chamber of Commerce for the Levant urged the State Department to defend the Open Door policy more vigorously in Turkey. It emphasized that the opportunities for the expansion of American interests in the Near East were "practically unlimited," provided there was a fair field open for individual enterprise. After the conclusion of peace, there would be the "economic structure of an empire to be developed."[10] In other words, the potential size of the profit was judged to be exceedingly large and, in the terminology of the period, "Open Door" meant the right of every nation, with adequate power to support its claims, to share in the mineral resources of any part of the world.

These estimates of the situation were reaffirmed by the Guaranty Trust Company in a booklet entitled: *Trading with the Near East—Present Conditions and Future Prospects*. The booklet stressed that in opening a branch in Constantinople, the company was coming to terms with contemporary economic realities. Before the war merchandise from the United States was a "negligible factor" in the business of that city. The presence of an American merchant ship was a "rare sight indeed." "Today one will find four or five American liners in the Golden Horn at all times." It also was pointed out that at the conclusion of the war a dozen important American corporations had permanent offices there, and many other American concerns were represented by local agents. In the exaggerated opinion of the company, the possibilities for trade with the Eastern Mediterranean, the Sea of Marmara, and the Black Sea ports from the United States were of "almost unbelievable proportions."[11]

In a peripheral way the Open Door policy was applied to Greece, for the strategic importance of her location and, to a lesser extent, her potential as a market were recognized by the Departments of State and Commerce even before the conclusion of the war. The gradual emergence of America's presence in Greece after 1917 was thus accomplished in an international milieu of conflicting economic and political interests. A major factor in this process of involvement was the participation of the United States government in the Tripartite Loan of 1918. However, before turning to this problem, it is necessary to review the international setting in which the loan negotiations were undertaken.

2
The United States and the First Abdication of Constantine

Soon after the First World War began, it became clear that the role of the Balkan front would be crucial. The Central and the Allied powers began to court Greece and Bulgaria in an effort to win them to their side. The attitude of the Greek and Bulgarian governments was important because Turkey, the Allies' primary objective, had signed a treaty with the Central Powers in August 1914, and had entered the war in October. Until the Bulgarian entry into the war Greece was considered a secondary factor in the Balkans. Initially, Great Britain and France advised the Greek government to remain neutral. One reason was the fear that Greece would add more to the Allies' responsibilities than her assitance would be worth. Another was their objective to secure the cooperation, or at least the neutrality, of Bulgaria which they viewed as a critical factor in the area.[1] Nevertheless, in August 1914 Greek Prime Minister Eleutherios Venizelos placed the Greek army and navy at the disposal of the Allies. The offer was refused in the hope that Balkan unity might be preserved. On 5 March 1915 the offer was repeated; this time for the campaign in the Dardanelles. Under pressure from the Russian government, which feared Greek designs on Constantinople and the Straits, King Constantine refused to give his consent. Venizelos resigned the following day. These events gave rise in England to the argument that the prolongation of the war was due in large part to the failure of the Allies to bring Greece into the war at the onset of the hostilities. One proponent of this theory was Winston Churchill.[2]

After Turkey's entrance into the war, attention was turned to Bulgaria. When Bulgaria followed the Turkish example and joined the Central Powers, Greece and Romania remained the only neutral nations in southeastern Europe. The belligerents then concentrated on them. After considerable diplomacy and for a high price, Romania joined the Allied side in August 1916. The loss of Bulgaria and Turkey to the Central Powers meant that the need to have Greece on the side of the Entente was crucial. France and Great Britain had begun to apply pressure on the Greek government to enter the war on their side.[3] Allied intervention in the domestic politics of Greece at this critical time became virulent. The political and personal animosities that it served to stimulate, as well as the constitutional crisis that it helped to precipitate, combined to bring the Greek state to the brink of national collapse.

The Role of Greek Politics

When hostilities began in 1914, the question of intervention or neutrality became a burning issue in Greece. In the beginning, both Constantine and Venizelos agreed that the uncertainty of the international and military situations dictated a policy of neutrality. It soon became apparent, however, that Greece's treaty obligations to Serbia would make a policy of neutrality difficult. On 1 June 1913 the two countries had signed a treaty of mutual assistance that committed each to go to the defense of the other should either be the victim of unprovoked aggression. The treaty was, in fact, used against Bulgaria in the Second Balkan War. There is little doubt that at the time all signatories considered the agreement a purely Balkan pact, aimed primarily at a revisionist Bulgaria which had emerged the loser from the two Balkan wars and would now certainly seize any opportunity to regain territories lost in those wars, as well as certain "unredeemed" lands in Macedonia and Thrace.

When Austria declared war on Serbia, the Serbian government broadened its interpretation of the 1913 alliance and asked Greece for military assistance. Constantine and Venizelos instructed their foreign minister, George Streit, to state that Greece would not permit an attack on Serbia by Bulgaria, but at the same time, the Greek government reserved

King Constantine and Venizelos at General Headquarters at Haidji-Beïlik (northern Greece) during the Balkan Wars. (Benaki Museum)

the right to interpret the provisions of the 1913 treaty in the light of existing realities. Greek authorities, including Venizelos, were inclined to interpret the treaty in its narrow sense—as a purely Balkan alliance. They found no difficulty, moreover, in concluding that the assassination of the Austrian Archduke Francis Ferdinand in Sarajevo constituted provocative conduct on the part of Serbia, and that Greece, therefore, was under no obligation to offer assistance.[4] Cooperation between Constantine and Venizelos, proved to be temporary. The two men eventually began to quarrel violently over the issue of Greece's neutrality.

As the first months of war passed, pressure to take sides became stronger. Kaiser William II tried every form of persuasion to convince his brother-in-law, Constantine, that it was to the advantage of Greece to ally herself with the Central Powers. The King answered that Greece's interests could be served best by the preservation of the status quo in the

17

Balkans. He stressed that it had never been the intention of the Greek government to help the Serbs in a general European war. William II was angered by this reply. He ordered the Greek minister in Berlin to inform Athens that Germany had made an alliance with Bulgaria and Turkey for the war against Russia and would treat Greece as an enemy in the event that she did not join Germany in the war. On a softer note he added that he was appealing to Constantine "as a comrade, as a German marshal . . . and as a brother-in-law to march together, hand in hand against the common enemy, Slavism [i.e., Russia and Serbia]." Constantine refused to be flattered or intimidated, and defended his neutrality on the grounds that the Mediterranean was at the mercy of the united fleets of England and France. "Without being able to be helpful . . . in any-thing," he replied, "we should be wiped off the map. I am compelled to think that neutrality is forced upon us."[5] Even the British conceded privately that the fear of an Allied victory was only one part of Constantine's dilemma. There were no assurances that the Central Powers would not emerge victorious. Whatever pro-Entente sentiments there might have existed in Greece in 1914 they were tempered in the aftermath of Germany's initial victories on the battlefield. There was a great deal of respect for German military strength in the country. There were few informed Greeks who sincerely believed that Germany could be de-feated. The natural inclination in these circumstances was to await events because, if Greece joined the Allies and the Allies were defeated, the consequences to Greece would have been disastrous.[6]

In the meantime, the Allies had begun to court the Greek government with the enthusiastic approval of Venizelos. The premier's initial cau-tion was short-lived. He was convinced that the war would be brief, that the Entente powers would emerge victorious, and that unless Greece acted immediately her opportunity to share in the spoils of war would be lost. This parting of the ways between king and prime minister marked the beginning of a schism that had devastating consequences for every aspect of Greek life. The split between the two men gave rise to a long series of complicated events and sordid tales of intrigue, the cumulative effect of which resulted in the polarization of the Greek nation into two hostile camps, each trying to destroy the other. One must look to the Greek civil war of the 1940s to find a political crisis with more destruc-tive and long-term consequences. The controversy can be reduced to the following generalization: King Constantine, finding himself in the posi-tion of being pressed simultaneously by the Allies and the Central powers, tended to follow the advice of his General Staff which urged him to remain neutral. Venizelos, on the other hand, had the support of the majority in the Chamber of Deputies for his foreign policy. As a consequence of this political division, relations between king and premier crumbled and became irreparable.

Unable to come to terms with Constantine, Venizelos on 6 March 1915 resigned his office, despite his parliamentary majority, whereupon the king exercised his constitutional right and decreed the dissolution of the Chamber of Deputies. In an apparent effort to infuse a spirit of compromise into the political scene, he gave the Premiership to Demetrios Gounaris, a Royalist, but also a man who had often led the opposition to some of the king's policies. General elections were held on 13 June 1915 in which Venizelos and his Liberal Party were returned with a majority of 185 seats out of 316. The king, who was ill at the time, used his illness as an excuse to postpone the handing over of the government to Venizelos and retained Gounaris in office. It was not until August that the ex-premier was allowed once again to form a Government.

Venizelos became relentless in his efforts to find some unassailable basis for joining the Entente. His opportunity came on 21 September 1915 when Bulgaria mobilized her forces and appeared ready for war. Serbia asked that Greece honor her treaty obligation and offer military assistance. So great was the concern over Bulgaria's mobilization that even Constantine momentarily compromised his neutrality and agreed with Venizelos that Greece, too, must mobilize and be ready to fight. Under pressure from his General Staff, however, the king modified his decision. He declared that the mobilization of Greek forces was defensive and that Greece would not depart from her neutral course. He assured the Bulgarian government that in case Bulgaria declared war on Serbia, Greece would not intervene, while Bulgarian leaders assured Constantine they had no designs on Greek territory. This declaration infuriated the Venizelists who believed that the king was bent on treating the Serbo-Greek alliance as a mere scrap of paper. The Royalists retorted that Serbia had been guilty of provocative conduct. On 4 October, the day Bulgaria declared war on Serbia, Venizelos repeated his intention in the Chamber of Deputies to honor Greece's treaty obligation and go to aid of the Serbian government. The Deputies approved the premier's policy by a vote of 147 to 110. Despite this parliamentary vote of confidence, Constantine called Venizelos to the palace the following day and asked him to resign. Venizelos believed that the king, in dismissing him earlier in the year, had acted within his constitutional rights.[7] By then, however, the will of the people had been made clear by the election results and Venizelos believed Constantine was guilty of undermining the constitution.

The hatreds and passions unleashed by this personal feud had a profound influence on the relations between Greece and the United States in the interwar period. Today, it is not uncommon to encounter an otherwise amiable octogenarian who, under subtle prodding, can become very excited as he proceeds to tell the "true" story behind the Constantine-Venizelos controversy. Many Greek-Americans in the United States attend church services in parishes and are members of societies and clubs which were originally organized along Constantinist or Venizelists lines.[8]

The Intervention of the Allies

As the pressures of war intensified, Constantine's intransigence could no longer be tolerated by the Allies. They concluded that the success of their war effort in northern Greece required a new regime in Athens. Accordingly, the French and British landed troops in Salonika early in October 1915. The German government's reaction to the Allied landing was surprisingly mild, partly because it understood the difficulty of Constantine's position. Nevertheless, in an attempt to justify German policy, the Kaiser pressed Constantine to make a public protest in all neutral states, and especially in the United States, by drawing an analogy between the Allies' violation of Greek neutrality and Germany's violation of Belgian neutrality.[9]

The Allied decision to take military action was reinforced by rumors emanating from Berlin which suggested that Greece was ready to join the Central Powers. The American ambassador to Germany wrote to the secretary of state of his suspicion that an arrangement had been made by which Greece would permit the Central Powers to attack the Allies in Salonika. Consequently, on 3 June the commander-in-chief of the Entente forces in Greece, General Maurice Sarrail, delivered a note to the Greek military authorities in Salonika in which he informed the Greek government that he had declared a siege for the whole of Macedonia.[10] Several days later the French increased their pressure by imposing a partial blockade on Greek shipping.[11] This action interned all Greek ships in Allied ports and prohibited the departure of Greek vessels from Salonika. The Greek ministers in London and Paris were informed that more severe measures were imminent.[12]

These developments lead to the conclusion that an attempt was being made to force the Greek government into general elections which would presumably be manipulated by Anglo-French personnel in Greece, thus ensuring the emergence of a regime dominated by Venizelos and his Liberals. Whatever the technical diplomatic considerations might have been, the blockade soon proved to be an effective punitive and coercive device, prompting Greek Foreign Minister Stephen Skouloudis to present to the Allies and all neutral states a bitter protest against such high-handed tactics. An effort was made to influence the attitude of the United States government.[13] The State Department, however, remained uncommitted, and merely requested more detailed information from the American legation in Athens.

On 21 June 1916 France and Great Britain increased their pressure when they presented to Greek authorities certain specific demands. These demands specified that the Chamber of Deputies must be dissolved, that there be complete demobilization, that new elections be held, and that there be police reforms. The last demand was made in order to end the persecution of Venizelists by the Royalists.[14] The Greek government yielded, though these concessions proved insufficient to placate France and Great Britain.

In the meantime, Venizelos had come to the conclusion that nothing short of revolution would force Constantine to change his policy of neutrality. After several weeks of preparation on his native island, Crete, he landed at Salonika on 9 October where amidst enthusiastic popular acclaim he took over the reins of a provisional revolutionary government that had been formed recently by a group of his closest supporters. These developments created the impression that two states had emerged—one at Salonika and northern Greece under Venizelos; the other in Athens and the south under Constantine. The Venizelist regime was recognized on 19 December by the Allies, though Italy and Russia, because of certain territorial aspirations in Asia Minor and the Straits respectively, did so with some misgivings.

American Policy towards Venizelos' Revolutionary Regime

The attitude of the United States towards Venizelos' provisional government remained vague and uncertain, but the State Department expressed interest in the events that led to the formation of the revolutionary regime. The position of the American government on the question of recognition became sensitive. The inclination of the State Department was to follow the example of France and Great Britain and grant official recognition. However, there were certain risks that attended the implementation of such a policy. In the first place, recognition would have led to the conclusion that the United States was turning its back on the Constantine government (which by all rules of international law was still the legitimate government of the nation) and was now becoming directly involved in the internal politics of Greece. There was also the matter of America's neutrality. Venizelos' government, with an army of only 3,000 troops in the field, lost no time in declaring war on Germany and Bulgaria, thus admitting his government into the ranks of the belligerents. It was not clear how America's role as a neutral would be interpreted in Paris and London if Washington recognized Venizelos' provisional government. Less important, but not unrelated, was the concern that the government in Athens would take retaliatory measures against American shipping in Greek ports and American firms conducting business in Greece.[15]

These difficulties were magnified when it became evident that there was a major difference of opinion between John E. Kehl, the American consul in Salonika, and Garrett Droppers, the American minister in Athens. In clear reference to Kehl, Droppers suggested that the Allied cause might be served best if Washington would send a sympathetic, but clearheaded, diplomatic representative to Salonika.[16] Kehl, who was able to witness by direct observation the excesses of the Allied troops and the strong-arm tactics of the French, tended to exhibit anti-Venizelist tendencies;[17] while Droppers was eager to extol the virtues of the Venizelists and to attack the Royalists for their purported duplicity.

The Venizelist Regime and American Recognition

These were the issues that occupied the attention of the Division of Near Eastern Affairs when on 3/16 November Nicholas Politis, the foreign minister of the provisional government, sent a message to Droppers in which he appealed to the American minister to use his influence in encouraging the U.S. State Department to accord recognition to the revolutionary government in Salonika with a view to sending an accredited diplomatic representative to Washington. "I presume," wrote Politis, "that the government of the United States, conforming with the practice regularly followed by it on analogous situations, has already tacitly recognized the Provisional Government as a government 'de facto'."[18] When Politis received no answer from Droppers he turned to Kehl for assistance.

Insofar as the United States government was concerned, the problem of recognition reduced itself to a single fundamental question: Can a regime whose creation is the result of the goodwill of foreign powers claim for itself the right to be recognized as a sovereign state. Unlike a de facto government which by its own power overthrows the regularly established authorities and replaces them with its own officials, or where a portion of the populace separate themselves from the parent state and somehow acquire the power to establish an independent government, Venizelos' provisional government was created essentially by the will and power of the Allies. Moreover, this de facto government was, at best, of undefined jurisdiction, encompassing a number of islands and certain loosely defined territories in northern Greece. There is little doubt that without the aid of British ships and French bayonets Venizelos' revolutionary movement would have been short and ineffective.

The State Department settled for a vague course of action by tacitly accepting the recommendation of Consul Kehl that the consulate at Salonika recognize the provisional government "as a matter of form" with the understanding that such semiofficial recognition was ample under the circumstances. Kehl was ordered to deal informally and unofficially with the provisional authorities if that became necessary. He was urged to exercise the greatest care and discretion in private and official dealings with Greek officials. This lukewarm attitude of the United States government was acceptable to the Venizelists initially. In fact, their minister of finance expressed the opinion that he considered the American consulate's relations to be "informal and unofficial. . . ."[19] The reason for Venizelos' willingness to conduct semiofficial diplomatic relations was his conviction that, despite Washington's reluctance, official recognition would soon be forthcoming. The necessary prerequisite, he reasoned, was for America to become a belligerent. When that happened it could be expected that the United States would follow the example of its European allies and recognize his regime. However, even after its entrance into the war the United States remained uncommitted, for in the final analysis unilateral action in matters pertaining to Greek politics was an option that was unavailable to the State Department. Nevertheless, the effort of Venizelos' agents to secure American recognition continued unabated throughout the winter and spring of 1916–17. Before turning to the efforts of the Royalists to secure American support, it is appropriate to describe briefly the temperament of the American minister in Athens and the way in which his view of Greek political life affected the conduct of Greek-American diplomacy.

Royalist Propaganda and Garrett Droppers

While Venizelos was attempting to gain the support of American officials, Constantine was taking every measure to gain the approval of Washington for his policy of neutrality. The Royalist press and the agents of the king undertook a propaganda campaign in Greece and in the United States which was designed to discredit the government of Venizelos. In the diplomatic conflict that developed, the American minister had the misfortune to find himself in the middle. It would have been a difficult position for anyone, but for Garrett Droppers, for whom the American legation and his entire tenure in Greece were rapidly assuming the role of a purgatory, the situation soon became unbearable. While he did his best to execute the policy of his government, he often found himself embroiled in political and personal controversies which at times diminished the quality of his work. These personality conflicts extended to the staff of the American legation.[20]

What incensed the American minister was not the fact that the Royalists should resort to propaganda in order to influence the attitude of the United States government. Much more disturbing to him was the virulent nature of the propaganda itself which was characterized by lying, duplicity, and by what he considered to be attacks on his integrity and professional ethics. His despatches to the State Department from the establishment of the revolutionary government to the departure of Constantine in June 1917 tend to betray a sense of bitterness and disillusionment. The difficulty lay in the fact that neither his training nor his temperament had equipped him to understand the workings of the Greek mind. Prior to his appointment by President Wilson as minister to Greece, Droppers had been a professor at Williams College in Massachusetts and was an authority on international law. On the basis of traditional American ideals, he had formulated certain definite and precise concepts relative to what rules of conduct constitute proper, civilized international law and politics. He was thus unable to come to terms with the painful realities of the moment. He seemed oblivious to the fact that the various belligerent nations were fighting for their very existence and that, under the circumstances, none of the governments would hesitate to use all the military and diplomatic weapons at its command.

Compton Mackenzie, who was in charge of the British secret service in Greece and a man with whom Droppers developed a personal feud, found him to be "like an American Minister in a novel or a play; and, so unerringly did he speak and behave . . . I ended by finding it hard to believe he was real." Moreover, his credulity, considering his training in history and international law, was little short of astonishing. For him "the American way of life" was the measure of all things. "Of course," he said to Mackenzie, "in America we can't understand this King business at all. To us it seems kind of madness for educated human beings to have kings."[21] He had written a book on international law, and his attitude on Greece during those difficult years remained that of an angry professor who was compelled to watch a lot of third-rate politicians deliberately tearing out page after page of his life's work. He wrote to the secretary of state that "The more I [see] of Europe the more I approve of the American tradition and the better I like Mexico."[22] This analysis of the American minister's temperament and demeanor might seem unfair, emanating as it does from the pen of one with whom Droppers never developed friendly relations. However, on the basis of the diplomatic correspondence, it seems to be an accurate summation of his outlook towards his work in Greece.

Droppers reciprocated with a scathing attack on Compton Mackenzie's honesty, professional competence, and personal morals. Describing Mackenzie's tenure in Greece as one of the saddest chapters in the history of Greek-Entente relations, he accused the Englishman of organizing, not an intelligence agency, but a band of "worthless scoundrels who use their power for infamy." He was seen "almost every night at some place of entertainment surrounded by his mistresses and often in a state of exhilaration, or at one of the well-known theaters of Athens with his harlots, occupying what was known as the "British Legation box."[23]

Another person with whom Droppers developed a personality conflict was Paxton Hibben, the Athens correspondent of the Associated Press who had distinguished himself by some excellent news reporting. When he arrived in Greece in the summer of 1915 he professed to be a Francophile but wished, nevertheless, to have an audience with the king. He turned for assistance to Droppers, who agreed reluctantly to make the necessary arrangements. Hibben emerged from the interview convinced that Constantine lacked the necessary perception to be a great statesman. Constantine's political astuteness must have had its effect, however, for it seems that, after further conversations with Hibben, he was able to transform the American correspondent into a passionate, uncompromising Royalist.[24] For the next five years Hibben would be one of Constantine's staunchest supporters in the United States, where he was relentless in his efforts to promote the Royalist cause in American financial circles and within the State Department.[25] Apparently, Constantine was able to convince Hibben that the United States government must be made to understand that for Greece neutrality was the wisest course of action and that the main obstacle to the implementation of smoother relations between Athens and Washington was Garrett Droppers. To lend weight to the latter assertion, the king mentioned a personal promise from President Wilson that as soon as Droppers' term of service in Athens was over he would be replaced.[26]

The American minister's initial reaction to this revelation was to believe Hibben. He assumed that Hibben was reporting what he had been told and that he continued to remain impartial in the conflict between the Royalists and the Venizelists. But as the Royalist propaganda in the Athenian press increasingly hinted at American intervention in Greek internal affairs, Droppers was led to suspect that the guiding spirit, if not the author, of most of the articles was none other than Paxton Hibben. The style in which they were written, and the nature of the detailed material they contained, suggested that only an American had the appropriate background to provide the necessary data; hence the origin of a feud between the two men, the climax of which led to the publication of Hibben's book *King Constantine and the Greek People*.

Written in June 1917, the book remained unpublished for three years. Hibben alleged that American authorities held up its publication and despite the fact that he had sent a carbon copy of the manuscript to the State Department, "No whisper of what was going on under cover reached the American people." There seems to be no documentary evidence to support this allegation, but the manuscript did become the source of pernicious gossip in Greece and the United States.[27] Hibben's account of French and British activities in Greece was inflammatory and promised to intensify the Royalist-Venizelist controversy by alienating pro-Ally elements in Greece and the United States. Hibben also commented on the conduct of the American minister which, in his view, was inconsistent with the behavior of a diplomat of a neutral nation. Droppers, who had acquired an advance copy of the manuscript, prepared a lengthy dispatch in which he insisted that his conduct was consistent with the policy of the United States towards Greece.[28]

The Royalists' Efforts to Obtain American Support

In the meantime, a concerted campaign was undertaken to induce Droppers to promote the Royalist cause. These efforts were often subtle and carefully orchestrated. They included "chance" meetings with avowed Royalists, evening parties at which groups of the king's partisans would be present, and invitations to afternoon tea parties at the house of the crown prince, where Constantine would often be a guest. On such occasions it was inevitable that private, informal chats between king and minister would be arranged.[29] On other occasions the efforts were much more direct. Successive delegations would appear in front of the American legation appealing to the American government to assist a people who were struggling "to abolish the chains of tyranny and recover their lost liberties." In response to these appeals Droppers remained correct and formal, but by his own admission, cold as well.[30]

The Royalists also reported to an intensive press campaign which was generally characterized by extreme partisanship, gross fabrications, and virulence. This campaign was effective enough to help create and prolong the myth that American military aid for Constantine's government was on the way. To the astonishment of Droppers, it was "amazing . . . what stupidities will be swallowed, hook, line, bob, and sinker, if only they appear in a well-prepared form." What he failed to realize was that the stress of war and political tensions were conducive to the creation of an atmosphere in which a poverty-stricken, semiliterate, and desperate people, in search of tranquility, would believe almost anything that offered hope. As conditions became increasingly critical, the Royalist press in Athens became more bold and irresponsible in its reporting of the news. Dramatic headlines told of American war ships, whose number increased daily, coming to rescue Greece from the fangs of French oppression. Finally, on 22 November 1916 the press bluntly stated that American military aid had been promised.[31]

Much speculation surrounds the source and organization of this propaganda. A popular coffee-house theory, to which Droppers subscribed, was that this campaign was the brainchild of German spies and money. What can be said with a fair degree of certainty is that the effort was a concerted one, or to use Droppers' words, "a frame-up," designed to keep up the courage of the populace and to make it appear that America, the friend of liberty, soon would appear to rescue Greece from the iron grip of the French and the British. But since such an eventuality was hardly a certainty, it was necessary to picture the United States government as a sort of international Don Quixote whose unpredictability might have a tempering influence on the Allies. The first step was simply to print an item as a mere conjecture, then as a rumor, then as a reasonable probability, and finally as a certainty; gathering size from day to day until the item seemed to be buttressed and supported by the most positive and official evidence. All this prompted Droppers to comment sarcastically on the uncanny ability of the Greeks to provide an unlimited supply of plausibilities to explain the inexplicable. In an effort to combat this irresponsible journalism, Droppers released a statement to the Greek and French press in Athens in which he denied reports that under certain conditions the United States would intervene on behalf of Greece. He insisted that he had no instructions on the subject from the State Department and therefore these reports were devoid of any basis in fact.[32]

The propaganda was not limited to Greece. It reached America, where it had its effect on almost every Greek-American community in the United States. The moving spirit was the Greek legation in Washington, though for whatever reasons Greek officials had in mind, it was the Greek consulate in Boston that undertook the actual effort to influence American public and congressional opinion. In April 1917, Greek Consul General D. T. Timagenis, sent a letter to a number of congressmen, several senators, and to many prominent Americans and Greek-Americans. He outlined in lengthy detail the Royalist position relative to the recognition of Venizelos. He expressed the hope that America would intervene to protect Greece's neutrality. Timagenis, who was a voluble participant of long standing in Greek-American affairs, also addressed a letter to Secretary of State Robert Lansing, identifying himself as both consul general and an American citizen, but emphasizing that it was in the latter capacity in which he was taking the liberty to write. The inherent contradiction explicit in his letter did not seem to concern him, though the same thing cannot be said of officials in the State Department. Since Alexander Vouros, the Greek chargé in Washington, had already presented the Royalists' side of the controversy, there were matters of protocol and legality to consider. Was Timagenis writing as the consul general of Greece or as a United States citizen? If as consul general, he was writing in violation of protocol; if as an American citizen, he had made statements that were false and misleading.[33]

Department officials took a dim view of the letter-writing activities of Timagenis, and Lansing lost no time in protesting to the Greek chargé. He informed Vouros of his surprise at the consul general's activities and stated that he could assume only that correspondence of this nature was outside the scope and channel prescribed for persons holding office under consular exequatur. Vouros promptly apologized for Timagenis' indiscretions and advised Lansing that the consul general had been admonished never again to resort to such a practice.[34] These events, in the meantime, had created considerable interest on Capitol Hill where members of congress began to press the State Department for a clear expression of its policy towards Greece. Under the circumstances the secretary of state was left with little choice but to postpone a definite commitment and to state that the matter was under careful study.

In the midst of these activities on both sides of the Atlantic, probably the most sober and dignified argument in support of Constantine's policy was put forward by Prime Minister Spyridon Lambros, a professor of history at the University of Athens. He conferred with Droppers on current and future Greek-American relations. Lambros mentioned the traditionally close commercial ties which were bound to increase as the Greek people became accustomed to the high quality of American goods. Conversely, Greek products, such as emery, magnesite, tobacco, and currants had a good market in the United States. Furthermore, postwar Greece could be expected to expand in all facets of her social and economic life. There would be a need for public utilities, harbors, docks, a whole new system of communications, engineering skills and, above all, capital. Why should America miss the opportunity to invest in Greece. A well-established American bank in Athens could serve to facilitate the introduction of American capital and to promote Greek business both in Greece and the United States.

Nor was the problem of immigration forgotten. Lambros suggested that the quality of immigrant traffic from Greece to the United States could be regulated, thus insuring a more productive class of immigrant who could encourage American tourists to visit Greece to the benefit of both countries. The prime minister then went on to speak in historical terms of the traditional ties that went back to the Cretan Revolution of

1866. He cited the establishment of the Hill School, which for many years was the leading institution in Athens for the education of girls, and the founding of the American School of Archaeology in Athens as examples of what could be done to implement friendly diplomatic relations between Athens and Washington. Closer intellectual ties, often offer a sound basis for the expansion of relations between nations. France and Germany already had implemented a system of exchanging professors with the United States. It seemed logical and desirable for Greece to do the same.[35]

This was the kind of language that Droppers could understand, and he was elated with the possibilities of these suggestions. He was so pleased to find someone with whom he could communicate that he was lavish in his praise of Lambros' ability to use the German language, to display high intellectual powers, to express himself with clarity and distinction, and to apply all the scholarly arguments at his command in support of Greek neutrality.[36] At the time, Droppers could do little more than offer a few words of comfort, though the conversation between the two men was not without its significance. When negotiations for the Tripartite Loan began, it became apparent that Lambros' eloquent arguments had made a favorable impression on the American minister.

The Departure of Constantine

In the meantime, events were beginning to move rapidly. With the formation of the Salonika revolutionary regime Allied pressure on Athens increased steadily. France and Great Britain initiated a new series of high-handed measures whose ultimate purpose was the overthrow of the King. On 10 October 1916, the day after Venizelos had landed in Salonika, the French submitted an ultimatum to Athens demanding the surrender of the Greek fleet. The government yielded. Several days later new demands were made that included the dismissal of the representatives of the Central Powers in Greece and the surrender of additional arms and equipment. The Greek government felt obliged to yield no more and refused to submit to these demands. France and Great Britain responded on 30 November by landing troops at the port of Piraeus. The following day Greek forces fired on the Allied troops as they marched towards Athens, forcing them to return to their ships.[37] In retaliation, on 8 December, the Allies imposed a blockade on a much larger scale than that imposed by the French several months earlier.

The result was the creation of a hunger blockade which produced great suffering for the populace and ruinous consequences for Greek commerce and shipping. As long as events in Greece moved along political lines, American policy was characterized by a watchful aloofness. However, when it appeared that the Allied blockade would have an adverse effect on American commerce in the Eastern Mediterranean, Lansing lodged a protest with the French ambassador in Washington. It is pertinent to the history of Greek-American relations in the interwar period to quote at some length the text of the State Department's protest because it reflects the fundamental tone that was to guide the department's attitude toward Greece after World War I. Reminding the ambassador that neither Greece nor the United States was a belligerent, Lansing wrote:

> I have the honor . . . to inform you inasmuch as this Government has been informed by the Greek Government that peaceful relations subsist between Greece and the Allies, the United States adheres to its traditional position which has heretofore been set forth in relation to the Cretan blockade of 1897, and the Venezuelan blockade of 1902, that the United States does not concede the right of a foreign power to interfere with the rights of uninterested countries by the establishment of a blockade in the absence of a state of war, and therefore reserves the consideration of all international rights and of any question which may in any way affect the commercial interests of the United States.[38]
>
> The United States, therefore, does not acquiesce in any extending of the doctrine of pacific blockade which may adversely affect the rights of states not parties to the controversy of discriminating against the commerce of neutral nations; and my Government reserves all of its rights in the premises.[39]

Hitherto France and Great Britain had not pressed for the abdication of Constantine. One reason was Tsar Nicholas II whose influence had restrained the Allies from demanding the king's dethronement. Another was the role of Aristide Briand, the French premier and foreign minister, whose moderation held back French extremists. Finally, the Allies were concerned about the attitude of the United States government, and about American public opinion, which would have been critical if the world had been compelled to witness two western democracies, ostensibly the champions of the principles of neutral rights and national sovereignty, in the act of using raw force to effect the illegal overthrow of a legitimate ruler. French War Minister Paul Painlevé told Greek officials

31

that French policy vis-à-vis Greece would be "tangibly reconsidered" as soon as the United States entered the war.[40] These obstacles were removed when Nicholas II and Briand fell from power and the United States entered the war. After April 1917 the Allies felt free to take the final steps.

On 14 June 1917 France and England gave Constantine the alternative of abdication within forty-eight hours or the bombardment of Athens. Late in the evening of the previous day George Streit had called on the American legation to announce that an ultimatum concerning the king's abdication was probably imminent. He urged Droppers to send a telegram to Washington requesting the intervention of President Wilson.[41] Despite his pro-Venizelist inclinations, Droppers' commitment to the principles of international law was an overriding consideration. Consequently, he was willing to use his influence to preserve Constantine's throne. He told Streit that he would give whatever assistance he could, but that the source of Greece's suffering was the division of the country into two hostile parties. Unless there was some evidence to indicate that a compromise was imminent, there was little that the American government could do. Streit replied that the king was ready to make any sacrifice, even to call back Venizelos.

Droppers was not impressed. He knew that Constantine had been advised to make every effort to reunite Greece by recalling Venizelos, but that he had refused to do so. Nevertheless, Droppers agreed to give whatever constructive assistance he could, after discussing the matter of the king's dethronement with C. C. Jonnart, special high commissioner of the Allies. The following morning (15 June) he set out to find Jonnart and to obtain from Streit positive assurances relative to the king's willingness to effect a reconciliation with Venizelos. These efforts proved futile because at 11:30 a.m. Streit called the American legation to inform Droppers that the ultimatum already had been delivered to Premier and Foreign Minister Alexander Zaïmis.[42] It was now too late, and there was nothing the American legation could do. Constantine chose to depart, leaving his throne to Alexander, his second son. On 27 June Venizelos became prime minister, and on 2 July he formally brought Greece into the war on the side of the Allies.

Constantine's departure did not constitute a true abdication of his throne. Jonnart's original demand was that formal articles of abdication be signed, but on the advice of his closest and most astute adviser, George Steit, the king refused. He was willing to leave the country with

Crown Prince George and to hand over the Royal power to his second son, Alexander, if the Allies would not compel him to sign the abdication papers. In a moment of weakness, Jonnart decided to make a concession to the pride of the deposed king, but in so doing he laid the foundation for a controversy that was to have a profound effect on Greek politics and on Greek-American relations when Constantine returned in 1920.[43]

While it cannot be said that Constantine was free of pro-German sentiments, there is no evidence to suggest that he had definite plans to enter the war on the side of the Central Powers. For better or worse, he sincerely believed that Greece had no alternative but to remain neutral. His position was extremely difficult because the nature of the forces surrounding him assured bitter opposition regardless of what policy he pursued. " 'Just imagine,' he wrote, 'what would have happened if I had joined the Entente. They would not have sent troops in sufficient numbers . . . and I alone against the Germans, Austrians and Bulgarians should have been crushed.' "[44] On the other hand, had he joined the Central Powers, the Allied blockade would have been imposed at a much earlier date with even more serious consequences for the Greek people and Greek shipping. When the inevitability of his departure finally became clear to the people, hysterical crowds surrounded the palace shouting, "Do not abdicate!" Even among Venizelists there were many who believed that the king was the victim of cunningly devised pro-German propaganda.

One month after Constantine's departure, King Alexander wrote to President Wilson to inform him officially of his accession to the throne. "I feel assured," he wrote, "that my reign will ever find a support in your sentiments and I beg you kindly to be convinced that for my part I shall exert my every effort toward drawing closer and closer the bonds so happily established between our friendly and allied countries."[45] President Wilson's reply was reassuring, but also noncommittal. He assured Alexander of the friendship of the United States government and of the American people, but made no other commitment.[46] These were the circumstances and the political climate in Greece when negotiations for the Tripartite Loan began in the summer of 1917.

3
The Tripartite Loan
of 1918

On 10 February 1918 the financial representatives of France, Great Britain, and the United States met in Paris, where they ratified a loan of 750,000,000 francs ($150,000,000) to the government of Greece (see appendix A). The purpose of this Tripartite Loan was to help Greece become a viable partner of the Allies in their war against the Central Powers. The participation of the United States government in this agreement signaled the beginning of a greater American interest in Greek internal affairs and is, therefore, a significant point of departure in the history of the diplomatic relations between the two countries. The loan also served to form a basis for the development of Greek-American political relations until 1940. The signing of this financial agreement and the ensuing controversies provided a semblance of unity and continuity for the diplomacy between the United States and Greece in the interwar period. Without an adequate appreciation of this fact the picture one obtains of Greek-American relations during the First World War and between the world wars is fragmented.

Negotiations for the Tripartite Loan

On 10 July 1917, Greek Minister of Finance Miltiades Negro-pontes, along with a delegation of government officials and Greek financiers, appeared at the American legation to inquire of the American minister about the feasibility of a loan to Greece for 100,000,000 drachmas ($20,000,000). Droppers was assured that France and England were prepared to furnish the money for munitions and supplies that would put the Greek army on a war footing.[1] What was needed was an additional loan that would stabilize the Greek treasury and bolster the government of Venizelos. Such an agreement would have the approval of the French and British governments which would probably be willing to allow the International Financial Commission (IFC) to guarantee its terms.[2] The loan would also pave the way for United States membership in the IFC, thus enabling the American government to keep in touch with developments that could affect its financial and commercial interests in Greece.

When Droppers raised the question of Greece's public debt and her ability to repay her loans, he was told that discussions on these subjects would be premature, since it must first be ascertained whether the United States government would agree in principle to the Greek request. It was suggested that an increase in taxes, the development of Macedonia's resources, the use of certain foreign capital surpluses, and a closer supervision of government spending would provide ample security. Moreover, since approximately 70 percent of the country's public debt was under the control of the IFC, there should be little concern about the ability of the Greek government to meet its obligations.[3]

In order to assure himself of the strength of the treasury, Droppers conducted his own investigation of Greek finances, and he discovered that as of 31 December 1916 the difference between the IFC's receipts and reimbursements represented a balance of nearly $7,000,000 which was transferrred to the Greek treasury. This sum and any future surpluses would not be under the control of the IFC, and could be used to satisfy the provisions of a new loan. Politis conceded that the public debt of Greece was large and that it bore heavily on private incomes of the population, but despite these handicaps he did not consider this financial burden as great as that of many other countries.[4]

Droppers was receptive to the idea of an American loan to Greece. He proceeded to describe with enthusiastic detail the great potential of untapped natural resources which, in his opinion, included an almost un-equaled richness of soil in Thessaly and Macedonia that was lying idle owing to the lack of capital, intelligent planning, and political security. The implication was clear. Here was an opportunity for American busi-nessmen and financiers to open new markets for their goods and services.

But one question remained. If France and England were willing to advance credits for arms and military supplies, what was to prevent them from providing for all of Greece's needs, including the settlement of her public debt and the stabilization of her treasury. When Droppers put this question to Venizelos, the prime minister pointed out that in reality his government was seeking two separate loans, each with its own pur-pose. France and England had particular reasons for wanting to put Greece on a war footing as quickly as possible. The Greek army had to be well-trained and well-equipped without delay if it were to prove a real asset on the Macedonian front. It was logical that, since French and En-glish military personnel had long experience in Greece and understood the problems that are peculiar to the Greek land and people, they were best suited for the task of training the Greek armed forces. Venizelos might have added that, considering the blatant pressures the Allies had applied to put him in office, they also had a moral obligation to assure that Greece would become a viable ally.

The credit of the National Bank of Greece and the state of the coun-try's finances, especially the inexcusable deficits left by incompetent ministries, were another matter. France and England had many claims upon what few disposable funds remained in the treasury, and the pre-mier was loath to ask their governments for further advances. The weakness of the country's economy was rapidly becoming a source of considerable popular discontent which, in view of the events of the pre-vious two years, could once again inflame the political atmosphere with serious consequences for Greece and for the Allied war effort. The pos-sibility of renewed political bickering was a source of concern, since the United States was now formally on the side of the Allies and would find it difficult to maintain its former aloofness from Greek domestic affairs. Thus, the preservation of internal political stability became the primary concern of officials in the State and Treasury Departments as they weighed the merits of the Greek loan request. Nor were they convinced that Venizelos was the man to insure internal stability. Droppers made an effort to reassure American officials. He expressed the view that Venizelos was able to grasp the political and social implications of the war better than any other Greek statesman. He possessed exceptional, lucid intelligence and excellent powers of expression: "To have such an ally on the side of the Entente is by no means a negligible element."[5] While this assessment of the premier's political acumen is correct, it should be noted that Greece was unified politically only insofar as martial law prevailed under the government of Venizelos.

Droppers also mentioned that R. C. Brackenthorpe, the British chargé d'affaires, had confided to him that he had learned of the Greek loan request, and he expressed the hope that Washington would favor the project as the loan was certain to facilitate the appointment of an American to the IFC. Such an appointment, he believed, would have a beneficial effect on the function of the commission because an American would be likely to have a more objective and disinterested point of view than the other members of the commission.[6] It is significant to compare the arguments of the British chargé with those advanced earlier by the Greek finance minister. Their striking similarity leads to the conclusion that the Greek authorities were acting with the approval, if not at the instigation, of the British legation. As early as 1915, Sir Edward Grey, the British foreign secretary, told Colonel Edward M. House, private diplomatic adviser to President Wilson, that it would be unfair to Greece to let her come into the war without some protection.[7] Presumably, such protection would be financial as well as military. If a Franco-British military loan could be combined with an American stabilization loan, the viability of Venizelos' government could be assured.

By early autumn, American officials had come around to the view that the needs of the Greek treasury were indeed genuine and that a loan to the Greek government under the circumstances was a practical and moral necessity. The specific terms did not present a serious problem, because there were ample precedents to serve as guidelines. What was troublesome was the persistence of three problems which had not yet been resolved: the matter of security, the benefits to be derived from the loan, and the danger that the United States might be drawn inexorably into the turbulence of Greek politics.

The problem of security had been considered from the outset and some specific methods of raising revenue had been discussed, but the Treasury Department remained skeptical. Droppers decided that such skepticism could be reduced by sounding a warning relative to the activities of American firms doing business in Greece. He reminded the

Treasury and State Departments that trade with the United States in Macedonian filler leaf tobacco was conducted almost exclusively by American organizations and averaged $5,500,000 per year. An excise tax on tobacco was already an established method of raising revenues for the payment of interest on loans. If the Greek government were compelled to seek a loan elsewhere, it was probable that its terms would be more expensive, with the result that the excise tax on tobacco would be increased greatly to the detriment of American firms. On the other hand, if the United States were to grant the loan, it would be possible to regulate the tax on tobacco, thus protecting American firms and simultaneously contributing to the security of the loan. If this formula could be applied successfully to tobacco, it could be applied to other commodities as well.

The loan to Greece would also help to open new business opportunities in that country after the war. But first the war had to be won, and the Greek armed forces were an important part of that effort. French military experts informed Droppers that Greece's aid in the war was expected to consist of 200,000 men (it eventually reached 250,000), while the use of Greek territory for purposes of transportation would minimize the use of sea lanes, so that Allied forces would be less susceptible to submarine attacks. The American minister then went on to extol the virtues of the Greek soldier with enthusiastic detail. In watching Greek troops drill under the most difficult conditions he was impressed by their energy, stamina, patience, and ability to subsist with minimal clothing and on small rations of the most simple food. Unlike his French, English, and German counterparts, the Greek soldier was less expensive to maintain. Furthermore, he was far better adapted to the climate of northern Greece and, unlike the Allied soldiers, he did not suffer from the fevers that were common to that part of the country. The enthusiasm and patriotism of the Greek forces were exemplary, for they "looked forward to the opportunity of wiping out the disgraceful surrender of Fort Rupel to the Germans and Bulgarians." These views were not merely the thinking of a zealous diplomat. They were shared by Allied military experts and by Colonel Edward Davis, the American military attaché, who requested that the American legation add his endorsement of the American minister's views.[8]

As a practical matter, an American loan to Greece at this time was almost unavoidable as it was obvious that, if the United States did not provide the money, some other power would probably do so on more expensive terms and with money borrowed from the U.S.[9] From the general tone of the correspondence it becomes obvious that the other power was an allusion to France or Great Britain. Thus, the loan the Greek government was seeking might ultimately be obtained without the United States reaping any of the benefits.

Finally, there remained the political phase of the problem. All American officials agreed that the loan should be guaranteed by the IFC. But this prerequisite gave rise to the question of whether American participation in the IFC was appropriate. There was reason to believe that the members of the commission would not object to the addition of an American member. But this raised fears that the United States government would find itself embroiled in the internal political squabbles of Greece. Droppers argued that this possibility was unlikely because the responsibility of guaranteeing the loan would be shared by the other members of the commission, while the actual collecting of revenues would be done by the Greek government and by Greek companies, not by American officials. Conversely, if the loan were not guaranteed by the IFC, the United States might still be forced to a much more energetic intervention in Greek politics in order to safeguard its interests. Thus, some instrument of control had to be devised which would be politically acceptable to the United States government.[10]

Negotiations moved very slowly, partly because of the complexity of the problem and partly because of the need to gain congressional approval. Droppers pointed out to Greek officials that an act of congress limited loans only to countries at war with Germany. It was necessary that the Greek government provide documented information to the effect that Greece was actually at war. The Treasury Department also had to consider in every case the military value of the country to which it would lend financial assistance. Venizelos became extremely anxious at the prospect of lengthy congressional debates, so with the aid of the French ambassador in Washington, who provided corroborating information, he was able to convince the State Department and Congress that Greece was at war against the Central Powers and that the lack of additional financial assistance was preventing him from effecting full mobilization.[11]

Throughout the autumn of 1917 the appeals of Greek officials became increasingly desperate in tone. They stressed the fact that prolongation of the war would increase human suffering and that, while the drachma was still relatively sound, the stability of the Greek treasury and the credit of the National Bank of Greece were, at best, tenuous.

Negropontes, now foreign minister, urged Venizelos to find a solution to the country's financial problem as soon as possible; if not in its entirety, at least in part, because there was a great demand for a wide variety of supplies for military purposes and for the basic needs of the population. Failure to do so, he warned, would lead to severe protests and unrest throughout the country.[12] In their desperation, Greek officials made many unrealistic promises relative to the size of the army and navy they could raise. They also hinted at French and British participation in the loan that would be entirely separate from other financial agreements between Greece and the Allies.[13]

By the autumn of 1917 it had become obvious to General Tasker H. Bliss (the American military representative to the Allied Supreme Council and one who was intimately involved in the negotiations), and to Colonel House, that the war was escalating. If Greece were to make a meaningful contribution to the war effort, financial aid must be given quickly. They pointed out to the Treasury Department that under the circumstances a loan to the Greek government was almost inevitable. In the meantime, the French and British ambassadors in Washington added their support by joining Greek Minister Venizelos and Droppers in a concerted effort to sway the Treasury and State Departments toward a favorable decision. Finally, after considerable indecision, American officials became convinced that the financial needs of the Greek government were indeed genuine, and they agreed to grant a loan. There were, however, certain conditions attached to the offer.

One stipulated that Great Britain must join France in giving assurances that Greece was at war against Germany. Another required the French and British governments to participate in the loan on the same basis as the United States government and to help in the creation of an Inter-Allied Financial Commission which would regulate the spending of the money derived from the loan.[14] France and Great Britain were to grant a separate loan specifically for the purpose of purchasing munitions and military supplies.[15] Finally, the British government was required to give assurances that its military presence in the Balkans would remain until the conclusion of the war.[16]

On the basis of these conditions, negotiations began to progress more rapidly, and an agreement was reached on 7 December 1917. On the following day Secretary of the Treasury W. G. McAdoo suggested to President Wilson that, in view of the recommendations of General Bliss and Oscar T. Crosby, chief negotiator for the United States government, the United States should join with France and Great Britain and advance one-third of the 750,000,000 francs.[17] The president approved, and on 10 February 1918 the financial representatives of France, Great Britain, and the United States met in Paris where they signed the loan agreement.[18] The legal basis of the Tripartite Loan rested on congressional authority granted under the Liberty Loan Act (24 April 1917) which provided that the secretary of the treasury could, with the approval of the president, make loans to foreign governments engaged in war with enemies of the United States.

After the agreement was concluded, a decision had to be made relative to the manner in which the proceeds of the loan would be made available to the Greek government. Upon the recommendation of the American delegate to the Inter-Allied Financial Commission, Consul General Alexander W. Weddell, who was also the American delegate to the Inter-Allied Military Commission, credits were established by the Treasury Department in favor of Greece totaling $48,236,629.[19] The credits were intended as cover for a note issued by the National Bank of Greece for a corresponding amount in drachmas. The French and British governments also opened credits in equal shares.

The opening of these credits generated considerable optimism within Greek financial and military circles. It was assumed that each cash advance could now be secured as the need arose with only a minimum of formality. On the strength of the promised credits the Greek government made available a bond issue and put into circulation bank notes with a counter value of 250,000,000 drachmas which were employed according to the agreement of 10 February 1918. The Greek government, in fact, expended the whole 750,000,000 for the agreed purposes, but because the Inter-Allied Financial and Military Commissions were disbanded in 1920 the whole amount was never formally checked.[20]

The pernicious effects of these irresponsible fiscal policies became evident in the autumn of 1919, when the integrity of the drachma began to show the first signs of weakness. The notes issued by the National Bank of Greece and the spending of the Greek government were backed not by gold and foreign currencies, but by the assumption that cash advances would soon follow the opening of the credits. Consequently, on 3 September 1919 the Greek government called upon the United States treasury to make cash advances on the basis of the credits that had been established. In a letter addressed to the secretary of state the Greek chargé, Michael Tsamados, referred to the fact that under paragraph 2 of

Article 3 of the Tripartite Loan, the Greek government could not have recourse to the credits unless the credit of the National Bank of Greece fell below 100,000,000 francs or until six months after the conclusion of peace. Nevertheless, he ventured to hope that the United States government, taking into consideration the critical economic situation in Greece, would waive its rights under Article 3 and allow the Greek government to have recourse immediately to the credits arranged for in the financial agreement of Paris. He went on to argue that "the United States being the *country having suffered least from the ravages of war, . . . it is to her, very naturally, that Greece turns to procure all that she needs*" to maintain her economy. "In order to make the payment of all her orders without running the risk of seeing her monetary unity depreciated, Greece has needs of credits in the United States [document's emphasis]."[21] Tsamados made it clear that the request was being made specifically for the stabilization of the currency. As an incentive to American officials he promised that these advances would be used to meet the payment of debts incurred through orders placed in the United States.

It is important to note that the Greek minister did not base his request on the specific terms of the Tripartite Loan, but rested his case on the fact that the United States "suffered the least from the ravages of War." He specified that the money would be used for domestic purposes, mentioning nothing about money to be used for the prosecution of the war as the loan had intended.

It is not possible to document precisely what Greek officials had in mind when they requested cash advances outside the limits set by the terms of the agreement, but a reading of the documents gives a number of clues. Apparently, the Foreign Ministry intended to use the credits established by the French and British governments to pay for the actual prosecution of the war, while the money derived from the American credits was to be used purely for purposes of fiscal stabilization and national rehabilitation. The correspondence shows that when the advances were finally approved, they were made not to take care of war expenditures, but to rehabilitate Greece. In fact, all the requests of the Greek legation mentioned that the money was to be used for rehabilitation and relief. This is a crucial point, because it left room for much interpretation relative to the true nature of the loan, and led to endless controversies after the war when the war debts of the Allies became a serious issue in the conduct of Greek-American diplomacy and in the national politics of the United States.

It was understood by both sides that the funds were to be used for purchases in the United States for goods to be consumed in Greece and that itemized, semimonthly statements showing amounts and the purposes for which such funds were used should be submitted to the Treasury Department.[22] Pursuant to this understanding, advances of $15,000,000 were made in three five-million dollar installments (15 December 1919, 16 January 1920, and 24 September 1920). The annual interest rate was set at five percent.[23] On 22 December 1920 the Greek legation once again applied for additional cash, but this request was not honored because the untimely death of King Alexander on 25 October changed the political situation in Greece and introduced a new and turbulent phase in the relations between the United States and Greece.

4
Political Relations from the Fall of Venizelos to the Destruction of Smyrna, 1920–1922

Perhaps the most surprising development in the course of Greek history during the first two decades of the twentieth century was the electoral defeat of Premier Eleutherios Venizelos on 14 November 1920 and the subsequent restoration of King Constantine. This unexpected turn of events prompted the State Department to reexamine its policy towards the new Greek government. From the legal point of view and on the basis of historical precedent, there was little reason for the United States to withhold its recognition. Indeed, from the outset the State Department was disposed to recognize Constantine upon the execution of certain diplomatic formalities. The American attitude, however, met with the immediate opposition of France, Great Britain, and Italy. At first, the Allied position consisted of the exchange of diplomatic notes and intimations that perhaps the Monroe Doctrine, in light of America's inclination to extend the Open Door policy to the Near East, should be reexamined. But when it became clear that American financial and commercial interests were at stake, the United States sent hints to its wartime allies that it was prepared to act alone. At this point France, Great Britain, and Italy dropped all pretense of moderation. They warned that if the State Department persisted in its intention to involve itself directly in the affairs of the Eastern Mediterranean, they would be prepared to play a more aggressive role in the Western Hemisphere. In these circumstances, the United States was left with little choice, but to follow the Allies' example in the formulation of its Greek policy from 1920 to 1922.

The Electoral Defeat of Venizelos

The failure of Venizelos to win a majority in the Chamber of Deputies in the elections of 14 November 1920 and the subsequent restoration of King Constantine combined to introduce a new and turbulent period in the history of Greece and of Greek-American diplomacy. An analysis of the factors that shaped the attitude of the United States government towards Greece in the 1920s must necessarily be preceded by an examination of two fundamental questions: Why did Venizelos, at the peak of his political power, suffer an unexpected defeat? and What historical precedents had been established by the United States relative to the recognition of new states and governments?

The conclusion of World War I found the Greek premier at the pinnacle of his career. After the war, his diplomatic skill proved to be invaluable to Greece. He was especially popular with the British because of his contribution to the Allied war effort. At the Paris Peace Conference he was the constant companion of Lloyd George, prime minister of Great Britain. Under his direction and with the support of the British, Greece was able to gain a great deal from her hostile neighbors in the Balkans and Asia Minor. The Treaty of Neuilly with Bulgaria (27 November 1919) and the Treaty of Sèvres with Turkey (10 August 1920) gave the Venizelos government control of much of the Aegean coast, almost to the gates of Constantinople. Much of this, however, was little more than a settlement on paper. When the Greek forces landed at Smyrna on 15 May 1919, they were to discover that it was one matter to win territory at the conference table and quite another to maintain control over it.

The nature of the opposition to the Greek landing was diplomatic and nationalistic. The presence of Greek troops in Asia Minor conflicted with Italian aspirations in the area, while the French, wishing to protect and expand their interests in Syria, were becoming increasingly Turcophile. At the same time, the specter of Turkish nationalism under the leadership of Mustafa Kemal compounded the difficulties. Stripped of large amounts of territory on both sides of the Bosporus the Kemalists believed that the very existence of their nation was threatened. They resolved to take desperate measures to protect Turkey's political and territorial integrity. Kemal and the leadership of the Turkish nationalist movement withdrew from Constantinople and established headquarters at Ankara in the central part of Turkey. In September 1919 they issued a manifesto in which they declared their determination to preserve the idea of Turkish nationality.

The domestic situation in Greece compounded the difficulties for Venizelos. Despite the existence of martial law, political opposition to the Venizelist regime persisted to the point where political assassination became an acceptable alternative to parliamentary debate for extremists on both ends of the political spectrum. Apart from party feelings, however, there were those who felt that the Asia Minor part of Venizelos' foreign policy was a fatal blunder. As early as January 1915 John Metaxas, acting chief of the General Staff, warned that a campaign in Asia Minor entailed insurmountable logistical difficulties and must not be undertaken without extensive support from France and Great Britain. There were those who believed that British interests coincided with those of Greece, and it was precisely for this reason that Greece's gains at the conference table were extensive. It was not generally thought among Greeks that Greece owed her triumph to Venizelos.

To these factors must be added the disillusionment of the people with the domestic policies of the Venizelists. During the premier's lengthy absences from Greece, internal affairs were left in the hands of lieutenants with inferior abilities. They seized the opportunity to strike back at their political enemies. The internment or exile of many influential politicians roused their families to bitter hatred, and the introduction of martial law infuriated much of the nation. One newspaper virtually advocated the assassination of the leading Royalists in Greece, and hinted at a military coup d'état to strengthen the position of the government.[1] As far as the Royalists were concerned, these coercive measures and implied threats constituted a reign of terror. Consequently, brilliant successes in foreign affairs were insufficient to combat the pernicious effects of domestic administrative incompetence. Corruption and petty politics became the guiding principles in the administration that bore Venizelos' name; causing him to quip: "I am not a Venizelist."[2] In view of these circumstances, Venizelos decided to hold elections in November 1920, partly because he wished to renew his mandate from the people and partly because elections had not been held since 1915. The political atmosphere was hardly conducive to the creation of optimism though the prime minister remained hopeful. He declared confidently that the elections would put an end to the uncertainties and that the Greek people would be free "to march towards the glorious future which has opened through its national success."[3]

An additional element in the total picture was the untimely death of King Alexander, 25 October 1920, as the result of a bite from a pet monkey. The king enjoyed considerable popularity and was a person with whom Venizelos had been able to work for the common good. His untimely death served to subtract a significant element of support from the political base of the Venizelists. Other factors that worked against the premier were the prolonged mobilization;[4] the political, military, and economic crises of the previous decade; and the painful memories of the privations endured during the Allied blockade. To ensure that these issues would remain alive, the Royalists undertook a propaganda campaign reminiscent of the bitter controversy which was waged over the issue of neutrality during the war.

The campaign was vicious and replete with virulent accusations and innuendoes by both sides. Nor were Greek-Americans immune to the pressures that attended the struggle for political power. In the United States events were leading up to a second and more violent phase in the conflict between Royalists and Venizelists. At the conclusion of the war the Royalists felt free to renew their attacks on France and Great Britain for forcing the departure of Constantine in 1917. Their strategy was to undermine the confidence of Greek-Americans in the prime minister by stressing the burdens that Greece had assumed by her occupation of Smyrna and the suffering endured by the Greek people during the Allied blockade. This propaganda was effective enough to alarm the Venizelists who did not hesitate to take retaliatory measures. Venizelos assailed Constantine as a plotter whose secret agreements with the Kaiser and the betrayal of Macedonia to the Bulgarians during the war brought untold suffering to Greece. "This conduct," he said, "inspired an immediate disgust in the people of Greece." The Greek charge in Washington vehemently rejected the allegations of the Royalists, and warned Greek-Americans not to be susceptible to the malicious reports being fabricated by the political opponents of Venizelos.[5]

Despite warnings from friendly and astute political observers, the Venizelists remained confident. Minister of Finance Negropontis went so far as to invite the British minister, Earl Granville, to his residence on the evening of the election, "if it would amuse [him]," and await the election results.[6] Such reckless optimism led Venizelos to declare his willingness to make the coming elections a personal contest between himself and Constantine. On 2 November he announced that candidates for office would be free to advocate the return of the King. This announcement was widely interpreted to mean that should the supporters of Constantine be defeated, the Glücksburg Dynasty, of which the King was a member, would lose all claims to succession. There was no hint, however, that Venizelos was contemplating the formation of a republic.[7] As the votes continued to be counted and the truth could no longer be denied, the cabinet met in special session on the morning after the election and through a spokesman declared: "It is evident that the Government was mistaken in its expectations. . . ." The final count showed that the Liberal Party (Venizelists) and its allies managed to win fifty-two percent of the popular vote, but because of a complicated formula in apportioning seats in Parliament, they were able to gain only 110 seats out of 370 in the Chamber of Deputies.[8]

Venizelos' defeat created a tense political climate in Athens, prompting the British to station four warships in the port of Piraeus. Feelings ran high and rumors of impending riots or a coup d'état by infuriated Venizelists were heard everywhere. Venizelos' secretary appealed to the American minister, Dr. Edward Capps, to station a United States destroyer at Piraeus, in the hope that the combined presence of British and American war vessels would have a mitigating influence on the pernicious gossip emanating from Athens. It is not clear precisely what action Capps took relative to this request, but within two days the American destroyer *Borie* arrived in Piraeus by orders of Admiral Mark L. Bristol, high commissioner to Turkey. Venizelos was determined not to sanction the use of violence by his followers, and so he chose to leave the country. On 17 November he and several of his ministers boarded a British yacht and left for Nice via Rome, where a few days later William Miller, the English historian and correspondent, "found him a broken man."[9]

The sudden change of fortune in the career of such a towering figure in Greek politics evoked amazement from London and Paris, satisfaction from Rome, and uncertainty from Washington. The United States government now had to come to terms with this unexpected turn of events.

The State Department began to search for precedents that could guide it in the formulation of a realistic policy toward Constantine whom the Royalists lost no time in restoring to the throne on 5 December 1920.

Historical Precedents in the Recognition of Foreign Governments by the United States

It is generally agreed that, by the end of World War I, there had been three stages in the development of the policy of the United States in recognizing governmental changes in foreign countries—the Jefferson, the Seward, and the Wilson doctrines.[10]

Before the beginning of the nineteenth century Thomas Jefferson, in his capacity as secretary of state, declared that it was not inconsistent with American principles to recognize any government which is formed by the will of the nation, if that will is substantially declared. In a letter to Gouverneur Morris, United States minister to France, he expressed the view that each nation has a right to choose as a form of government whatever organ it thinks proper. The will of the nation is the only thing to be considered. Nor did this point of view exclude revolution as a valid means of effecting a change in the government of a state. Jefferson believed that radical action was at times desirable. " 'I hold,' he wrote, 'that a little revolution now and then is a good thing and is as necessary in the political world as storms are in the physical. . . . It is a medicine necessary for the sound health of government.' "[11] Jefferson believed in the continuity of state life and in the desirability of entering into formal relations with whatever party ultimately gained the ascendancy. It was the element of control rather than the method by which the change was effected that appeared to him to be the ultimate test in determining the legitimacy of a government.

By the middle of the nineteenth century the views of Jefferson were expanded to include two additional conditions of fact: the ability and willingness of a government to discharge its international and treaty obligations and the general acquiescence of its people. Popular acquiescence was defined as the willingness of the citizens to pay taxes, render military service, and obey the new government. Insofar as these precedents were to affect the relations between Greece and the United States, perhaps the most significant summation of America's traditional recognition policy was made in March 1913 by Alvey Adee, second assistant secretary of state, when he wrote: "The form of government has not been a conditional factor in such recognition. In other words, the de jure element of legitimacy of title has been left aside."[12]

The only significant deviation from Jefferson's doctrine occurred during the American Civil War, when the British questioned whether the term "acquiescence" could realistically be applied to the Confederate states. It fell upon Secretary of State William H. Seward to modify Jefferson's policy by stating that a revolutionary government could be considered legitimate only after it had clearly demonstrated that it maintained itself by the will of the people rather than by the force of arms.[13] The Seward Doctrine had no significant lasting influence because it was specifically designed to satisfy a temporary need. Insofar as it came to apply to Greece, it proved a convenient argument for withholding recognition from the Plastiras-Gonatas Revolutionary Government immediately after the Asia Minor debacle in September 1922.

The third major stage in the recognition of new governments was the result of the revival of the doctrine of legitimacy originally formulated by the Holy Alliance in the early nineteenth century. The twentieth-century version of that concept differed from the original in that legitimacy was now proclaimed in the guise of republican constitutionalism. Its author was Dr. Carlos Tobar, foreign minister of Uruguay, who suggested in 1906 that a new regime should not be recognized until a constitutional reorganization of the nation had taken place. The Tobar Doctrine was prompted by the perpetual state of political chaos in the republics of Central America. Under the prodding of the United States and Mexico, Tobar's ideas were embodied in the Central American Treaty of 1907, which prohibited the installation of a new regime until freely elected representatives of the people had constitutionally reorganized the country. It remained for President Wilson to make the first application of the Tobar Doctrine to American foreign policy.

With the advent of Wilson's administration there was a radical departure from Jefferson's principles in respect to the Central American republics and to all Latin America, but particularly in respect to the Republic of Mexico. In 1913 and in 1920 governmental changes were effected as the result of bloody coups d'état. President Wilson steadfastly refused to recognize either regime because of the violence which attended its rise to power. In his sympathy for the development of constitutionally guaranteed freedoms among the peoples of Latin America, President Wilson's feelings did not differ from other presidents before him. But he did differ from the practice of his predecessors by introducing the direct involvement of the United States government. This was the point that Greek authorities stressed when they sought to gain American recognition for the governments of Constantine and his successor, George II. If Washington felt free to act independently in countries of the entire Western Hemisphere, they asked, why could not the same policy be followed in the case of Greece. The answer lay in the conflicting aims of the Allies in the Near East and in the connection between the Monroe Doctrine and the Open Door policy.

The Recognition of Constantine and Allied Policy in the Near East

The issue of Constantine's recognition has little intrinsic historical value. Its significance lies primarily in the manner in which it served to reflect and delineate the global issues that preoccupied the Great Powers during the first quarter of the twentieth century. The First World War and its aftermath generated strong forces that came into play in the race for commercial expansion and territorial realignment. When viewed as a microcosm in this general struggle, the problem assumes a greater significance and helps to explain the intensity with which the Great Powers addressed themselves to its solution.

Historically, France harbored considerable envy of the prestige that Great Britain had acquired in Greece. France was envious of British naval supremacy in the Aegean and of Britain's commercial interests in Greece and Turkey. Above all, the French were fearful of the power which a "protectorate" over an enlarged Greece would give the British in the Eastern Mediterranean. Psychologically, they longed for the prestige that France had enjoyed in the East during the sixteenth and seventeenth centuries. Commercially, they hoped to supplant the British in the markets of the Near East. Politically and practically, they wished to reduce their commitments in Syria and in Cilicia (southern Turkey), a burden which increasingly had been made difficult by their inability to compete with the British navy. The French government also was anxious to arrive at some agreement with Kemal Ataturk that would give France a predominant position in Turkey. Consequently, French policy was directed at the destruction of the Treaty of Sèvres. To the extent that Constantine's return and the recognition of his government might serve to maintain the treaty by unifying the Greek nation politically and militarily, his restoration was to be resisted.

51

Italy's aspirations were similar to those of France, though its military weakness imposed upon the Italian government a more subtle and diplomatic approach in the pursuit of its objectives. Italy maneuvered for a position in Turkey without any political or military responsibilities. This policy gave promise of direct confrontation with neighboring Greece, and so Italy strived for the creation of a weak, not hostile Greek state. At times, when it appeared that there were fundamental disagreements between the French and Italian governments in their policies towards Constantine, those disagreements were superficial and transitory.

Great Britain's Greek policy was necessarily less well-defined. The idea that prompted support of Greece was the need to protect British access to India and the Far East via the Mediterranean and the Suez Canal. Since the Congress of Vienna (1815), Britain had supported Turkey as the first line of defense in the Eastern Mediterranean. When Turkey joined the Central Powers in the First World War, Britain fell back on a second line—a line from Smyrna to Salamis. Geographically, the strategic position of Greece was ideal for the purposes of British foreign policy. Politically, Greece was sufficiently strong to save the British government expense in time of peace and sufficently weak to be subservient in time of war. Thus, the treaty of Sèvres would be an immense asset if it could be preserved in the face of French and Italian efforts to destroy it. In these circumstances, Great Britain was confronted with a dilemma. By striving to protect its interests in the Eastern Mediterranean, Britain would either offend or play into the hands of France. Conversely, Britain could be supportive of French and Italian aims, but not without compromising its position in Greece and Turkey. In an effort to resolve this dilemma, Britain's Greek policy between 1920 and 1922 was often nebulous and contradictory.[14]

The Return of Constantine and the Allied Response

Immediately after the elections of 14 November 1920 the Allies began to search for methods with which to prevent the restoration of Constantine. Despite their traditional support of Venizelos, the French saw the defeat of the ex-premier as an opportunity to solidify their position in the Near East. The Italians were anxious to expand their influence in Asia Minor and were receptive to French suggestions that coercion ought to be used to prevent the king's return. The British were not eager to bring about any fundamental changes in the status quo in the Eastern

Mediterranean, nor were they disposed to see the unconditional restoration of Constantine. The British foreign minister, George N. Curzon, proposed that the Allies continue to support Greece and even to recognize Constantine if Constantine would agree to contract no loans without the approval of the IFC; conclude no political or military convention without the consent of the Allies; undertake no unilateral peace negotiations with Turkey; and dismiss all military officers and officials accused of pro-German activities prior to 1917. Under pressure from the French, however, this proposal was aborted.[15]

It was decided that before any hard ultimatum was presented the attitude of Greek authorities should be ascertained by issuing a warning somewhat general in its tone, but very clear in its implications. On 3 December the French legation, acting on behalf of the Allies, delivered a note to the Greek Foreign Ministry stating that while the governments of Great Britain, France, and Italy had always demonstrated their compassion for the Greek people and had supported their interests, it was with "painful surprise" that they were witnessing recent events in Greece. They did not wish to interfere in the internal affairs of Greece, but at the same time they felt compelled to declare publicly that the restoration to the throne of Greece of a sovereign whose attitude during the war had had a detrimental effect on the Allied war effort could only be considered by them

> as a ratification by Greece of the hostile acts of King Constantine. This fact creates a new, unfavorable situation in the relations between Greece and the Allies, and consequently the three governments declare that they reserve for themselves complete freedom of action in order to regulate this situation.[16]

When the Foreign Ministry failed to offer a satisfactory reply, another note was delivered, describing precisely what retaliatory actions the Allies were prepared to take, including the cessation of all financial aid.

Despite these attempts to intimidate the Greek government, a plebiscite was held on 5 December to decide whether Constantine should be restored to his throne. Although the Venizelists abstained, there were still 1,010,343 votes cast. According to official figures, 999,960 votes (99 percent) were recorded in favor of the king and 10,383 against. While these figures hardly can be accepted as authentic, there is no doubt that public opinion was overwhelmingly in favor of Constantine's return.[17] Three days later France and Great Britain officially informed the Greek government that they would no longer continue their financial support. For political reasons this information was withheld from the people. That decision proved to be a fatal mistake by the Royalists who were to see six of their members executed for treason in November 1922 after the catastrophic campaign in Asia Minor. One of the charges brought against the Six was their failure to inform the country that, in the event of Constantine's return, all French and British financial assistance would be withdrawn.

The American Attitude towards the Regency of Admiral Coundouriotis

On 17 November 1920 Admiral Paul Coundouriotis, in his capacity as Regent, accepted the resignation of Venizelos and administered the oath of office to Demetrios G. Rallis as prime minister. There followed a complicated series of political maneuvers within the government and the court, replete with intrigue and legal hairsplitting that left considerable room to doubt the sincerity and stability of the new government. It was not certain that the Royalists were prepared to honor the commitments nor acknowledge the obligations incurred by Greece during the tenure of Alexander.[18]

The situation became further complicated as political and civil strife increased in intensity. It was now the turn of the Royalists to seek revenge. After the departure of Venizelos there was a noticeable relaxation of discipline among soldiers and police. In the words of the American minister, Edward Capps, "Athens entered upon an orgy of demonstrations" in which numerous soldiers and policemen participated. Political prisoners were released, including the officers who had been imprisoned for the surrender of certain Macedonian garrisons to the Bulgarians during the war. Many high-ranking officers of the army and navy were discharged and replaced by Royalists. Practically all civil service and diplomatic officers of Venizelos' government resigned or were removed. Capps was moved by these events to label Rallis' ministry "semirevolutionary" and to question its claim to legitimacy.[19] Officials in the State Department shared his misgivings and chose to consider the matter of recognition in the most careful way. A crucial factor was the attitude of France, Great Britain, and Italy.

From the point of view of the Allied governments there were three alternatives open to them. One was to accept the inevitable and recognize Constantine as king by the will of his people, without extending to him or to Greece their friendship or cooperation. Another was to withdraw their ministers before his arrival in Greece, leaving chargés d'affaires to carry on the day-to-day business with the Greek government. Finally, they could allow their ministers to remain and carry on formal relations with the government, but ignore the king, the Royal family, and the court. The French and British preferred the second course and the Italians preferred the first. At first it was suggested by the French that the return of Constantine be forbidden, but the Italians would not agree. Unable to arrive at a definite agreement in time, the three powers compromised their positions and selected the third alternative, which was probably the worst of the three. The contradictions inherent in this decision led to serious diplomatic problems between Great Britain and the United States. A meeting was held in London between Lloyd George, Count Sforza, Italian minister of foreign affairs, and Georges Leygues, premier of France, at which a spirit of moderation prevailed and, on 19 December, Constantine was permitted to enter Athens amidst great popular enthusiasm and demonstrations of support.[20]

Anticipating the hostility of the Allies, Constantine once again attempted to use American influence as a protective shield from the punitive measures he expected to incur. Before leaving Switzerland he issued a statement from Lucerne in which he appealed to the sense of fairness of President Wilson and the American people in actively seeking their support. He dismissed his Germanophile reputation as the result of domestic political intrigue and wartime propaganda. He declared his willingness to forget the past and to establish friendly relations with the Allies. He wished to remind the American people that he was, after all, the sovereign of a legally elected government. "I feel more than ever," he said, "as the President of the United States must feel. I, too, have been elected by vote of the people to the high office which I am about to fill and which I formerly occupied by the single constitutional right of heredity."[21]

The Return of Constantine and the American Response

Upon his arrival in Athens Constantine issued a proclamation which contained the usual platitudes, but he made no mention of Venizelos' work. Constantine's failure to be specific on this point prompted American officials to wonder about the new government's attitude towards the credits issued to Greece under the Tripartite Loan of 1918 and all other agreements undertaken during the reign of Alexander. On 28 December, Norman H. Davis, the acting secretary of state, wrote to President Wilson that recent events in Greece raised the issue as to what attitude the United States government should take towards King Constantine. He informed the president that although new credentials technically would be necessary when the new monarch was installed, the department's legal advisers had reached the conclusion that the government of Greece, as it existed under Venizelos, could legally be considered as continuing.[22] This was a clear expression of the Jeffersonian doctrine which put much of its emphasis on the continuity of state life. It was also an indication that the State Department was inclined to consider seriously the issue of recognition.

It is certain that if the matter of legality had been the controlling factor, recognition would have been prompt. The problem, however, was more complex. Overall economic policy, U.S. relations with the Allies, and the chaotic state of Greek politics were important considerations. For these reasons Davis found it necessary to add that Great Britain and France had decided not to grant additional credits and that the French embassy had "suggested" the same course of action by the United States. It was imperative that a decision be made as soon as possible, because the Greek legation was pressing the Treasury Department for a fourth advance of $5,000,000.[23]

In the meantime, the Foreign Ministry in Athens accelerated its efforts. Rallis ignored the technicalities of diplomatic protocol and appeared repeatedly at the American legation to discuss mutual problems with Capps, when it would have been more natural to hold these discussions in the Foreign Ministry (Rallis was also foreign minister). He made a favorable impression on the American minister who suggested to the State Department that the moment was opportune for the opening of discussions regarding a number of issues on which the Foreign Ministry and the State Department had failed to reach agreement. He stressed that the Greek government was endeavoring to establish close and friendly relations with the United States and, in view of the attitude of the Allies, was counting upon American support. Capps urged that State Department to take advantage of the situation. The position of the United States government now became sensitive, since it had to formulate its policy toward Greece within the framework of its financial self-interest and against the wishes of France, Great Britain, and Italy. When the

Division of Near Eastern Affairs inquired of President Wilson what America's Greek policy should be, he replied that he saw no reason why recognition should not be granted as soon as Constantine returned and made a formal announcement of his accession to the throne. New credentials would then be sent. Capps was instructed to proceed on this basis in his discussions with Greek officials. But only one week later these orders were rescinded, and Capps was advised that in the event Greek authorities requested information relative to Washington's attitude he should state that he had no instructions.[24]

The explanation for the sudden change of policy lies in the attitude of the British government. Hitherto, it had been primarily the French who had used their influence to convince the State Department to withhold its recognition. The sources also suggest that Capps informed the British minister in Athens of the United States government's intention to follow an independent policy. It appears, therefore, that the British were caught by surprise. The British government's attitude was not merely an expression of personal antipathy for Constantine. There was apprehension in London that the king would attempt to undermine the war effort in Asia Minor and to nullify the financial agreements of Alexander. Partly as a consequence of British influence, but primarily because of American self-interest the State Department confronted the Greek legation with certain specific questions. It wanted to know if there was a new status quo, if the present regime recognized the legitimacy of Alexander's government, and if agreements undertaken during the absence of King Constantine were considered valid.[25] The Foreign Ministry responded with evasive replies.

By mid-January, it had become clear that the Royalists had decided to develop a line of reasoning designed to treat Alexander's tenure on the throne as a mere interlude in the reign of his father. They argued that Constantine had never ceased to be King because he had never signed formal papers of abdication. He had only to choose the time and occasion that seemed to him most appropriate for returning to Greece and assuming his Royal prerogative. It is true that Constantine did not abdicate to the extent of signing a legal document. But, Jonnart agreed to go along with the proposal with the understanding that the abdication was complete and final in spite of the fact that the formal act was not executed. Whether Constantine and his counselors viewed this episode in the same light, at the time, is uncertain and probably doubtful.[26] The momentary weakness of Jonnart in making this concession to the pride of the deposed king furnished a very good basis for Constantine's claim to legitimacy.

The new ministers forged ahead, applying their theory whenever and wherever possible. They were inclined to issue a sweeping decree invalidating every act of the Greek government during Alexander's tenure, but since this action would have negated the benefits derived from the Treaties of Sèvres and Neuilly, they did not dare to do so. Instead, they resorted to piecemeal legislation in order to revoke such acts as suited their purposes. It was this particular aspect of their policy that disturbed the Treasury and State Departments, as well as American businessmen. "Athens," wrote Capps, was "full of contractors vainly seeking to learn where they stand."[27]

Despite these reservations and the hostile opposition of France and Great Britain, the State Department was prepared to act independently if it seemed that decisive action was essential to the protection of American interests in Greece and Turkey.[28] Consequently, when the Greek chargé, George Dracopoulos, officially informed the United States government on 12 January of Constantine's accession to the throne, he was called to the Division of Near Eastern Affairs for a candid discussion of the main issues on which the two governments had not reached agreement. He was told that while the United States accepted Constantine's return in principle, no reply could be given to his note until a formal announcement, signed by Constantine and addressed to the president, was received by the State Department. He was confidentially informed, however, that after consultation with President Wilson, the United States government "was inclined to consider favorably the recognition of King Constantine" as soon as the Greek monarch complied with the department's request. Secretary of State Bainbridge Colby assured the Greek chargé that the American attitude towards Greece was friendly and sympathetic. The secretary then made the surprising revelation that the government of the United States did not agree with the policy of France and Great Britain towards Greece. Colby said that he considered the Greek people to be free to follow whatever political course they chose, and he respected their wish to have Constantine on the throne. It was not his country's desire to interfere in the internal questions of Europe. Dracopoulos was also informed of the American government's willingness to consider additional credits for Greece under the terms of the Tripartite Loan, if the recognition problem could be resolved and if the money would not be used to maintain the Greek army in Asia Minor. Following the conversation with Dracopoulos, Davis advised Capps that, in the opinion of the State Department, Constantine's accession to the throne and Venizelos' overthrow were the result of a legal plebiscite. American recognition, therefore, should not be refused.[29]

Although these discussions were held under the guise of strict confidentiality, subsequent events indicate that the Wilson administration wanted to make its position well-known in order to leave no doubt where it stood in relation to the Eastern Mediterranean and the Near East. On 15 January the *New York Times* published an article in which the essential parts of the discussions with Dracopoulos were outlined. The position of the State Department was stated tersely. The attitude of the United States was not associated with that of the British and French governments, and the United States was considering the problem of recognition independently.[30] Greek officials were elated. Rallis went about spreading the good news by announcing the imminent recognition of the United States government and the release of the remaining American credits.

In view of the dominant role exercised by the Western powers in Greek affairs, the United States government's efforts to assert itself might appear fanciful. However, American officials were becoming frustrated by their inability to act independently and by the interminable petty obstacles that hampered their freedom of action. Undersecretary of State Leland Harrison reflected the sentiment of his colleagues when he questioned the wisdom of America's Greek policy. The time had come for the United States to ask itself if continuing to follow the line of France, Great Britain, and Italy was in the best interests of America, or whether recognition would put the United States in a stronger position in Greece, and thus give it a commercial advantage over the other three Powers.[31] Every possibility was explored in order to find an escape from the dilemma.

In late January the State Department renewed its efforts to obtain a firm commitment from the Greek government relative to the status of Alexander's reign. The Division of Near Eastern Affairs informed the Foreign Ministry once again that, since the United States government had recognized Alexander as King of Greece,[32] the question of Constantine's succession could only be decided between chiefs of state. This interpretation required that Constantine address a formal communication to President Wilson, informing him of his accession (or reaccession, if that word suited the king better) to the throne. The demand by the State Department that "accession" or "reaccession" be used in any formal communication was not mere legal hairsplitting. It would be an admission that a legitimate government had existed prior to the king's restoration.[33]

The validity of the American position was recognized by Premier Rallis who promised Capps that he would attempt to persuade the king to write a letter to President Wilson that would include every guarantee the State Department was seeking. After considerable hesitation, Constantine, in what he hoped would be interpreted as a form of capitulation, sent a letter to the president in which he wrote: "I . . . have assumed the throne as a result of having been summoned by the unanimous suffrage of the Hellenic people. [I hope that you will be] gratified to see my accession and that you will be disposed to accord me your highly valued friendship in the exercise of my royal dignity."[34]

Constantine's announcement had a positive effect, for it appeared to clear the way to serious negotiations. The Greek chargé was received unofficially on several occasions at the State Department and was assured that any communications, written or oral, he cared to make would be given immediate attention, since the question of recognition was being given serious consideration. On 15 March the New York Times reported that active negotiations had begun and that recognition was imminent.[35] To this series of events was added the resignation of Minister Capps on the day of President Warren G. Harding's inauguration, only one day after the Greek chargé had delivered Constantine's letter to the State Department. The combined effect of these circumstances, especially the departure of Capps, produced considerable optimism among Royalists who interpreted these developments as the first steps toward recognition.

The attitude of the United States also was influenced by the need to resolve several outstanding issues. Most important were the impeding negotiations relative to a commercial treaty which would give the United States most-favored-nation treatment, the settlement of war debts, and the expansion of American capital in Greece. Regarding the second point, American officials admitted that the United States was morally obligated to grant the remaining credits and the only way it could justify its failure to do so would be the continuance of nonrecognition. "This course seems to be small and unworthy of us," wrote the undersecretary of state.[36]

Allied Efforts to Influence American Policy

Throughout the spring of 1921 the Royalist press complained that Constantine's failure to gain American recognition was the result of a tacit understanding between the United States and the Allies, which in practical terms amounted to a Monroe Doctrine for the Eastern Mediterranean. This assertion was justified by historical precedent and by events taking place behind the scenes. Traditionally, the United States refrained from active political involvement in the Near East, while Great Britain played a key role in support of the Monroe Doctrine. In Mexico, where there were ample opportunities for justifiable intervention and where Britain could have led a coalition of disgruntled European governments seeking redress to various claims, it acted as a restraining influence and followed a policy that was supportive of American interests. With this historical relationship in mind, officials in the British Foreign Office approached the State Department in a spirit of moderation and appealed for American support of Allied policy in Greece.

During the first week in January, Sir Auckland Geddes, the British ambassador in Washington, visited the State Department in an effort to convince American officials that the United States should join France, Great Britain, and Italy in applying economic pressure to bring about the fall of Constantine's government. Geddes was willing to accept American support, even in a nominal sense, because he understood Washington's reluctance to become involved in the domestic politics of Greece. He added that it was not necessary for the United States government to declare its opposition openly. He said that the U.S. could effectively withhold recognition through the use of a wide variety of procrastinating devices. What the British wanted was a promise that no further credits or new loans would be granted to Greece. The withholding of American financial assistance would complete the economic blockade already implemented by the Allies. Without financial aid, Constantine's government would collapse because the Asia Minor campaign had begun to have serious consequences on the Greek economy.[37] The State Department's reply was sympathetic, but vague—it understood the Allies' position, and the matter would be studied in light of American interests in the area.

In the meantime, France and Italy were becoming anxious. Unlike the British, who traditionally enjoyed closer ties with the United States and had a merchant marine which surpassed the American commercial fleet, the French and Italians were limited in the number of ships they could build. These nations had emerged from the war with their economies greatly weakened. Yet, both had definite maritime aspirations. It was with considerable alarm that they watched the expansion of the American commercial presence in the Mediterranean. Their feelings were best expressed in the words of an Italian writer in reviewing an American book on the role of modern navies. The author ventured the hopeful, but complacent, opinion that British-American cooperation, together with naval supremacy, would best insure the peace of the world. " 'Peace of the world,' the reviewer echoed, 'why not rather the enslavement of the world?' "[38] Thus, the Italians assisted the French in their attempts to involve the British in a joint effort to control the commercial penetration of the United States in the Near East via the Monroe Doctrine.[39] The background to the problem is as follows.

After the downfall of President Porfirio Diaz in 1911, Mexico was convulsed by a revolution that reduced the country to a state of collapse by 1914. Numerous leaders and regimes had succeeded one another with the result that drastic economic measures were undertaken to save the country from complete economic chaos. Foreign holders of petroleum lands saw their titles suddenly converted to fifty-year leaseholds under an increasingly complex and burdensome tax system which ultimately bankrupted the country. The revolution brought about the suspension of interest and amortization on Mexico's bonded public debt, nearly all of which was held by foreign nationals. Since the suspension of payments had continued for almost two decades, accumulated interest rapidly augmented the total indebtedness. French citizens held the largest share of this debt, followed by the British and the Americans.[40] When General Álvaro Obregón was elected president on 5 September 1920, he sought American recognition by offering his personal assurances for the security of American property and American citizens in Mexico and for the repayment of loans held by American bondholders. His promises, however, were ambiguous and bound only himself and his administration. Under these circumstances the United States refused to recognize the Mexican government. France and Great Britain followed the American example and withheld their recognition. In the broadest sense, therefore, the issues inherent in the recognition of Obregón were not unlike those which related to the recognition of Constantine.

The French became especially aggressive in their efforts to sway

American policy. They made it clear that France would "deplore" recognition of the Greek government and that "severe consequences" would follow a unilateral American action in this regard. American officials tried to persuade the French embassy that domestic pressures from a variety of sources were being brought to bear on the United States government to appoint a minister to Greece. Jules Jusserand, the French ambassador in Washington, reminded the undersecretary of state, Henry P. Fletcher, that he had kept his government from recognizing Obregón, despite pressure from French interests in Mexico. Fletcher acknowledged the French government's restraint in this respect, but expressed the hope that some compromise might be arranged. Jusserand refused, however, to waiver and continued to apply diplomatic pressure. The uncompromising attitude of the French was only partly due to diplomatic considerations. Their feelings toward Constantine bordered on hatred. Government officials in Paris readily admitted to the American ambassador their intense dislike for the Greek king, whom they held responsible for the "massacre" of French troops near Athens in December 1916.[41]

State Department officials next turned to the British legation in Washington. They complained that the British government was exploiting both the Mexican and the Greek situations unfairly. It was pointed out that the presence of a minister in the British legation in Athens permitted London to carry on diplomatic relations with Constantine's government in fact, if not in name. The British retorted that the magnitude of the financial commitment in Mexico by British nationals gave Great Britain the right to protect the interests of her citizens. The presence of a minister in Athens, on the other hand, was in complete accord with her role as a Protecting Power and as a member of the IFC. The British representative acted in a ministerial capacity in matters relating to Britain's dual role in Greece. In all other instances the minister carried on only the functions of a chargé d'affaires.[42]

The British government's attitude was not the result of uncompromising intransigence. Despite many public disclaimers, Great Britain was willing to recognize Constantine, if some compromise could be arranged. The Foreign Office was interested in strengthening Greece so that she could play an effective military role in Asia Minor. Ultimately, it was Franco-Italian hostility, political opposition at home, and negative public opinion that proved decisive in Britain's Greek policy.[43]

Eventually, American officials were forced to acknowledge their inability to act independently. The chief of the Division of Near Eastern Affairs, Warren D. Robbins, admitted to the undersecretary of state that the attitude of the Allies was the overriding consideration. He wrote in part:

> Mr. Vouros' desire to bring the matter [of recognition] formally to the attention of the Secretary [of State] seems to me inopportune, for he bases the failure of the United States to recognize the Government of King Constantine upon a misunderstanding. As you are well aware, this is not the case. We have known for some time the points which he again sets forth. It does not seem as if there were any points of international law which would warrant our refusing to recognize Constantine but the matter hinges entirely, as I see it, on international policy wholly distinct from international right.[44]

Allen W. Dulles later admitted that the "Greek precedent indicates the importance of general policy upon recognition." No definite rules can be fixed, for "while circumstances may justify recognition, there is no legal duty to accord it."[45] Despite the fact that the government of Constantine had satisfied every legal and doctrinaire requirement, recognition remained elusive.

The Greeks' anxiety reached its climax when, in the spring of 1922, Premier Demetrios Gounaris practically begged the American chargé, Jefferson Caffery, to inform the State Department that in return for American recognition, the Foreign Ministry was disposed to meet "practically any terms" of the United States government.[46] As the months passed, Greek representatives in Washington watched with dismay at the refusal of the United States to act independently in the face of Allied pressure. They were led to believe repeatedly that recognition was imminent, only to see each opportunity slip by as one obstacle after another presented itself. Greek representatives in Washington were aware of the broad and complex issues inherent in the problem of recognition, and they attempted to instill in their superiors at the Foreign Ministry an appreciation of the fundamental role of Central America. It is evident that they were not entirely successful. Neither Constantine nor the Foreign Ministry was oblivious to the problem, but each failed to comprehend its full significance. George Baltatzes, for example, found the American attitude "totally unexpected,"[47] when there was ample evidence to the contrary, while Constantine criticized the United States by asking: "What relationship does Mexico have with me?" As late as April

1922 John Gennadius, a special envoy of the king who had been sent to the United States to defend the Royalists' side, was at a loss to explain Washington's attitude. He could understand how European entanglements forced the Allies to withhold their recognition, but the United States was "perfectly free" to act independently.[48] One must assume that these attitudes betray a serious lack of appreciation for the forces which were helping to shape the policies of the European powers.

Latin-American Interest in Greek Politics

Political events in Greece from 1920 to 1922 had an impact of considerable proportions. But because Greece always has been a small country, it is natural to underestimate the importance of issues which were at the center of Constantine's recognition. The fact is that not only Europe and the United States, but much of Latin America took an interest in the matter. One reason was the desire of Greece and several Latin American nations to establish closer commercial ties. Another was the hope that American recognition would produce retaliatory action by European governments in the Western Hemisphere. In that event, the Monroe Doctrine would be weakened to the advantage of Latin American governments. The Greek minister in Rio de Janeiro reported that Brazil and the other South American nations generally were eager to recognize Constantine but they needed some sign from Washington, "for if the United States offers recognition, all the Republics of South America will follow without hesitation."[49]

By 1921 the Greek legation and the Foreign Ministry began to change their strategy. They attempted to circumvent the executive branch and to present their case directly to Congress and the American people. The emphasis shifted to the United States, where the struggle between Royalists and Venizelists reached new levels of intensity and violence.[50] The diplomatic correspondence from January to September 1922, is extensive but it does not contribute substantially to the issues. By July 1922 the deterioration of the Greek military effort in Asia Minor would intervene to change the strategy of the State Department. Secretary of State Charles Evans Hughes noted, in a speech before the Council on Foreign Relations, that separate action by the United States at such a crucial point in time hardly could have been interpreted in any other way than as an expression of support for Constantine's militaristic policy in Asia

Minor and as an indirect participation in the politics of the Near East.[51] Thus matters stood until the destruction of the Greek army in Asia Minor, the burning of Smyrna, and the second abdication of Constantine introduced a new phase in Greek-American diplomacy.

Constantine abdicated and left Greece for the last time on 27 September 1922, believing he had been betrayed. He harbored a strong resentment against the United States. In a lengthy interview with an American correspondent, he gave full vent to his frustrations by attacking what he considered to be the hypocrisy of the United States government. He said in part:

> Why didn't . . . [America] recognize me? What kind of a republic is she? I cannot understand the policy of America. Many of the difficulties with which Greece has met can be attributed to the fact that America did not recognize me. Why didn't she recognize me?—Because of the stupid issue of Mexico.[52]

On 11 January 1923, he died in Palermo, bringing to an end one of the most turbulent political careers since the creation of the modern Greek State.

The significance of Greek-American diplomacy from 1920 to 1922 is essentially a reflection of two developments. First, during this period more involved political relations between Greece and the United States were initiated. The controversy surrounding Constantine's restoration was simply one catalyst in that process. Second, the connection between the Monroe Doctrine and the Open Door policy, as it concerns Greece, reveals an American interest which is generally underestimated. The steady expansion of American influence in the Eastern Mediterranean in the face of strong Allied opposition is indicative of the fact that Greece was becoming a factor in the United States government's overall Near East policy.

5
Constantine and the Forced Loan of 1922

By the spring of 1922 Greece's Asia Minor campaign had taken its toll in terms of human life and financial resources. The national treasury was nearly empty, and the country was facing economic chaos. The financial plight of the Greek government was intensified further by the virtual cessation of remittances from Greek immigrants in the United States.[1] After credits were established by France, Great Britain, and the United States under the terms of the 1918 Tripartite Loan the Venizelos government printed additional currency equal to the face value of the loan. When British and American advances were stopped after the elections of November 1920, the detrimental consequences of this short-sighted fiscal policy gradually began to surface. The financial boycott of Constantine's government which attended the nonrecognition policy of France and Great Britain was in large measure responsible for the difficulties in which Greece found herself.

From October 1921 to March 1922 all efforts to raise a loan in British and American markets failed. The Greek government, therefore, was left with no alternative but to seek a solution within the limits of the country's resources. The imposition of new taxes or the printing of new money were unacceptable alternatives—in each case the solution was worse than the problem itself. It was under these circumstances that Minister of Finance Petros Protopapadakes conceived his unique plan to force the Greek citizenry to loan the government a portion of its cash holdings.

Background to the Forced Loan

Before turning to the Forced Loan and its effect on Greek-American relations, it is necessary to give some attention to the events which preceded it. The background to this problem is as pertinent to the general topic of this work as it is to the technical nature of the loan itself. On 2 October 1921 Demetrios Gounaris, the prime minister, and George Baltatzes, minister of foreign affairs, traveled to London at the invitation of the British government to negotiate a loan for the prosecution of the war in Asia Minor.[2] The need was acute, partly as a result of the Allied financial blockade and partly as a consequence of the summer offensive undertaken by Constantine's government. Since a new government loan or additional advances under the Tripartite Agreement were out of the question, the Greek leaders sought British permission to negotiate a private loan in the London market. Article 4 of the 1918 loan agreement stated that Greece could not offer any new guarantees for a foreign loan without the permission of the three lending nations and not until all obligations arising from that agreement had been liquidated.

The British government saw the opportunity to rid itself of the troublesome credits (a balance of £5,500,000 remained on the books) and to provide indirect assistance to the Greek war effort,[3] while simultaneously avoiding the thorny problem of recognition. On 22 December, an agreement was reached by which Gounaris and Baltatzes were given permission to seek a loan in the British market on condition that the Greek government renounce its right to the remaining credits and that most of the money be spent in the purchase of British products.[4] Article 2 was especially significant. It stated: "The Greek Government agree that no part of the proceeds of any loan raised in Great Britain shall be applied towards repayment of [the $15,000,000] advances made to the Greek Government by the Government of the United States of America."[5] The unilateral action of the British and the inclusion of Article 2 in the pact were received by the State and Treasury Departments with indignation and concern. The State Department protested to the British government by pointing to Article 4 in the Tripartite agreement, and assumed that the Greek representatives had been reminded of the necessity to gain the consent of France and the United States before offering any security for a new loan.

American apprehensions centered on the prospect that the State Department would be placed in an embarrassing position, if British firms profited from the British-Greek arrangement, while the procrastination of the United States resulted in a loss of business for American financial institutions. Although it was against American policy to make loans to unrecognized governments, the State Department undoubtedly would have been subject to criticism if one of the results of the nonrecognition policy of the United States, which was designed not to offend Great Britain, had been not to stop the British themselves from effecting a profitable arrangement. This point was sensitive in view of the fact that American banking firms had the same opportunity to profit from a Greek loan. The State Department also resented the action of the British government, whose membership in the IFC and whose freedom to influence Greek politics gave it an advantage not available to the United States.

These considerations prompted the economic adviser to the Division of Near Eastern Affairs, Dr. Arthur N. Young, to recommend that, in the event the British-Greek agreement was formalized, American recognition of Constantine should be immediate, without reservations, and without consulting any other power. Ultimately, the British loan failed to materialize. There is little doubt that American protests were at the center of that failure,[6] though other factors played a part. The opposition in Parliament, the hostility of the British press, and the negative attitude of British public opinion combined to defeat the entire scheme. The role of France and Italy was negligible because there was sufficient opposition to the agreement to make their intervention unnecessary.

It is not clear why the British government agreed to take unilateral action in a matter that would probably meet with serious opposition. However, the available sources permit certain reasonable, though hypothetical, conclusions. The British felt responsible for the Greek presence in Asia Minor and wished to do something about it. Since another government loan would have met with the opposition of Parliament and since French and Italian support was out of the question, a private loan seemed to be the logical alternative. Given the State Department's inclination to follow the British example in matters affecting the politics of

Greece, it is probable that London believed it could confront Washington successfully with an accomplished fact. By mid-February, however, it had become obvious that opposition to the loan was too strong. In response to urgent appeals by Gounaris, Curzon answered that the conclusion of a loan in the British market was improbable, if not impossible.[7]

The Greek Economic Mission to the United States

While the negotiations in London were taking place, the Greek government attempted to influence public opinion in the United States and, at the same time, to secure a loan in the American market. By autumn 1921 Constantine had become convinced that he must by-pass the American legation and make a direct appeal to American public opinion, to the United States Congress and to the Harding administration. Relations between the court and the American chargé d'affaires, Barton Hall, were strained. Hall's attitude towards the king and his family was hostile and often lacking in tact; a fact that made him a controversial figure within the diplomatic community in Athens and in the Division of Near Eastern Affairs. Consequently, Constantine turned to an old friend, Paxton Hibben, who was serving as an official of Near East Relief in New York.[8] Hibben was asked by the Greek legation to act as an intermediary between the Foreign Ministry and American officials. He was instructed to lay the case of Greece before the State Department and to reiterate the Greek government's determination to honor all agreements of Alexander's government. On 27 October Hibben had separate interviews with the secretary of state, Charles Evans Hughes, and the chief of the Division of Near Eastern Affairs, Warren Robbins, but both remained unimpressed. Robbins argued that in view of the recent Greek offensive in Asia Minor, the recognition of Constantine and an American loan to the Greek government could only be construed as siding with Greece against Turkey.[9] This pronouncement is significant because it shows that after the summer of 1921 the issue of recognition was no longer based on legal considerations alone, but on American interests in Turkey as well.[10] Hibben remained undaunted and continued to promote the case of the Royalist government through his connections in the State Department and in American financial circles.

On a more official level Constantine's private campaign in the United States consisted of a three-man economic mission headed by John Gennadius, special envoy of the Greek government and former minister to Great Britain, and Stamos Papafrangos, special envoy and solicitor to the National Bank of Greece. The third member of the group was Brainerd P. Salmon, chairman of the American Chamber of Commerce in Greece, whose role was unofficial, but integral, because he represented the interests of American firms in Greece. The idea of an economic mission was apparently the brainchild of Paxton Hibben who also made specific recommendations relative to the persons who should serve on it.[11] Papafrangos was the expert on finances, and so he was involved primarily in loan negotiations. Gennadius concentrated his efforts on the political question of recognition, while Salmon used his extensive contacts within the business sector to promote the growth of Greek-America commercial relations. The three problems were interconnected, so that each man complemented the efforts of the others.

The three men had reasons to be optimistic. Influential persons in the American government and in the private sector were pressing the State Department to look with favor upon the appeals of the Greek government. The Department of Commerce was interested in trade with Greece. The assistant director of the Bureau of Foreign and Domestic Commerce, L. R. Robinson, acknowledged the diplomatic problems posed by the nonrecognition policy of the United States, but he recommended that the question could be reopened in view of the unilateral action of the British. He stressed that Great Britain and the United States were "neck and neck in competition." He was also apprehensive about the possible detrimental effects of the British-Greek financial agreement. These sentiments were echoed by Salmon, who pointed out to the State Department the difficulties encountered by American business in the absence of a minister in Athens. The State Department agreed with this assessment, but could do very little since, under existing circumstances, recognition was primarily a political question and a matter of major policy.[12]

Numerous appeals also were made by banking firms wishing to participate in a private loan to Greece. They made clear their intention to seek assurances from the Greek government that not a single dollar would be spent for war purposes.[13] The secretary of commerce, Herbert Hoover, agreed with the administration's desire to promote the use of American money abroad for productive purposes, but under prevailing conditions it could be expected that any loan for national rehabilitation would release funds which could be used for the prosecution of war. The loan would constitute indirect support of Constantine's militaristic policy in Asia Minor and, in practical terms, a direct American involvement in Greek military affairs.[14] Hughes reinforced the secretary's estimate of the situation by reiterating the United States government's intention not to view with favor a loan to an unrecognized government.

In the six months after October 1921 the Greek delegation went about its business at a hectic pace. Their activities generated considerable interest and helped to fuel a second round in the Constantine-Venizelos controversy that probably surpassed in intensity the turbulence of the first one. The Royalist strategy centered on the thesis that the rise of Venizelos to power was the result of British and French intervention. The Greek people had been deprived of their constitutional rights. The United States government and American Greeks, therefore, had the moral obligation to support Greece and to raise their voices in protest against such undemocratic practices.

The Role of Venizelos in the United States

These activities coincided with the presence of Venizelos in the United States. He arrived from London in late October for what was ostensibly a vacation and a honeymoon trip.[15] His arrival also coincided with the opening of the Washington Conference on Limitation of Armaments. This coincidence and the presence of the Greek economic mission had obvious political implications which alarmed Secretary of State Hughes. He suggested to the British Ambassador in September that the British government intervene to postpone the trip, but this effort failed.[16]

The secretary's concern proved well-founded. Venizelos traveled widely and took full advantage of the "banquet circuit" in areas where there were high concentrations of Greek-Americans. As the months passed, his activities assumed an increasingly political character. His supporters in America were enthusiastic in response to his speeches. They interpreted his visit as a prelude to the emergence of a new Venizelist regime in Greece which would have not only the traditional support of the Allies, but of the United States as well. This optimism was given impetus by the personal meeting on 11 April 1922 between Venizelos and the secretary of state. The Venizelist Greek-American newspaper, *Ethnikos Kerix* (National Herald), published a distorted article in which it reported a promise by Hughes that under no condition would the government of Constantine be recognized by the United States.[17]

Greek officials watched these developments with dismay and became anxious lest their efforts prove futile both in London and Washington. Possibly as a gesture of submission, Gennadius made what was surely a major concession. He admitted that the British agreement had abrogated the Tripartite Loan and declared his government's willingness to accept the consequences of that abrogation. It is more realistic to suppose, however, that for the moment the Foreign Ministry had written off the balance of the 1918 credits and was seeking a private loan as the logical alternative. This rationale is reflected in the attitude of government officials in Athens. The acting minister of foreign affairs told Caffery that Greece was ready to renounce all claims on the balance of the American credits if the United States were willing to give its consent to a new loan in the American market.[18] The State Department, however, remained adamant in its refusal to be drawn into a scheme with unforeseeable consequences. In these circumstances the Greek government was left with no choice but to seek a radical solution to its financial difficulties.

The Forced Loan and Its Effect on American Citizens

On 22 March/4 April, Minister of Finance Petros Protopapadakes spoke before Parliament. He painted a bleak picture of the military situation and the state of the public treasury; then he proposed a controversial plan of funding fiduciary currency by literally forcing the Greek people to lend their government a portion of their cash holdings. The novelty of the operation caused somewhat of a sensation in American and European financial circles.[19]

The Forced Loan was carried out literally by a stroke of the scissors on 25 March/7 April, when the law was drafted, enacted by the Parliament, promulgated, and put into force. All persons possessing bank notes of 5, 10, 25, 500, and 1,000 drachmas were required to appear at their nearest bank to receive new currency which was printed in two equal parts. One half, bearing the picture of the founder of the Bank of Greece, constituted legal tender and was given to the original holder. The other half, bearing the imprint of the Royal Crown, constituted a twenty-year bond at 6½ percent interest and was retained by the bank. In this way the circulating currency was reduced effectively from 3,200,000,000 drachmas ($1,454,545,454) to 1,600,000,000 drachmas ($727,272,727).[20]

It was necessary to insert numerous special clauses in the law to reduce the Draconian effects of its provisions. One was to permit the settlement of all debts existing on 7 April in old currency, provided that such settlement was effected within three months (later reduced to eight weeks). Another was to require the National Bank to make loans upon the collateral security of the bond halves. In addition, saving deposits were excluded if they satisfied certain technical requirements. Finally, foreigners were exempted provided that they applied formally for exemption to their respective legations within ninety days after 7 April. It was this provision which was at the center of much of the controversy surrounding Americans. The law was of special interest to American importers and exporters, primarily because of the expansion in Greek-American commercial relations since the beginning of World War I. While in absolute terms the increase in trade was not extremely large, in relative terms it possessed considerable potential for future growth. The total trade between the two countries increased from $5,000,000 in 1914 to $51,000,000 for the calendar year of 1921—an increase of more than 1,000 percent.[21]

The haste with which the Forced Loan was implemented gave rise to many difficulties and technical problems. The main issue was the fundamental nature of the loan. It was intended strictly as a piece of municipal legislation directed at the domestic market. However, the ambiguity of its provisions resulted in inconsistencies which led to international complications. The unforeseen consequences of the law compelled the Greek government to attach amendments on a piecemeal basis, with little attention to the rules of elementary logic. The result was a maze of contradictions and wide disparities between theory and practice which taxed the talents of the State Department's financial advisers.

The effects of the Forced Loan upon American commerce and American citizens living in Greece were the cause of much distress. Debts owned to foreigners, whose legal residences and business operations were abroad, had to be paid in full legal tender. However, foreign debtors who had established themselves in Greece could not enjoy the privilege of paying in old currency during the ninety-day grace period. These provisions meant that foreign creditors would be in possession of drachmas whose value during and after the grace period would not be diminished by the effects of the Forced Loan. On the other hand, foreign debtors residing in Greece were not exempted in any way. There were immediate protests from American and European businessmen who charged that they were being forced to participate in the solution of a financial problem that was purely domestic. Consequently, special arrangements were made for the exemption of drachmas belonging to citizens of foreign countries who were in Greece on 7 April. These people were given ninety days to declare their respective legations in order to qualify for their exemption; however, the deadline for the fulfillment of this requirement was extended several times.

The issue was complicated further by three remaining problems. First, no provision was made for the exemptions of currency held abroad by foreigners or by naturalized American citizens of Greek descent who were merely visitors in Greece at the time. Second, the status of Smyrna remained unclear and controversial. Third, foreign bank accounts in Greece and accounts in Greek banks abroad could be "blocked" in order to control the supply of foreign currency in the national treasury. These factors combined to cause great friction between the American legation and the Greek government.

The problem regarding Greek currency held abroad was the most serious. Many American citizens of Greek origin had savings accounts in branches of Greek banks in the United States and elsewhere. The Greek government argued that all drachmas circulating abroad, either in the possession of individuals or in bank accounts, were being used for purposes of speculation. They constituted a commodity which could not be exempted from the provisions of the law. That this line of reasoning was a contradiction that negated the municipal character of the law was a technicality which was not permitted to interfere with the matter of expediency. Consequently, many depositors abroad found their savings accounts temporarily blocked.

Smyrna represented a peculiar problem. There were a large number of American firms in Smyrna, and they did not come under the protection accorded to foreigners in Greece proper. In the view of the Greek government, the Greek-occupied sector of Asia Minor had not been annexed to Greece formally, and could only be considered foreign territory for the purposes of the Forced Loan. To exempt foreigners in Smyrna would be impractical inasmuch as such action would constitute a precedent which would have to be followed in all countries of the world. State Department officials protested by emphasizing the domestic character of the loan, which gave it no greater legal force in Smyrna than in any other part of the world. The only legal controlling factor, they argued, was the Treaty of 1830 between the United States and the

Ottoman Empire. Under Articles 1 and 3 of the treaty, American merchants in Smyrna " 'shall not in any way be vexed or molested and shall not be disturbed in their affairs.' " But the Greek government could not be persuaded to alter its policy, which resulted in high tensions among those in the diplomatic corps. The situation was aggravated further by revelations showing that Greek authorities in Smyrna had made certain exceptions in favor of British commercial interests to the detriment of American business. In conjunction with more than a dozen of his colleagues, Caffery signed a collective note protesting such a discriminatory policy.[22] Before any definitive solution to this problem could be reached, the catastrophe in Asia Minor intervened to make the entire question academic.

The American legation also had found itself embroiled in the controversy surrounding the status of naturalized Americans of Greek origin who were temporarily in Greece. Hughes advised Caffery to request that Greek authorities grant to this class of persons the same exemption accorded to other foreigners. The ministers of finance and foreign affairs were reluctant to go along with Caffery's request for the justifiable reason that it would be too difficult to control fraud. Nevertheless, Caffery persisted in his appeals. Finally, the Foreign Ministry agreed to help alleviate the financial plight of naturalized Americans. Gounaris asserted that the Greek government did not consider the United States to possess most-favored-nation treaty rights in connection with the Forced Loan, but he would be willing to grant favored treatment to American citizens and companies if the American legation would undertake the responsibility of controlling fraudulent claims to exemption. The Greek government reserved the right to pass final judgment on any claim it deemed excessive.

Greek authorities also objected to American efforts to exempt all Greeks holding American passports because many persons were in Greece ostensibly for the purpose of visiting friends and relatives while, in reality, they were engaged in private business. It seemed unfair that these entrepreneurs should attempt to avoid entirely the participation of their bank notes in the Loan.[23] Eventually, a compromise was reached whereby only those Greeks who had become American citizens before 1914 would be exempted.

The American legation, in close cooperation with the several consulates in Greece, did an effective job of drawing up authentic lists of persons and firms to be exempted. Blocked accounts also were released gradually from the restrictions of the law. Smyrna represented a serious problem because of a fire which had destroyed practically all pertinent files. After more than a year of tedious work, the process was completed and compensation was made to the general satisfaction of both sides. On 22 October 1923, Ray Atherton, who had replaced Caffery, sent a note to the foreign minister which formally ended the controversy. The note read: "The Legation takes this occasion to express the appreciation for the courtesies of the Royal Foreign Office in the settling of American citizens and concerns for exemption from the Forced Loan."[24]

Because of the technical nature of this episode, the Forced Loan of 1922 can be seen easily as an aberration in Greek-American relations during the interwar period. The opposite, in fact, is true. From this incident arose guidelines which influenced Greek-American commercial relations for the next two decades. A careful reading of the contractual agreements of the period attests to this fact.[25] The American commercial attaché pointed to the significance of the problem in April 1922 when he wrote: "There is little doubt that one of the most serious problems which our commercial relations with Greece are now confronted is [the Forced Loan]."[26] American participation in this affair was basically an introduction to the technical pitfalls inherent in the process of doing business in Greece. The lessons learned from this experience proved a valuable asset for American corporations and financial houses which undertook business ventures in Greece during the ensuing two decades.

In 1926 another forced loan was imposed by General Theodore Pangalos; however, it was more limited in its application and much less significant in its international implications. The law affected only one-fourth of the notes in circulation, it involved no blocked accounts, and it was contained within the geographical limits of the country. The most important controversy that arose was a difference of opinion between the Foreign Ministry and the State Department regarding the status of American diplomatic officials in Greece. After the fall of Pangalos and the return of Venizelos in 1928 the matter was settled speedily.[27]

6

Political Relations from the Destruction of Smyrna to the Promulgation of the Greek Republic, 1922–1924

The period from the autumn of 1922 to the spring of 1924 represents a new phase in the political relations between Greece and the United States. It is a time during which the issue of recognition remained at the center of Greek-American diplomacy, though the forces which came to dominate this problem were different.

When a revolutionary government was established in Greece after the destruction of Smyrna in September 1922, two fundamental questions arose which affected relations between the new regime and the State Department. One involved the legitimacy of the new status quo; the other concerned itself with the prospects for lasting domestic tranquillity. The problem of legitimacy was treated on the basis of established United States policy relative to the recognition of the Central American republics. Internal political and social stability proved a far more difficult problem to resolve. Political executions, the uncertainty surrounding the negotiations at Lausanne, the emotional issue of the monarchy versus the republic, and British-French rivalry in the New East forced the State Department to assume a policy of noncommitment. The Greek Foreign Ministry was relentless in its efforts to soften the attitude of the

United States government and to hasten the recognition of the new revolutionary regime. American recognition was finally granted in January 1924, after the British government tacitly gave its permission by granting its own recognition. When the promulgation of the republic was given popular sanction by a plebiscite on 13 April 1924, the way was opened for the appointment of a minister to Greece and the restoration of normal diplomatic relations.

The Establishment of a Revolutionary Government in Athens

On 7 May 1919 the Allies, with the approval of President Wilson, gave Venizelos permission to land troops in Smyrna, ostensibly for the purpose of protecting all Christians in the area.[1] Eight days later the Greek landing was accomplished under the protection of Allied warships. Soon afterwards, with the expressed approval of the Allies, the Greek forces extended their area of jurisdiction to include not only Smyrna, but an ample hinterland as well. The landing eventually was given the force of legality by the terms of the Treaty of Sèvres in August 1920.

In the beginning there was considerable optimism that this military venture would succeed. Greece enjoyed the support of the Allies, the Greek army gained important victories in the battlefield, and the Turkish government in Constantinople was impotent and unable to offer resistance. Three years later the Greek forces were being driven into the Aegean, Smyrna was burning, and three thousand years of Hellenism in Asia Minor were coming speedily to an end. Why a Greek army, superior in numbers to the Kemalist forces and decidedly not inferior in equipment could have permitted such a cataclysmic series of events to transpire is still being debated. Undoubtedly, one reason is the psychological impact of the landing and occupation. The presence of Greek troops gave impetus and popular support to the Kemalist resistance movement. Another factor was the poor military planning of the Greek General Staff in permitting the formation of a front 200 miles long, which covered a line from the Sea of Marmara to Chivrill in southern Turkey.[2] Finally, there were conflicting commercial and territorial interests among the Allies. This served to deny to the Greek forces the support of the very governments which had sent them to Smyrna in the first place.

By July 1922 the tide of battle had begun to turn in favor of the Turkish forces. Kemal directed a main attack that broke through the Greek lines and opened the way to Smyrna. On 8 September the Greek headquarters evacuated the city, and the Turkish cavalry entered triumphantly the following day. Nearly 30,000 people perished in the wake of the Greek retreat, and over 200,000—without food, water, or shelter—thronged to the shore seeking to escape a martyr's death.

In Athens the political situation became chaotic as King Constantine sought vainly to find someone who could form a viable ministry. Soldiers were returning, destitute refugees were flowing in, and the government was on the verge of bankruptcy. In these circumstances two colonels—Nicholas Plastiras and Stylianos Gonatas—decided to take matters into their own hands. On the islands of Chios and Mitylene they established a revolutionary regime in the hope of salvaging something from an apparently hopeless situation. On 26 September an aircraft dropped leaflets over Athens, signed by Colonel Gonatas, that demanded the abdication of the King in favor of Crown Prince George. Thus, for the second time in five years, Constantine found himself faced with an ultimatum demanding the surrender of his throne. The next day he abdicated. He urged his followers not to oppose the "Revolution" and to rally around the young king. That afternoon a group of generals, constituting provisional authority, installed themselves in the capital. The following day the revolutionary forces, consisting of 12,000 troops, made an orderly entrance into the city. Within hours a Revolutionary Committee—headed by Plastiras, Gonatas, and naval Captain Demetrios Fokas[3]—entered Athens and assumed authority.

Initial Efforts to Obtain American Recognition

Once again the State Department was faced with an unforeseen situation at the center of which lay the problem of recognition. At first, it appeared that recognition of the new regime would not be hampered by insurmountable obstacles owing to the friendly attitude of the British legation toward the new king, George II. One of the first acts of the British minister in Athens was to make an appearance at the palace and sign his name to the guest book. Though this action did not constitute official recognition, it was a hopeful sign of happier relations in the future. It was evident, too, that the new government was prepared to take whatever steps were necessary to renew normal diplomatic relations with the Western Powers.[4] Before his arrival in Athens, Plastiras made it clear that a fundamental reason for the Revolution[5] was the reestablishment of friendly relations with Greece's traditional allies. When Constantine abdicated, the Revolutionary government helped to orchestrate a series of rallies in which wild enthusiasm was expressed in favor of the Allies. All Greece then waited for Allied appreciation, but none came. In fact, Venizelos received a cold reception in Paris and London, when he attempted to solicit the financial and political support of the French and British governments for the new regime. Both military and civil leaders were at a loss to understand what more was expected of them. They went so far as to suggest that King George could be removed easily and replaced by someone who would be agreeable to France and Great Britain. When these efforts failed, the Revolutionary leaders turned to the American legation and made a number of "pathetic attempts" to get the support of the United States government.[6]

What the Revolutionary Committee needed most was time to establish domestic peace, but with the revision of the Treaty of Sèvres a certainty and the Lausanne Conference looming on the horizon (it began on 21 November), the French and Italians did their best to perpetuate political instability in Greece in order to strengthen their position in the impending negotiations. They made a few vague promises and contributed money to all the major political parties in order to maintain a high partisan spirit and, as Caffery put it, "to keep the pot boiling." The British, on the other hand, wanted normal conditions restored. In late September, the British minister in Athens recommended the immediate recognition of George II in order to stabilize the country and to forestall a further swing to the left. However, conservative opposition at home, French and Italian aspirations in Turkey, as well as the tenuous political position of the king combined to place definite limits on the government of Lloyd George and on the State Department which, despite serious reservations, continued to follow the lead of the British.[7]

In the meantime, Revolutionary authorities made serious efforts to elicit a favorable attitude from the American legation. On 22 October a sixteen-member committee, composed of prominent citizens of Athens and Piraeus, organized a large public demonstration outside the American legation and in the name of the Greek nation presented a resolution to the American minister, Jefferson Caffery, which stated that the Greek people had accepted enthusiastically the principles of the Revolution and approved the forcible abdication of Constantine with the understanding that he should never be recalled under any circumstances. They also declared their "unshakable belief" that Greece's future lay beside her traditional friends and allies. Finally, they were prepared to recognize the new international realities by pledging their support to the refugees from Asia Minor. Caffery refused to be drawn into any of these activities, but at the same time he was quick to suggest that the State Department take advantage of the situation and enhance America's growing influence in Greece. He urged that recognition be granted at once "without adjournment and without subterfuge. This is the end we are seeking—the sole end of our diplomatic efforts." Officials at the State Department agreed, but the fact remained that united action in the matter of recognition was one of the few things the United States had to offer to the Allies in the Near East. A unilateral action by the United States at this critical point in time would have been a direct affront to Great Britain, upon whom the United States depended for support for its policy in the Western Hemisphere.[8]

Political Executions and the American Response

While the State Department was attempting to assess its position in relation to the new status quo that was emerging rapidly in Asia Minor, another crisis arose to complicate further the relations between Athens and Washington. This was the trial and execution of the "Six." Although the Revolutionary Committee initially established a civilian government to placate the Allies, the heads of the various ministries were treated merely as chairmen of governmental departments. On 18 October the military authorities issued a manifesto, stating that the Revolution was above party politics and that it would punish those who had been responsible for the catastrophic defeat of the Greek army in Turkey. Five days later it was announced that a military tribunal would be convened for this purpose. The most important figures were Demetrios Gounaris and Nicholas Stratos, both former prime ministers; Petros Protopapadakes, minister of finance; George Baltatzes, foreign minister; and Nicholas Theotokes, minister of war during most of the Constantinian restoration. The sixth member of the group was General George Chatzeanestes.

There is no doubt that, had it not been for the intervention of the British and French ministers, a number of Royalists would have been shot immediately upon the arrival of the Revolutionary Committee in

Athens. Both ministers urged that the accused be tried within the framework of the existing judicial system.[9] Given the long history of Allied antipathy for Constantine it is not surprising that Plastiras and Gonatas were disconcerted at the strong negative reaction their scheme elicited from the two most influential legations in Athens. Both men gradually softened their positions and urged upon their followers a more prudent course of action. At the center of this change of attitude was the demand that the ex-ministers be tried by a civil court, not by a military tribunal. Under some intensive prodding by foreign diplomats, the Revolutionary authorities publicly promised to conduct the trial in a manner to be determined by the National Assembly.[10]

Gonatas proposed that in the event of a conviction, clemency, and by implication life imprisonment, should be considered as an alternative to capital punishment. Plastiras also developed serious misgivings, and only under the most intense pressure from high-ranking Venizelist officers and after considerable personal agonizing did he agree to convene a court-martial.[11] Though a guilty verdict was a foregone conclusion, Plastiras apparently expected the court to recommend mercy in order to appease the Allies. It is obvious that he misjudged the mood of the extreme Republicans, most of whom believed there was no alternative to a "final solution." No doubt, the leaders and close supporters of the Revolution feared the power of the ex-ministers, particularly the popular Gounaris, and they could not resist the temptation of eliminating their opponents with a single stroke. The time was favorable for a political purge, since it could be accomplished under the guise of legal action. There was also great pressure from army officers and refugees to find a scapegoat. Many Venizelist officers believed that the execution of a few ministers would satisfy the bloodlust of the mob and would prevent the people from turning against those who had embarked originally on the Asia Minor campaign. But the deciding factor with those in authority was the conviction that it was impossible to restore discipline in the army and punish, with the necessary severity, deserters and others guilty of military crimes unless an example were set in the highest places.[12]

Fifteen specific indictments were brought against the defendants, though in reality the trial centered on two major points. One charge was gross incompetence in the conduct of the military campaign in Asia Minor, which in the view of the prosecution constituted "high treason." The other indictment pointed to the defendants' failure to notify the people that, in the event of Constantine's restoration in 1920, British and French financial assistance would be terminated. Before the trial the British legation tried to obtain assurances that no death penalties would follow a conviction. The Foreign Ministry was receptive to this suggestion if Great Britain would guarantee that the accused would be banished from Greece, never to return. The difficulties inherent in this undertaking were too great, however, and the British declined.[13]

When it became evident that a trial by a military tribunal was inevitable and that extremist elements within the officer corps and Venizelist Party would not be satisfied by anything short of the death penalty, almost every legation in Athens protested vigorously to the Foreign Ministry. The British and Italians threatened intervention.[14]

The role of the French legation in this matter was entirely negative. Constantine had been driven from the throne, Greece was humiliated and ruined financially, Turkey was victorious, and the British policy of saving the most essential parts of the Treaty of Sèvres had failed. The success of French policy, it appeared, was complete. The efforts to save the ministers was seen in Paris as a movement that promised to undermine and embarrass French policy in the Near East. Consequently, the French press undertook a propaganda campaign designed to provoke the extremists within the Venizelist Party and to ensure the elimination of the Royalists' leadership. The Revolution was held up as a comedy staged in order to win the sympathy of the Allies. The proof was that there had been no bloodshed. This propaganda was not without its effect. The fact that the ministers eventually were executed is to be attributed in no small degree to the abstention of the French legation from showing any interest in their fate.[15]

The possibility of foreign interference did not serve as a tempering influence. Instead, the political situation became more volatile, while the populace looked on with fearful uncertainty. The Revolutionary authorities also realized that the Allies, especially Great Britain, would never abandon Greece completely. Allied protests were viewed by extreme elements among the Venizelists as intimidating bluffs. Even if Great Britain were to break off diplomatic relations, they reasoned, she would soon find some pretense to restore them. The British Minister, F. O. Lindley, was told in the most terse language that his repeated protests in behalf of the defendants constituted interference in the internal affairs of Greece and that " 'the exemplary punishment of the acused constitutes an explicit demand of public opinion.' "[16]

The speed with which events were unfolding was beyond the comprehension of many persons. There was almost a complete breakdown of all social restraints and discipline in many parts of Greece. The countryside was full of brigands, demoralized soldiers, and wandering refugees to the extent that traveling became very dangerous. The Revolutionary Committee realized the seriousness of the situation, but lacked the moral and material means to cope with the problem. Faced by internal dissension and the possibility of foreign intervention, Plastiras hoped that the State Department would intercede to soften the impact of any punitive measures the Allies might be contemplating. On 2 November he and several members of the Revolutionary Committee appeared at the American legation to offer their gratitude for the aid given to refugees by American relief organizations. The group then solicited Caffery's views regarding the arrest and impending trial of the political prisoners. The opinion of the people of the United States, Plastiras said, was welcomed in everything affecting the Revolution and the efforts of Greeks to return their country to its previous prosperity. He wished America to know that every effort would be made to ensure a fair trial.[17] Caffery, following the specific orders of the secretary of state, replied that an unfortunate impression would be created in the United States if arbitrary measures were employed to try the accused and that the "springs of American charity [vis-à-vis the refugees] were likely to dry up if the executions took place."[18]

All warnings notwithstanding, the trial was held, and arbitrary measures were indeed used.[19] Nor was serious attention given to rules of evidence. The Foreign Ministry, with the apparent approval of the British legation, withheld from the defense certain secret documents showing that even before the elections of November 1920 the British prime minister had informed Venizelos of France's and Italy's decision to disassociate themselves from the Asia Minor campaign. Furthermore, these documents contained evidence of conversations between Curzon and Greek officials in which the former emphasized Great Britain's desire to have the Greek forces remain in Asia Minor. In other words, this evidence supported the central thesis of the defense that Allied policy towards Greece vis-à-vis Asia Minor did not change after, but before, the restoration of Constantine.[20] Why the British, whose clarion call for a fair trial was the loudest, should have withheld such vital information is not clear. Their minister in Constantinople confided to Admiral Bristol that his government felt considerable responsibility for the fate of the defendants, since British encouragement had been the principal factor in the retention of the Greek army in Asia Minor after the spring of 1922.[21] It is probable that the British government believed it could suppress the evidence to avoid embarrassment while simultaneously using its influence to prevent judicial murder. Whatever the complete truth of the matter, last-minute efforts to save the condemned men failed.

Throughout this ordeal considerable pressure had been put on Venizelos to intervene. The former premier, however, procrastinated. He argued that he was now outside the government and he could not interfere. The British decided to prod him into action. They sent Commander Gerald F. Talbot, a former naval attaché at Athens, to confer with Venizelos who was representing Greece at the Lausanne Conference. From there he hurried to Athens, but he arrived one hour too late. The evidence indicates that Venizelos' efforts to save the condemned men were somewhat less than enthusiastic. Talbot, however, was not too late to save the life of Prince Andrew who had been convicted of disobeying orders while engaged in the Asia Minor campaign. In retrospect, it is clear that, even if Venizelos had demanded clemency, it would have been a futile gesture because Plastiras had promised to abide by the court's verdict with no regard for the wishes of the ex-premier or the appeals and threats of the British minister.[22] The trial was concluded on 27 November 1922, and the next morning the six men were taken to Goudi, a short distance outside Athens, and shot.

The executions had immediate repercussions. From almost all the capitals of Europe came severe condemnations. The outstanding exception was Paris. Unlike Great Britain, which immediately recalled her minister, France kept her legation intact. The French government cautioned that the failure to withdraw its minister did not necessarily constitute a general approval of the executions. Nevertheless, a sampling of the Parisian press suggests an opposite conclusion. Not a single newspaper condemned the action of the Revolutionary government. The best Le Temps could do was an expression of regret for the loss of human life. Perhaps the most candid summation was given by the Journal des Débats which editorialized as follows: "Let us be sincere with ourselves. If a European court-martial had condemned and shot William II and his accomplices, would we have protested? Then how can we reproach the Greeks with having done that which we have demanded should have been done with the criminals of Germany?"[23]

Official and public reaction in the United States was extremely negative. Hughes ordered Caffery to avoid any statement which might be interpreted as an interference in the internal affairs of Greece, but at the same time he instructed him to reiterate to the Greek authorities that the executions had caused a most unfortunate impression in the United States. Furthermore, he was to advise the Foreign Ministry orally and unofficially that it was in the interests of the Greek people to avoid further action which would impede the work of refugee relief or embarrass American agencies in their efforts to meet the emergency in Greece.[24] The State Department's action had the support of President Warren G. Harding who approved of the discreet manner in which the matter was being handled. "I am especially delighted to know," he wrote, "that this becoming action is being taken without parade of the fact in the press."[25] Foreign Minister Apostolos Alexandris, speaking in behalf of the Greek government, expressed considerable concern over American opinion towards the executions, and he promised that any action which might further alienate American public sentiment would be avoided.[26]

Among Greeks in the United States, reaction to the harsh display of revolutionary justice was varied. As usual, opinion was divided along Royalist-Venizelist lines. In the country as a whole, however, the executions generated strong negative reaction. Scathing attacks were directed against the Revolutionary authorities and against the United States government for not taking a more direct hand in the proceedings. The State Department was inundated with protests and criticized in many magazine and newspaper articles. The *New York Times* editorialized: "The consequences of the recall of Constantine were plain enough two years ago to anybody who wanted to look for them. If it was a capital offense to bring Constantine back, about two-thirds of the Greek voters ought to commit suicide."[27]

To those criticisms were added the remarks of Paxton Hibben who was now serving as an official of the Near East Relief in New York. He sent a telegram to President Harding in which he stated that grave responsibility rested upon his administration, especially the State Department, "for the present sinister events in Greece." He chided the president for not having granted an early recognition to the Greek government. He urged him to request from the Foreign Ministry a mission empowered to grant whatever assurances the State Department required, since under the circumstances, the Revolutionary authorities were in no position to bargain. Hibbin reiterated his attacks in an article for *Current History*. He lamented the fact that President Harding had lost an opportunity to take the practical step to ensure peace and to save the lives of millions of Christians whom Americans were now called upon "to succor out of [their] charitable pockets."[28]

American public opinion also was influenced by sensational and inaccurate journalism to which even the *New York Times* succumbed. It reported that part of Stratos' skull was picked up by a boy who wandered the streets of Athens seeking to sell it as a souvenir. The same article also reported that one of the defendants died in the van on the way to the place of execution from heart failure. But the authorities would not be denied. They propped the body, and shot a man who was already dead! The truth of the matter is that it was a member of the firing squad who died of heart failure as the order to fire was given.[29]

These attacks on its foreign policy and the undesirable effects of irresponsible journalism were more than the State Department could tolerate. Hughes retorted angrily that he had no sympathy for the arguments of self-proclaimed statesmen and for the permeating hysteria of the moment. The United States could not feel responsible for the reversals experienced by any particular regime in Greece. On the contrary, the American policy of withholding recognition had been amply justified by events. The United States had done all it could by instructing its chargé in Athens to give his informal disapproval of the trial and the executions. To have taken a more direct hand would have been tantamount to an involvement in the internal politics of Greece.[30]

In 1929 Venizelos admitted that the executions had been a mistake, but that, under the circumstances, they were inevitable. Probably the definitive words were spoken in 1949 by General Pangalos, a leading figure in the convening of the court-martial and the prosecutor during the trial, who declared in an interview: "The condemned men did not commit premeditated treason, as they had been accused; they were inevitable and necessary sacrifices on the altar of the motherland during those critical times."[31] Such is the nature of military coups in times of national catastrophe. They often require sacrifices to act as an emotional catharsis. To be sure, the executions had the long-term effect of perpetuating and accentuating fierce political animosities, but their immediate effect was a sobering one. They represented a new and shocking experience in Greece. The death of the six men, therefore, served as a form of martyrdom, which probably prevented civil war and surely prevented further executions.

It is not difficult to assess the role of the United States government in such an emotional issue. One might be inclined to be critical of the lukewarm admonitions of the State Department, especially in light of Caffery's statement that "it was none of my business."[32] The opposite, in fact, is true. The British chargé reported that Caffery "attempted to profit from his exceptional position in order to save the ex-Ministers; but the Revolutionary Committee were deaf to all arguments."[33] In the minds of many persons the position of the State Department seemed to border on callous indifference. But given the determination of the extreme Republicans to have their revenge and the inability of the European powers to exert their influence, there was little that American officials could have done. Venizelos and Pangalos probably were correct when they suggested that the overwhelming nature of the crisis contained within it the seeds of an inexorable fatalism.

This episode seemed to justify, for the moment, the nonrecognition policy of the United States. However, it should be noted that, while Greek-American formal diplomatic relations remained strained, American relief work was conducted on a grand scale with the direct support of the American legation and the approval of the State Department. Secretary Hughes explained the absence of recognition did not indicate an unfriendly attitude toward the Greek people. The role of American agencies in assisting the refugees was clear evidence to the contrary. This humanitarian work could not have been carried out more effectively even if formal relations had been resumed.[34]

When one examines the extent to which Greek and American officials went to maintain informal contacts with one another and the avowed determination of the State Department to abstain from a direct involvement in Greek politics, the absence of formal diplomatic relations does not loom quite so large. Throughout the period from November 1920 to June 1924, when an American minister was again accredited to the Greek government, unofficial and commercial relations continued without interruption. Illustrative is the testimony of Caffery who wrote: "In fact, all during my stay the several Greek Governments I had to deal with, at a time when we recognized none of them, were most helpful. I was able to settle a mass of 'back claims'." Nor was contact with the court nonexistent. On various occasions Caffery had informal meetings with the king and queen, during which a very cordial atmosphere prevailed.[35] The absence of formal recognition did not drive the two countries further apart. On the contrary, the pressures of international events served to bring them closer together, despite the existing state of diplomatic affairs. The American policy of nonrecognition, however, did prevent the solution of many mutual problems dividing the State Department and the Foreign Ministry. In the period from December 1922 to June 1924, five interconnected issues dominated the political relations between Greece and the United States: The Lausanne Conference, French propaganda in Greece, the restoration of civilian government, American policy toward the republics of Central America, and the promulgation of the Greek Republic.

The Lausanne Conference

The United States was not a participant in the Conference at Lausanne, but it sent unofficial observers to look after American interests in the Near East. Despite the informal nature of this country's presence, American officials often played a significant role in the proceedings. No one was certain in what condition the Greek state would emerge from the proceedings. Pending the conclusion of the negotiations, the United States decided to adopt a wait-and-see attitude.[36] This policy, however, was maintained with considerable uneasiness. The reason was the conviction that France was attempting to emerge from the conference with the lion's share of the spoils at the expense of her wartime ally, Great Britain. Relations between the two countries had been strained for some time. British officials harbored feelings of resentment and suspicion against the French who on 11 January 1923, with the aid of Belgian troops, proceeded to occupy the Ruhr. They justified their action with the fact that the Allied Reparations Commission declared Germany to be in default of its deliveries of timber and coal. The British government refused to participate, declaring that the Franco-Belgian action was not authorized by the Treaty of Versailles. The French, for their part, were active reviving anti-British feelings which had lain dormant for more than a generation. Thus, both London and Washington became suspicious over what they envisioned to be the scheming designs of the French Foreign Ministry. Even before the execution of the ministers, Dulles expressed his apprehension. He declared that while he did not think it would be wise to recognize George II previous to the conclusion of the Lausanne Conference, the United States government should have the matter carefully in mind so as not to be the last to take this action.[37] These words were written with France primarily in mind.

French Propaganda in Greece and Its Effect on United States Policy

The suspicions of the State Department were strengthened when a sudden xenophobia, aimed primarily at the United States and Great Britain, began to manifest itself in Greece. A series of restrictive and petty measures against foreigners were passed in rapid succession. These included the exchange of small amounts of currency, restrictions on travel, and unusually stringent measures in obtaining permits and other documents required in the conduct of business. The American vice-consul in Salonika reported that considerable circumstantial evidence pointed to a foreign power as the moving spirit behind this trend. That power, he believed, was France.[38] The mood of the populace suggested a well-conceived plan of indoctrination. Paradoxically, then, there was a sudden rise in anti-Americanism at a time when all Greece was extolling the unselfishness and compassion of the American people relative to the relief work being done in the country.[39]

The situation was aggravated further by the Greek Foreign Ministry which was aware of the concerns entertained by the State Department. In August 1923 Apostolos Alexandris, minister of foreign affairs, informed the American chargé, Ray Atherton, that French recognition was imminent. He added that he had been advised of the intention of Belgium, Poland, and Czechoslovakia to follow the French example. While officials in the State Department were attempting to assess the plausibility of the foreign minister's allegations, French Premier Raymond Poincaré intervened to erase all doubts. In the first week of September, he announced his government's decision to recognize George II, though he was careful to remain vague about the date the recognition was to be granted. This decision was prompted by the desire to please Queen Marie of Romania, the king's mother-in-law. But the Corfu incident intervened and the matter was temporarily set aside. The American military attaché in Greece expressed the opinion that this move on the part of France would probably cause other governments to follow suit.[40]

It was clear that French recognition would strengthen the Venizelists' control over the government, while simultaneously enhancing the position of the king whose hold on the throne was, at best, tenuous. Both governments denied that any special benefits would accrue to either side. However, the diplomatic realities of the moment told a different story. France emerged from the Lausanne Conference with little to show for her efforts. The gains she expected to make did not materialize, and her prestige in Turkey had been diminished. As a result of this diplomatic setback the French government evidently saw the need to be on good terms with Greece in order to be able to use Greece as an ally against the Turks in the final settlement of its Near East problems. Furthermore, France was in need of friends for her plans in Central Europe.[41] Like Bismarckian Germany after 1870, she sought to build an alliance system to preserve the status quo in postwar Europe and to prevent the resurgence of the Hapsburg dynasty. Consequently, she searched for a link with the Little Entente comprising Czechoslovakia, Yugoslavia, and Romania. The French government tried to gain admission of Greece in the alliance, in the hope that it could exploit the dynastic ties between Greece and Romania to further its aims in Central Europe.

These circumstances produced a self-assurance which Alexandris did not attempt to disguise. The American chargé was made to understand that the Greek government assumed American recognition would not be forthcoming until elections had been held. The tone of the conversation suggests that the foreign minister was willing to wait. Atherton could not agree more. He cautioned the State Department not to allow the threat of French intervention to stampede it into recognition. The Greek people had demanded the return to civilian rule for some time. To recognize a government that might be inclined to postpone elections indefinitely would serve to diminish American popularity in Greece. From a Balkan viewpoint, the United States should "insist" that constitutional governments be established "thereby tending to avoid internal and/or alleged international groupings."[42]

Atherton was justified in his skepticism. Since the dissolution of Parliament on November 1922 the military authorities had done little to allay the apprehensions of the populace. Threats of coups and counter-coups, saber rattling by military officers with political ambitions, economic uncertainty, humiliating defeats, and social upheaval combined to produce a national neurosis. There were also controversies surrounding the manipulation of the electoral system. Certain technical changes were introduced to allow local politicians to influence the voting pattern in "unsafe" districts and thus ensure an anti-Royalist majority in Parliament. The Government also sought to secure favorable election results by exploiting the refugee vote, while a special electoral college was created to control the voting pattern of the large Jewish community in Salonika.[43] For these reasons general elections had been delayed, but eventually they were scheduled tentatively for 28 October 1923.

Despite Atherton's cautious advice, officials in the Division of Near Eastern Affairs were uneasy about the prospect of French recognition. Most had committed themselves to the idea that continuing to follow the British example was valid only so long as all the major powers continued to withhold their recognition. Allen W. Dulles, Chief of the Division of Near Eastern Affairs, was especially concerned that the United States might be duped into a position of waiting for some undefined future event to occur without being able to explain clearly either to Greece or to the people of America the procrastination of the United States government.[44] At this point American policy in Central America emerged once more to influence the attitude of the United States government.

Central America and the Recognition of George II

State Department Economic Adviser Arthur N. Young, who fifteen months previously had joined Dulles in urging Hughes to recognize Constantine, offered a dissenting opinion.[45] He shared Dulles's concern, but in view of recent treaty agreements with the republics of Central America and in light of the volatile nature of Greek politics, he advised a wait-and-see policy.[46] On 7 February 1923, under the prompting of the State Department, a Treaty of Peace and Amity was signed in Washington between the five republics of Central America. Article 2 provided that no government in Central America which came into power via a coup d'état would be recognized by the other four until freely elected representatives of the people had constitutionally reorganized the country.

The question then arose whether it would be appropriate and wise to apply this principle to the recognition of European governments. In the case of Central America, elections were a necessary prerequisite to recognition, since power theoretically was derived exclusively from the people. Under the implications of the Monroe Doctrine the United States had assumed a certain responsibility with respect to these republics. Europe, however, presented a different problem because the State Department often had to deal with monarchs who were not elected, but held power by virtue of hereditary right. As a consequence of this fundamental difference there appeared to be no serious inconsistency in adopting for European governments a policy different from the one followed with respect to the republican governments in Central and South America. It was this distinction that had enabled the State Department to recognize the Bulgarian and Italian governments, both of which had emerged by extraconstitutional means. The fact that the king in each case had accepted the new government tended to give the new regime a certain legality from the point of view of the European governmental system. The case of Greece seemed to be no different from that of Italy or Bulgaria.

Dr. Young emphasized that his reluctance to recommend recognition for George II was not based on questions of legality, but on overall policy and the prevailing political uncertainty in Greece. He stressed the inadvisability of applying Article 2 to the governments of Europe, since such action would result in constant interference in European affairs.[47] Atherton's admonitions prevailed, however, and Article 2 was given tacit application throughout the autumn of 1923.

The Abortive Coup d'état of the Royalists

During the period when this soul-searching was taking place, an abortive countercoup took place in Greece which seemed to put new light on the entire subject of recognition. The officers of the army and navy had learned early in their military careers the fatal secret that a handful of armed men could change a government.[48] The Treaty of Lausanne hardly was concluded when Greece was confronted with an unexpected crisis. On 29 August Mussolini's Italy bombed the island of Corfu on the pretext that Greeks had murdered General Enrico Tellini and four members of his mission to the International Commission which was delimiting the Greek-Albanian frontier. Twenty-seven days later the crisis was over, but not before a decision by the League of Nations had forced Greece to pay Italy 39,000,000 francs as an indemnity for the death of the Italians.[49] The national humiliation of Corfu played into the hands of the Royalists. They began to conspire with some Venizelists who had their personal reasons for resentment. On 21 October a coup d'état was attempted, but it proved abortive and ill-conceived. The uprising was crushed quickly. Insofar as Greek-American relations were concerned, the only effect of the revolt was to weaken the position of those in the State Department who had been urging the speedy recognition of the Greek government. More important, however, was the fact that the revolt gave impetus to the fortunes of those liberal elements who were calling for the abolition of the monarchy and the establishment of a republic.

The Restoration of Civilian Rule and the Promulgation of the Greek Republic

It is impossible to say precisely when the idea of a republic began to germinate. For nearly a quarter of a century references to socialism, workers' parties, and republicanism were frequent in private conversations. At times these issues drew the attention of the press and inspired the publication of scholarly journals for the dissemination of socialist and republican ideas.[50] In practical terms, republicanism had its origins in 1915, when King Constantine dismissed Venizelos from office despite the prime minister's large majority in the Chamber of Deputies. When Venizelos founded his own regime in Salonika many of his followers openly advocated the establishment of a republic. During the reign of Alexander, the republican idea remained dormant due to the exigencies of war. Constantine's restoration in December 1920 served to revive republicanism with renewed intensity and vigor. Early in 1922 seven prominent Venizelist politicians, including three deputies, issued a manifesto advocating a republican regime. Despite a clause in the constitution prohibiting the arrest of deputies without the consent of the Chamber, and after a mock trial, these officials were sentenced to imprisonment for three years. This was a fatal mistake for the Royalists because it made the republican idea a living issue and in essence created the Republican Party.

With the defeat of the Greek army in Asia Minor, an opportunity presented itself which found the Republicans as yet unprepared, primarily because of their own inability to reconcile the differences between the conservative and radical wings within their party. Consequently, the accession of George II met with comparatively little opposition on the part of the Venizelist-Republican Party as a whole, although Plastiras accurately voiced their views when he said that the monarchy was on its last trial.[51]

A second opportunity came in October 1923, when the Royalists organized a countercoup against the Revolutionary government. King George, who ruled at the pleasure of the Revolutionary authorities, refused to denounce the revolt. This attitude eventually was temporarily to cost him his crown. The Republicans were loath to allow another opportunity of establishing the Greek Republic to slip through their hands, and so they pressed and schemed for the immediate overthrow of the Glücksburg Dynasty. The interval which elapsed before the republic was promulgated was prolonged only by the efforts of Venizelos to act as a moderating influence in that transition. Venizelos had long been a Republican in theory, but he had doubts about the wisdom of establishing the republic before the people should have progressed further in their political sophistication. His turbulent relations with Constantine, however, gave impetus to his republican sensibilities, and he now declared that the Greek people were probably ready for a republican form of government.

By November 1923 the question of a republic was no longer academic. The debate centered not on whether Greece should have a republican form of government, but what form the republic should take and by what method it should be implemented. Under national law the Parliament could not be called into session until eighteen days after general elections which had been rescheduled for 2 December. There was great demand, however, that it meet on 9 November to debate informally the abolition of the monarchy. The entire issue gave promise of aggravating political divisions in Greece to the point where irreparable harm would be done to the country's national interests. At this point Venizelos intervened from Paris in an effort to stabilize the situation. He attempted to persuade his followers to build a political edifice on stronger foundations than on a coup d'état carried out under the aegis of military authorities. He sent a telegram in which he supported the formation of a republic, but he beseeched all those who had any respect for his opinion to be mindful of Greece's dependence on the goodwill of the Western Powers and to strive for a peaceful solution to the problem by permitting the people to decide the issue through a plebiscite.[52] Three weeks later he reiterated his admonitions in greater detail by stressing the adverse effects of another coup d'état in Greece. He pointed to the balance of the 1918 credits, the refugee loan under negotiation, the philanthropic and relief work being conducted by foreign agencies, and the overall dependence on foreign financial and technical assistance for the settlement of the refugees.[53]

These admonitions notwithstanding, great pressure was put on Plastiras to promulgate a republic immediately. The main supporters for the summary overthrow of the Glücksburg Dynasty were Generals Theodore Pangalos and George Kondyles, Admiral Alexander Chatzekyriakos, and Alexander Papanastasiou, leader of the Republican Union Party. They made vigorous attempts to sway Plastiras to their point of view. They promised to obey without hesitation every wish of the leader of the Revolution, to serve as mere corporals, to participate in politics, or to return to private life. At the same time, they made certain that rumors were circulated intimating the possibility of a coup d'état, if their demands were not met.[54] Plastiras was not a statesman, but he was shrewd enough to see through these empty promises and to appreciate the validity of Venizelos' arguments. In spite of faltering health, he traveled throughout Greece to test public opinion and to ascertain the mood of the armed forces. Thus, Plastiras, who a year before was considered an uncompromising revolutionary, now generally was regarded by Greeks of all political inclinations as a moderate, who was upholding the constitution by demanding elections.

Plastiras was not transformed suddenly into a doctrinaire libertarian. He was reacting to foreign influences with which he was confronted. British interference in the domestic affairs of Greece at that point in time was exceedingly heavy-handed. Venizelos was told by British authorities in Paris that an ill-advised course of action by the government in Athens would have serious consequences for the refugee loan under negotiation. The British legation involved itself in Greek politics to the point of offering confidential advice to the king whose popularity was already very low. Even smaller legations (e.g., the Serbian and Romanian) advised against a hasty decision regarding the overthrow of the dynasty. By contrast, the French legation continued to woo the Revolutionary authorities, primarily for the purpose of undermining British and American influence.[55] The effect of these admonitions was immediate. A coup was averted, but it was postponed only until after the elections, when neither Colonel Plastiras nor Colonel Gonatas had the strength, or perhaps even the courage, to resist any longer the pressure from the military, Republican elements within the government.

During those critical months the American role tended to assume a political character as a result of strenuous efforts by Greek officials to draw the United States into a more direct involvement on the question of the dynasty's future. Plastiras and Kondyles often sought the advice of Atherton, while contacts between the Foreign Ministry and the American legation were close and frequent. At the same, emissaries of the king made repeated efforts to gain the sympathy and support of the American legation. The position of the American chargé thus became very sensitive. Atherton refused repeated invitations to appear at the palace as a guest of the Royal family for fear of making his relations with the people in power difficult. Nevertheless, discreet contacts with the court were maintained through the use of intermediaries.[56]

The reason why the principal powers continued to withhold recognition was not understood by the Greek populace, or by many informed persons in Greece and abroad. It was presumed that France and the United States would be glad to see a Republic established in Greece, but this could hardly be expected of Great Britain. The fact that the United States, Italy, and Great Britain had severed relations with the government responsible for the execution of the former ministers and could not, therefore, recognize or have any relations with a king over that same government was a crucial point which was not fully appreciated. Despite efforts by the Foreign Office to clarify its position in the Greek press, the erroneous impression created was that the British government objected to King George and that his continued presence on the throne was the primary reason for Great Britain's policy of nonrecognition. This was a weapon which the Republicans used repeatedly against the king throughout the autumn of 1923.[57] This misunderstanding was strengthened by inflammatory statements of British officials in the British press, in which they gave vent to their old grievances against Constantine, and by the unexpected declaration of Venizelos that he considered the Greek people more prepared for a republic than a crown democracy. Considerable speculation was inspired by these statements, and Republican propaganda sought to exploit the situation as much as possible. Contradictory rumors were circulated in Athens which implied that Great Britain was ready to establish a republic in Greece, as she had done in Germany and Austria, and to replace George II with a British Prince.[58] This propaganda was not without its affects. It helped to poison the political atmosphere, and in no small measure contributed to the king's demise.

The elections were held on 16 December. The Royalists abstained in protest of what they termed government persecution. The field, therefore, was left open to the Venizelist Liberals and Republicans who won an overwhelming majority. Encouraged by their victory at the polls many army officers now began to press for the immediate abolition of the Glücksburg Dynasty. Gonatas initially demurred, but ultimately decided that the king's departure was necessary in order to have a peaceful debate on the dynasty's future. On 19 December, the third anniversary of Constantine's restoration, George II and his queen left quietly "on a leave of absence" for Romania. In his farewell letter he described his withdrawal as provisional, but twelve years were to pass before he would set foot again on Greek soil. On 21 December Admiral Coundouriotis was once again appointed Regent, pending final outcome of the dynastic question.

Considerable space was given in the press to the fact that the American legation had refused to be drawn into the controversy, despite the intense efforts of the Royalists. A deliberate effort was made to exaggerate the effect of the American attitude. *Demokratia*, an organ of Papanastasiou's Republican Union, literally rhapsodized about the "aggressive role" of the United States in promoting the concept of self-determination through its refusal to intervene on behalf of the king. All efforts to save the dynasty failed because all nations, "following the leadership of America, let it be understood that foreign interference in the internal affairs of Greece would not be tolerated." The editor of the *Chicago Tribune* (Paris edition) declared the United States' intention "to approach the Washington representatives of the powers and to stress that it would view most unfavorably their involvement in the internal affairs of a small nation."[59] These press releases were an effort to induce the American legation to make any public statement which could be construed as a vote of confidence for the republic. Greek authorities believed that because of their own republican form of government American officials would welcome a republican regime in Greece, but they were waiting for some signal from Great Britain. They were partly correct. While British influence was certainly an important factor, American policy was not based on considerations of political doctrine. The legitimacy of the government, its viability, and its ability to honor international agreements were always the overriding considerations.

Whatever the hopes of George II when he left Greece, few people expected him to return, for it was generally believed that even if the monarchy were retained, the throne would pass to a new dynasty. Bewildered by the situation in which they found themselves, the Greek people instinctively turned to Venizelos, the statesman whom they had repudiated and, in effect, expelled three years previously. Urgent appeals were sent to the former premier to return to stabilize the political situation. Venizelos declared his determination to remain out of politics and never return to his country. The American vice-consul in Salonika expected him to remain true to his word, for he remembered only too well the fickleness of the Greek voters. Then, somewhat prophetically, the vice-consul added: "He is much too big for the country and the country will never be able to understand and appreciate him. Within a year he will once again be forced to leave." When an invitation to return, free of any restrictive conditions, came from the Gonatas cabinet and the Parliament, Venizelos reversed his decision and accepted the offer. Before leaving Paris he appeared at the American embassy to inform the American ambassador of his decision to return to Greece. He reiterated his pledge to permit the newly elected Parliament to determine the fate of the monarchy through a national plebiscite. He declared his intention to reenter public life temporarily, but solely for the purpose of restoring political stability in his country. He intended to postpone the plebiscite two or three months in order to allow passions to subside and thus ensure a fair election.[60]

The Parliament met in January 1924 with considerable pomp and ceremony. Plastiras gave a lengthy farewell address in which he reviewed with pride the accomplishments of the Revolution and publicly praised the United States for its role in the settlement of the refugees. Amid cheers of "Long Live the Republic! Down with the King!" he announced the resignation of the military government and the return to civilian rule. On 11 January, exactly on the first anniversary of Constantine's death, Venizelos once again became premier to the great relief of the Western Powers and the Greek people who hoped that a new era of internal peace might lie ahead.

This sense of optimism was not well-founded, for it failed to allow for the presence of strong and irreconcilable elements within the Liberal and Republican Parties. There were those who feared that Venizelos would not pursue the immediate overthrow of the dynasty with vigor. In fact, it was precisely for this reason that Venizelos' tenure as Premier was so short. Unable to come to terms with the extreme elements in his party, he resigned on 3 February. It was recognized also that loyalty to the crown had not been obliterated from the popular mind and that in the event of a plebiscite, the people would probably choose to bring back the king. Despite these uncertainties, the British government was impressed with the premier's efforts to restore constitutional liberties to the Greek people. They were motivated also by the necessity to remain on top of the political situation in Greece. Consequently, on 15 January, four days after the ascendancy of Venizelos to the premiership, Great Britain officially recognized the new government of Greece.[61]

The Dynastic Question and the Role of Henry Morgenthau

These circumstances raise certain questions regarding the role of the American chairman of the Refugee Settlement Commission, Henry Morgenthau.[62] Throughout the autumn of 1923 the British minister had made no effort to disguise his support of the king. It appears, however, that his pro-Royalist sentiments were less an expression of sympathy than concern for another "revolution" which the British legation might not be able to control. These apprehensions were justified by events taking place behind the scenes.

On 18 January Morgenthau was invited to a party at Papanastasiou's apartment where General Kondyles and Admiral Chatzekyriakos were present. He was taken aside and informed of a conspiracy by uncompromising Republican officers to effect a revolution. This revelation was remarkable considering that British recognition was less than one week old and that American recognition was surely imminent. Morgenthau was surprised. The three men appealed to Morgenthau, as a friend of Greece and as president of the Refugee Settlement Commission, to understand their position. The immediate overthrow of the Glücksburg Dynasty was essential to the stability of the country. But its elimination by peaceful means was impossible because the majority of the Liberal Party would not consent to it. King George had no sympathy for the refugees and no real understanding of the Greek people. During the preceding decade, the Glücksburg Dynasty had demonstrated its impotence and its insensitivity to the country's needs. As long as the Republicans were preparing to get rid of a particular dynasty, why not eliminate the monarchy? The Greeks were capable of governing themselves, and the best government for that purpose was a republic. Venizelos had blundered in dealing with Constantine. They were determined that he should not repeat his mistake with George II.

Morgenthau listened sympathetically to their disillusionment with Venizelos' politics and informed his hosts that he, too, was a confirmed republican. He promised to do all he could to promote the establishment of the Republic. He pointed out, however, that as a practical matter the sympathy of Great Britain, France, and the United States was essential to Greece in her present refugee crisis. This sympathy would be compromised if the Greeks failed to have an orderly plebiscite or should fail to abide by its results. Political stability was at the center of the refugee problem.

On 29 January Morgenthau gave a dinner for members of the government and the Refugee Settlement Commission. Venizelos was to have been present, but he had been disabled that morning by a heart attack during a stormy session in Parliament. At the end of the evening's activities the minister of foreign affairs, George Roussos, the Greek minister to Rome, Constantine Karapanos, and Venizelos' personal secretary, G. A. Michaelopou, called a private meeting in which Morgenthau's views on the dynastic question were solicited. The inclusion of an outsider in discussions relating to such a sensitive issue of internal politics undoubtedly was inspired by the need to cope with the refugee problem. The welfare of the refugees was vital to the economic and political stability of Greece.

In the opinion of Morgenthau three possible courses lay before the government. One was to preserve the status quo. This was clearly out of the question and was treated only academically. A second was to ask the electorate, through a plebiscite, whether it wished to change from a monarchy to a republic or whether it wished, while retaining the monarchial system, to change the dynasty. Finally, the Parliament could declare the republic immediately, and seek the ratification of the electorate after the fact. There was no doubt in Morgenthau's mind that the sentiment for the republic was so pervasive that nothing short of the immediate elimination of both the monarchy and the dynasty would satisfy the country.

The three men were inclined to agree with this analysis as a matter of judgement, though with varying degrees of enthusiasm. Uppermost on their minds was the attitude of Great Britain. The monarchy, though largely sentimental, remained a real force in British policy. After several hours of discussion on this point, a decision was made to obtain the views of the governments of Great Britain and the United States, for fear of jeopardizing the refugee loan negotiations and the relief work of British and American agencies.[63]

In order to avoid official involvement on the part of the three governments, it was decided to sound out the British government through

Montagu Norman, governor of the Bank of England and an intimate friend of Morgenthau. A coded cablegram was sent stating the problem as follows: It was imperative that political and financial stability be restored in Greece. Virtually all members of Parliament agreed that the Glücksburg Dynasty be eliminated immediately and unequivocally without regard to any political considerations. Subsequently, a plebiscite would determine if the country should be governed by a monarchy or a republic. "I have been asked," wrote Morgenthau, "how Great Britain and the United States would view this proposition. Can you ascertain for me your government's attitude."[64] In other words, whatever the will of the Greek people, the fate of the Glücksburg Dynasty was sealed. Norman replied the next day that ". . . assuming that in your opinion [the] proposition would insure domestic settlement and political stability we consider you may expect sympathy here."[65] Government officials were elated, for it appeared that Norman's telegram would free Venizelos to act immediately and decisively in eliminating the dynasty. Venizelos' initial reaction was positive, and he agreed to reexamine his position. He told Morgenthau that he was willing to go so far as to meet with Papanastasiou to discuss ways in which political differences might be removed. These assurances, however, proved mere delaying tactics because two days later Venizelos resigned.

In the meantime, parts of Morgenthau's and Norman's telegrams were published in the Athenian press, causing a veritable furor. Norman's reply was interpreted as a demand by Great Britain for the ousting of the dynasty and as an endorsement of the Republican Party. Morgenthau felt obliged to publish their full text to correct this misconception. But in the virulent political atmosphere that prevailed, the opposite effect was achieved. The cablegrams intensified the political debate and, in Morgenthau's words, "undoubtedly contributed materially to crystallizing public opinion. They removed the strongest objection to the immediate declaration of the Republic by direct action of the Parliament."

The British minister in Athens was angered at Morgenthau's overall initiative and by the distorted image of British policy that these telegrams produced. Morgenthau's attitude throughout his presence in Greece, had been directed towards a change in regime. He was now using his role as chairman of the Refugee Settlement Commission to force the issue. The British minister informed the Greek government that Morgenthau's activities were not a reflection of British policy. The harm was done, however, and no effective remedy could be taken.[66]

The State Department also took a dim view of Morgenthau's self-styled personal diplomacy. Morgenthau retorted that since he had been appointed to his present position by the League of Nations, Washington was in no position to question his activities. Instead, he proclaimed his indispensability to the Greek government. He gave himself most of the credit for the success of the Refugee Settlement Commission, and he asserted that while in Greece he was given complete authority which amounted to dictatorial power. He attempted to instruct Greek officials in the making of foreign policy, and hardly let an opportunity pass to expound upon his political views in the press. He went as far as to give speeches, replete with parables and allegories, that bordered on political catechism. In the process, he succeeded in infuriating and alienating the very governments upon which Greece depended for political and financial support. Morgenthau, in whom messiahship was not lacking, was to some degree justified in manifesting this quality. In the popular mind, he was a veritable hero and savior. One Greek official called him "The most unforgettable American I have ever known," and proceeded to dedicate a book to his memory.[67]

Even more significant is an episode which occurred on 25 March 1924, the day on which the republic was promulgated. The Parliament met and, as was the practice since his arrival in Athens, Morgenthau was given the "courtesy of the floor." This honor permitted him to sit beside the official stenographer where he "could see and hear and be part of the whole proceedings." As the establishment of the republic was formally announced six white pigeons were set free as a symbol of new freedom and rising aspirations. One pigeon was caught and handed to Papanastasiou. The premier attached a card to the bird's leg, and had it sent to Morgenthau. On the card was the inscription: " 'To the Father of the Greek Republic!' "[68] By Morgenthau's own admission this was hardly accurate. However, the episode is illustrative of the influence that American officials and private citizens often had in Greek affairs. The British chargé described Morgenthau's role on the question of the dynasty as "a tremendous propaganda campaign" which helped to produce a strong "American hold on Greek affections."[69]

American Recognition

Immediately after the recognition by Great Britain, Greek officials in Athens and Washington began to press the American legation and the

State Department to follow the British example. Dulles responded by recommending to the secretary of state that immediate steps be taken to accredit a minister to the Greek government as it was becoming increasingly difficult to justify a policy of nonrecognition.[70] On 25 January Hughes informed President Calvin Coolidge that the time had come to settle a number of outstanding issues between Greece and the United States which had been held in abeyance in the absence of formal recognition. The secretary pointed to the remaining credits from the Tripartite Loan of 1918, the Greek government's indebtedness to the United States, and the necessity to negotiate a new commercial treaty with Greece as the most pressing problems facing the two countries. "In view of this situation," he wrote, "I wish to suggest for your consideration the desirability of resuming on a formal basis the relations between the United States and Greece."[71] The same day the President replied: "The recommendations you make . . . are approved."[72] American recognition was officially granted on 29 January 1924. The appointment of a minister was withheld until elections should give popular sanction to the promulgation of the republic. This occurred on 13 April when a plebiscite made the transition in government final by a margin of more than two to one.[73]

The recognition of the Greek Republic by the United States was greeted in both countries with great satisfaction. A long and difficult period had ended, and the future of Greek-American relations seemed bright. To commemorate the occasion, the *New York Times* included a lengthy article in a Sunday supplement entitled: "New America in Old Greece." The article was intended to introduce American readers to the character of modern Greece, the role of Greek immigrants in the United States, and the benefits to be derived by both sides through cooperation and mutual trust. The ensuing years largely justified this sense of optimism, but not without considerable difficulties along the way.

Perhaps the most pervasive element in Greek-American diplomacy during the early 1920's was the role of expediency in the conduct of foreign affairs. Then, as now, overriding considerations of policy ultimately were the decisive factors. Between 1920 and 1922, for example, when the element of de jure clearly was applicable to the recognition of Constantine but contrary to American interests, considerations of legality were conveniently set aside. With the establishment of a revolutionary regime in Greece in 1922 and with the uncertainties to which it gave rise, the United States government reversed itself. The element of de jure became central to its refusal to grant recognition to George II. To be sure, the problem was far more complex, given the opposition of France and Great Britain, but when viewed in its broadest terms, this generalization is applicable to the period from 1920 to 1924.

7
Refugee Settlement: American Philanthropy in Action

The destruction of Smyrna in September 1922, and the subsequent expulsion of approximately 1,500,000 Greeks from Asia Minor, introduced a new element in the relations between the United States and Greece. The Great Powers suddenly were faced with a refugee problem whose magnitude imposed upon them the necessity to undertake emergency relief measures on a scale which, at that time, had no recorded precedent in modern history. Of the victorious Allied Powers only the United States had the financial resources to make a major contribution. Almost instinctively Greece turned to America for help. The response of the United States government and the American people was swift and positive. Food, clothing, medical supplies, and financial assistance were provided on a scale that had a profound effect in mitigating the suffering and trauma of uprooting. The role of American philanthropy during those critical years comprises one of the brightest chapters in the history of Greek-American relations in the twentieth century. It gave rise to strong pro-American sentiments which, despite the pressures of more recent international politics, have not been eradicated entirely.

The Political Background

The financial boycott of Constantine's government was but one element in the military defeat of the Greek forces in Asia Minor. Allied territorial ambitions, political instability in Greece, and a variety of other factors have been examined in previous chapters. In this tragic affair there are three general sets of responsibilities to examine. One is the role of the Allies who encouraged Greece into a participation in the war promising, in return, Smyrna. Another is the policy of Venizelos who committed his country to an ill-advised, ill-conceived military venture. Finally, there is the hypocritical attitude of Venizelos' successors who attempted to continue a military policy of which they always had expressed the most emphatic disapproval. The present chapter will address itself solely to the first point, insofar as it relates to the American role in the defeat of the Greek army in Asia Minor. It should be noted, however, that foreign guilt for the Asia Minor catastrophe lies overwhelmingly with the French and British governments. A discussion of the responsibility of the United States government is appropriate at this point in order to place the main elements of the problem in their proper historical perspective.

The role of the United States at the Paris Peace Conference was somewhat peculiar because America entered the war late (April 1917) and because the United States government had not been a party to the secret treaties for the dismemberment of Turkey, which were concluded among the Allies during the war. These circumstances, together with the Bolsheviks' subsequent renouncement of those agreements, created a situation in which American statesmen became participants in the radical revision of the original arrangements. This was the crux of the problem as it concerned the conduct of Greek-American diplomacy at the peace conference.

President Wilson went to Paris apparently forgetful of the *Realpolitik* that animated the negotiators at the conference table and not sufficiently aware of the difficulties inherent in the revision of agreements in which he had taken no formulating role. Apart from his famous twelfth point, relating to the self-determination of nations, he cannot be said to have had any particular bias in favor of claims put forward by the Greek delegation. His advisers, however, viewed the entire issue in more precise terms. They did not look with favor upon Greek claims to western Asia Minor, southern Albania, and eastern Thrace. They opposed

President Woodrow Wilson (*back row, center*) and Eleutherios Venizelos (*front row, far right*) at Sèvres during treaty negotiations following World War I. (Benaki Museum)

strongly the cession to Greece of Smyrna on the grounds that its population was primarily Turkish, not Greek as Venizelos insisted. Furthermore, the city constituted a natural and indispensable outlet for the export of goods from Central Anatolia. To deprive Turkey of such an important port would be prejudicial and contrary to the spirit of the fourteen points on which the conference was based.

The American attitude might appear to be a contradiction of Wilson's policy, since the Greek landing at Smyrna on 15 May 1919 had been accomplished with the approval of the American president. At that time, however, Wilson was in conflict with the Italians over the disposition of Fiume and other territories surrounding the Adriatic Sea. Moreover, he had serious misgivings relative to Italian aspirations in Asia Minor. When he gave his consent to the occupation of Smyrna he acted unilaterally and for tactical considerations, without consulting American experts on the Territorial Commission on Greek Affairs.

Two closely related problems were the issues of eastern Thrace and southern Albania. On 1 March 1919 the peace conference's commission on territorial acquisitions had voted to cede the whole of eastern Thrace to Greece, except for a small area east of the town of Chataldja which was to serve as a buffer between Constantinople and the Greek frontier. Lloyd George and Georges Clemenceau, the French premier, agreed but immediately they met with the opposition of Wilson. The American position was based on the fact that the liberation of eastern Thrace from Turkey in the First Balkan War had been accomplished through the sacrifices of the Bulgarian armed forces. To exclude Bulgaria from a generous portion of the spoils of war and to deprive her of access to the Aegean would be unjust. Despite pressure from the British and the French, the appeals of Venizelos, and notwithstanding a Senate resolution (21 January 1920) in favor of the Greek claims, Wilson refused to alter his position. His obstinacy brought the negotiations on the Turkish Treaty to a virtual standstill. To eliminate the impasse the Supreme Council went over the president's head, and by a majority vote ceded eastern Thrace to Greece. The United States also opposed Greek claims to southern Albania on the grounds that the population was Albanian, not Greek.

The other part of the settlement with Turkey involved the creation of an independent Armenian state whose territorial integrity no European country was prepared to guarantee. Since the United States had no political entanglements in the Near East, the idea of an American mandate for Armenia was introduced as the logical alternative. Despite the objections of his secretary of state and his military advisers, Wilson was receptive to the proposal, but Congress was not. From a political and military point of view, the reluctance of Congress is understandable, though there is good reason to speculate whether a colossal tragedy could have been averted had there been an American presence in Anatolia to act as a mitigating influence.[1]

The American Response to the Destruction of Smyrna.

The devastation which attended the defeat of the Greek army in Asia Minor had few precedents in recorded history. As the Kemalist forces made their inexorable march westward, they followed the path of several hundred thousand refugees desperately trying to reach the western coast of Asia Minor in the hope of saving themselves from the advancing armies. In Smyrna, approximately 250,000 Greeks and Armenians (about 100,000 from the interior and 150,000 local residents)[2] gathered at the quay where the drama that unfolded was worthy of the cataclysmic aura in a Biblical tale.

In the panic that resulted, Allied consuls attempted to give formal assurances to the Greeks and Armenians that they need not fear for their lives. Only George Horton, the American consul general in Smyrna, refused. He was aware that the vindictive passions in the Near East, the isolationist mood of the United States Congress, the misgivings of President Harding, and the serious state of disarray within the Greek armed forces permitted him no such optimism. Horton informed the State Department that he could not assure the Armenians and Greeks that they would remain safe.[3] On 4 September Horton cabled Admiral Bristol in Constantinople begging him "in the interests of humanity and for the sake of American interests" to mediate with Mustafa Kemal for amnesty to permit the orderly withdrawal of Greek troops from Anatolia and possibly avoid the destruction of Smyrna. The State Department "was not inclined," however, to do more than to send destroyers for the protection of American lives and property.[4] Acting Secretary of State William Phillips replied: "The situation would not appear to justify this government assuming the role of voluntary mediator."[5]

The Allies, faced with impending chaos on a massive scale and determined to look after the safety of their own nationals, were not eager to consider schemes for the evacuation of refugees. The British and French landed marines to guard their consulates, while the Italians assisted the Turks in patrolling the city. For his part, Admiral Bristol issued strict orders to his officers to avoid any action which could be interpreted as cooperation with Turkey's enemies, a policy that met with the approval of the acting secretary of state.[6]

Yet, despite this official aloofness, the Americans were the only ones who truly considered the fate of the refugees. Even before the departure of the Greek authorities on 8 September, Horton took the initiative. With the cooperation of leading American citizens, businessmen, and social and humanitarian groups he organized a Disaster Relief Committee to distribute food among the destitute.[7] When 6,000 bags of flour were discovered in an American warehouse, the committee took possession of it, and after obtaining money and private motor vehicles from its members, bakers were hired and within a day the Americans had a respectable relief organization at work feeding refugees. When the American Consulate burned during the great fire (13–14 September), Horton

Guarding the bread line in Constantinople, ca. autumn 1922. (*National Geographic*)

remained undaunted. He moved his headquarters to an adjoining building and continued his work without interruption.

Admiral Bristol agreed to cooperate, though not without some prodding by the British high commissioner.[8] When the committee cabled to Constantinople for funds on 6 September, the Admiral felt free to grant the request on condition that the entire operation be accomplished as discretely as possible. He suggested to the State Department that $50,000 be transferred specifically to the American Red Cross in Constantinople to avoid the impression that the United States intended to undertake relief work in Smyrna.[9] But when the true magnitude of the crisis could no longer be denied, Bristol met with the managing director of the Near East Relief, the director of the Red Cross Russian mission, and several other representatives of American organizations in Smyrna to decide what course of action should be taken. It was agreed that a relief unit should be dispatched to render whatever emergency assistance the political and military situation might permit. The group took along large supplies of bread, flour, milk, and medicines. It arrived in Smyrna on the morning of 9 September, only hours before the Turkish troops entered the city.[10]

The zeal of the Disaster Relief Committee was contagious to the point where, at times, American sailors and legation officials were led to take illegal actions in behalf of the refugees. One evening sailors from an American ship smuggled bags of flour to the quay from where it was taken to a nearby cemetery, and a makeshift bakery was quickly established.[11] A Greek friend of Jefferson Caffery has written:

> I also remember with gratitude the "mistaken" activities of Jefferson Caffery who, despite the orders of his government relative to the observance of strict neutrality, responded to our appeals and sent light American naval vessels to several sensitive points on the shores of Asia Minor which were crammed with thousands of women and children.

Caffery reports in his memoirs that American naval personnel "assisted hundreds of thousands to escape by helping to get vessels to carry them away."[12]

With the outbreak of the Smyrna fire on 13 September, the official American attitude began to change quickly. Faced with a catastrophe of large proportions and with the threat to its citizens and commercial interests, the United States government could no longer hide behind a veil of neutrality. While neutrality continued to dominate Washington's official policy, the State Department actively sought the support of the Allies in a cooperative effort to contain the effects of the disaster.

As the first refugees began to trickle into Greece they were lavish in their praise for the alacrity shown by American sailors in their efforts to render whatever assistance they could.[13] The Greek press was also at a loss for superlatives to express the gratitude of the Greek people. In the florid and overdrawn journalistic style of the Near East, each newspaper tried to outdo its competitors in heaping praise upon the United States and its diplomatic representatives.[14] Without attempting to minimize the role of the Greek government, it is safe to say that after 13 September the American Navy,[15] American relief agencies, and the State Department were the most important factors in the efforts to effect emergency relief and speedy evacuation. There is a considerable body of primary and secondary evidence which attests to this fact.[16] The British chargé, C. H. Bentinck, described the American effort as one that surpassed all other efforts put together, excepting the Greek. Greece, he wrote, owed to "America a debt of gratitude which [it] is to be presumed will not be quickly forgotten." Dr. Fridtjof Nansen, high commissioner with the League of Nations for refugees, wrote to Bristol: "I am well aware that

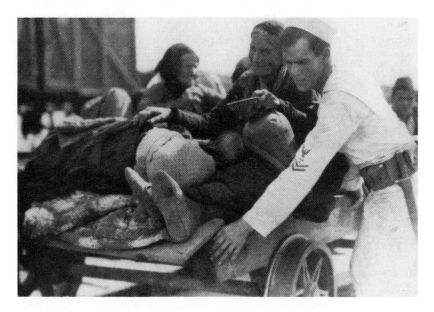

American sailor evacuating refugees on a hand truck in Smyrna, September 1922. (*National Geographic*)

the real direction of this evacuation lay in your hands and it is to you that the credit is due for the wonderful way in which it was carried out.[17]

Refugee movement on such a massive scale was something new. With the possible exception of the Armenians, rarely had so many people been forced to migrate in such large numbers. Greece, already exhausted by a decade of foreign and domestic turmoil, found herself confronted by a gigantic task. A country of approximately 5,000,000 people had to shelter, feed, and settle about 1,500,000 of her destitute countrymen. Except for Israel, no other nation in the twentieth century has achieved so much as Greece in absorbing so many of its uprooted brethren.

However, it was one matter to transfer refugees across the Aegean and quite another to assure their survival. To save hundreds of thousands from the Turkish sword and then lose most of them to pestilence, hunger, and exposure would have magnified the tragedy. Emergency relief was only a temporary solution, though it was not clear who would assume the burden. Even as Smyrna burned, the Greek and Allied gov-

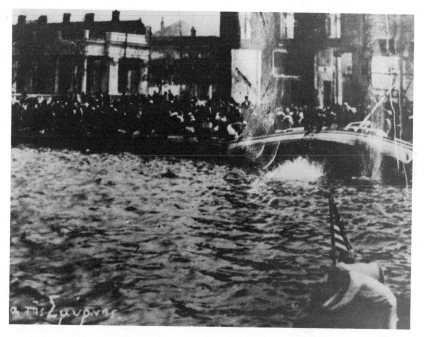

American sailor rescuing refugees in Smyrna during the great fire. (Benaki Museum)

ernments began to anticipate the question. The European powers appeared to be seeking ways to avoid the responsibility of relief by assuming that the Americans would take the initiative. The minister of public assistance, Apostolos Doxiades, made an impassioned plea to the American Red Cross. "To be or not to be?" he asked. "That is the question." The time had come for America and other nations to decide whether the Greek nation must live or die. "My hopes," he said, "center on America. The existence of my country, I believe, is in her hands."[18] On a less dramatic note Venizelos expressed the same sense of urgency. In October 1922 he gave an interview to the *International Interpreter* in which he expressed his gratitude to the United States for the emergency relief work of American agencies. This humanitarian undertaking must not be interrupted. Europe was too exhausted by war and political convulsions to render sufficient financial support. And so it was to America, primarily, that the Greek people now looked for economic assistance. With an eye to the looming refugee problem, he added: "There is one point which I particularly wish to stress, and it is that we need help in the organization of relief as much as we need funds."[19]

Bristol and the State Department emphasized that no American involvement would take place unless it was accompanied by Allied and Greek willingness to share in the task. The Allies must not avoid their responsibility, because they were largely responsible for the difficulties in which Greece now found herself.[20] President Harding was agreeable to the possibility of continued American assistance, but expressed the same reservations as Admiral Bristol. Nevertheless, it is clear that the State Department was ready to take the initiative should the procrastination of the Allies endanger the lives of the refugees. Bristol was instructed to submit his own plan if he reached an impasse in his discussions with the Allied representatives relative to a general program of relief.

The response of Admiral Bristol is significant, because it served as the basic guideline in the overall policy of the United States toward all aspects of the refugee problem. Most important was the necessity for Greece to demobilize in order to release funds for the reimbursement of her soldiers and for the settlement of her refugees. If Greece agreed to place herself on a peace footing, Bristol was willing to recommend assisting her with funds to care for her demobilized army and her refugees. This assistance would be given with the understanding that the Greek government would handle all relief work in its country and that American relief organizations would not be drawn into operations in Greece, which would mean large expenditures of money on a more or less permanent basis.[21] These views met with the approval of officials in the State Department who instructed Caffery to convey to the Greek government the spirit of Bristol's ideas.

After receiving assurance from the Allied governments that the United States could expect their cooperation and financial support, President Harding, at the request of the Near East Relief, called a conference at the White House on 7 October to formulate plans for coordinating the work of American relief organizations and for the creation of a national committee to assist in raising funds. The chairmanship was assigned to the president's personal secretary, Will Hays. The result of the conference was a formal agreement outlining the organizational structure of the relief effort.

The American Red Cross (ARC) and the Near East Relief (NER) were recognized as the primary agencies for the task. The two organizations were to act jointly under the general direction of the Red Cross. The ARC was to deal with the emergency in Europe and the NER was to oversee the relief work in Asia, though the latter organization eventually found itself doing considerable work in Greece. A special fund, known as the Near East Emergency Fund, was created. The money was to be raised by a nationwide appeal, endorsed by the president and a special committee composed primarily of the chairmen of leading American philanthropic and governmental organizations.[22] On 8 October, President Harding issued a statement to the press in which he made known the full text of the White House agreement. He concluded by expressing the hope that "the heart of the American people will respond generously in enabling these agencies of relief to meet the crying emergency."[23] On 25 November (Thanksgiving Day) the fund-raising drive began officially, and it lasted a little over one month. The goal was $20,000,000.[24] The relief work was carried on almost exclusively by the ARC, the NER, other American philanthropic agencies, the Greek government, and European governments and private groups.

The Work of the American Red Cross

Up to June 1918 relief work in Greece had been confined almost exclusively to the vicinity of Salonika because of the need to assist in the care and rehabilitation of returning soldiers and because of recurring epidemics of malaria and other related diseases. Several months later a Red Cross Commission for Greece was appointed. To Greece belongs the distinction of having had the first ARC child health center in Europe, which was devoted exclusively to preventive medicine. The preparatory work was begun in March 1919 under the direction of Dr. Edward Capps and completed in July of the same year.[25]

For the next three years the Red Cross was active in helping Greek families whose relatives in the United States had fought with the American forces in the First World War. These people were supplied with garments, blankets, and medical care. Self-help groups were organized under the direction of Red Cross representatives, physicians, and volunteer workers to teach the rudiments of sanitary living, good nutrition, and child care. Special attention was given to orphans to help complement the work of the NER. Approximately twenty child health centers were built at strategic points throughout Greece. The result was a dramatic decline in child mortality. Young people were trained to render paramedical services. The ARC was also instrumental in changing the image of Greek women by advancing their role in public welfare work. By 1922 women had become an indispensable element in all social work carried on in the country.

Every effort was made to instill in the refugees a sense of self-sufficiency. Clinics, schools, equipment, and supplies were turned over to various local agencies as soon as they demonstrated their ability to do the work themselves.[26] All activities were carried out with the energetic cooperation of the Greek government, the American legation, and the American consulates.[27] Following the defeat of the Greek forces in Asia Minor the ARC was the first foreign organization to arrive in Smyrna to assist with the refugee problem. The NER was already established there. On 13 October the NER vice-chairman, A. Ross Hill, and a group of experienced personnel sailed for Greece. At the same time, nurses serving in other parts of Europe were directed to proceed to Athens. By 29 October an effective Red Cross unit was established and in control of relief operations.

It was understood from the beginning that Red Cross assistance was a temporary measure to serve the needs of the refugees until the time when the Greek people would be able to help themselves. It was chiefly because of this policy that the ARC unit never exceeded forty-five Americans. With this small group and a large number of Greeks, an efficient system was organized under which 533,000 refugees were fed daily. During the winter months the number reached 860,000 per day. Approximately 24,000 tons of food, clothing, blankets, shoes, and medical supplies were distributed during the period when the ARC was officially in charge of relief work in Greece.[28]

The extensive use of the Greek people in the relief effort was not without its beneficial results. Both native Greeks and refugees were compelled to accept the inevitability of national self-rehabilitation. The process of assimilation, a very sensitive and difficult problem, was helped along by the ability of the ARC to demonstrate to the Greeks the need to cooperate with one another for the sake of simple preservation.[29] Consequently, when the Red Cross withdrew on 30 June 1923, there remained an extensive relief organization composed of Greeks who were able to function after the departure of the Americans. Tables 1, 2, 3, and 4 give a good summary of the ARC's accomplishments. By any standard of measurement it is not an overstatement to describe the role of ARC as massive. From September 1922 to 30 June 1923 the most extensive single foreign activity of the Red Cross was that by which it met the emergency following the defeat of the Greek forces. During that period ARC expenditures were approximately $3,000,000.[30]

The Work of the Near East Relief

Next to the ARC, the NER performed the largest service in rendering aid to the refugees. At the time of the Smyrna disaster, it was the only relief agency in the area. Soon afterwards, the Turks forced the NER to leave the country and to abandon its Greek and American orphanages in Anatolia. The only recourse that remained was the transfer of the orphans from Asia Minor to Greece. Under the leadership of Admiral Bristol and primarily through the use of American vessels, a systematic program of evacuation was begun. By 1923 the number of children in Greek orphanages reached approximately 25,000. They were housed in every conceivable place where they could be fed and sheltered. In addition to the buildings provided by the Greek government, the NER built an elaborate orphanage on the island of Syra which was capable of accommodating 2,500 children.[31] This orphanage was the largest and most complete institution of its kind in the Near East.

Next to the immediate need for food and shelter the most important requirement was medical care. There was hardly a child who did not have at least one serious disease which, more often than not, was communicable. To meet this emergency, well-equipped hospitals, clinics, and dispensaries were established in each of the orphanages (see Table 5).

Education was the next priority. The need for vocational training was especially critical, since Greek males between the ages of eighteen and forty-five were detained in Turkey, ostensibly for the purpose of fulfilling their military obligations, though in reality they comprised a sizeable group of hostages. Consequently, the future of most refugee families rested on the shoulders of the young people, many of whom were catapulted from childhood to adulthood in a matter of months. By September 1924 the NER's orphanage schools were fully equipped and able

TABLE 1

American Red Cross Operations in Greece
Recapitulation of Medical Program

Months	No. hospitals equipped	No. hospital beds supplied	No. patients treated	No. ambu-latoria	No. ambulataria cases treated	No. cases typhus	No. cases smallpox	No. cases cholera	No. cases typhoid	No. cases malaria	No. other contagious diseases	Death from typhus	Death from smallpox
November	0	0	0	1	3,000	234	215	0	1	200	3	81	25
December	2	33	120	13	21,185	96	467	0	11	392	696	13	56
January	10	486	735	14	23,742	1,031	650	0	78	2,627	948	266	114
February	9	380	1,215	16	36,434	1,329	433	0	15	3,622	868	152	46
March	10	220	1,818	5	35,510	1,594	436	0	38	9,112	937	308	18
April	15	500	2,631	13	39,814	1,056	201	0	22	13,317	1,029	51	11
May	4	45	1,763	3	39,708	739	63	0	40	25,307	128	37	0
June	9	87	1,499	6	34,150	12	6	0	23	20,200	240	2	0
Total	59	1,751	9,781	71	233,543	6,091	2,471	0	228	74,777	4,849	910	270

SOURCE: American Red Cross, *Annual Report for the Year Ended June 30, 1923*, 64.

TABLE 2

American Red Cross Operations in Greece
Recapitulation of Feeding Program, November 1922–July 1923

Month	No. refugees (gov't. figs.)	No. adults fed	No. children under 3 years old	No. sick invalids and convalescents fed	No. nursing and pregnant mothers fed	Total no. refugees receiving A.R.C. food	Total no. rations fed	No. feeding stations established	No. milk stations established
November	850,277	170,384	4,478	1,323	250	176,435	5,293,050	4	8
December	850,277	359,079	15,127	7,972	1,847	384,025	11,904,775	52	25
January	850,277	426,991	27,809	7,010	2,192	459,002	14,229,062	20	13
February	850,277	461,683	20,597	9,967	2,409	494,656	13,840,424	25	21
March	889,093	495,654	24,462	10,775	2,349	533,240	16,530,440	17	31
April	889,093	487,796	29,411	10,257	2,301	527,965	15,838,950	15	53
May	889,093	454,481	32,075	12,032	2,607	524,195	16,343,045	8	8
June	889,093	317,791	28,934	8,670	3,179	368,584	11,057,520	1	1
July	889,093	324,240	28,732	8,655	3,147	364,784	11,308,304	0	0
Total							116,345,570	142	160

SOURCE: *American Red Cross, Annual Report for the Year Ended June 30, 1923,* 64.

TABLE 3

American Red Cross Operations in Greece
Recapitulation of Sanitary Program

Month	Total no. refugees (gov't fig.)	No. vaccinations by A.R.C.	No. typhoid and paratyphoid inoculations by A.R.C.	No. cholera inoculations by A.R.C.	No. vaccinations by other agencies	No. typhoid and paratyphoid inoculations by other agencies
November	850,277	0	0	0	0	0
December	850,277	3,600	0	0	0	0
January	850,277	24,000	500	0	22,450	25,100
February	850,277	28,475	7,569	7,569	62,110	60,600
March	889,093	16,044	27,964	27,964	92,714	89,086
April	889,093	19,992	30,329	30,329	64,146	52,964
May	889,093	12,973	17,532	11,887	6,057	7,741
June	889,093	9,850	7,167	7,167	1,000	5,000
Total		114,934	91,061	84,916	248,477	240,491

SOURCE: American Red Cross, *Annual Report for the Year Ended June 30, 1923,* 65.

TABLE 4

American Red Cross Operations in Greece
Recapitulation of Sanitary Program

Month	No. cholera inoculations by other agencies	Delousing plants established by A.R.C.	Bathing plants established by A.R.C.	No. refugees deloused by A.R.C.	No. refugees bathed by A.R.C.	No. refugees deloused by other agencies	No. refugees bathed by other agencies
November	0	1	1	800	800	3,000	3,000
December	0	5	5	4,700	4,700	0	0
January	25,100	11	11	9,100	9,100	27,453	27,453
February	60,600	15	12	54,179	64,179	2,810	2,810
March	89,086	24	21	83,511	93,661	22,939	27,939
April	52,964	9	6	120,543	120,543	19,676	19,676
May	7,741	1	1	89,555	89,555	28,938	28,938
June	5,000	0	0	37,095	37,095	7,700	7,700
Total	240,491	66	57	399,483	419,633	112,516	117,516

SOURCE: American Red Cross, *Annual Report for the Year Ended June 30, 1923*, 65.

TABLE 5

Infant Mortality Rates in NER Orphanages, 1923–25

Year	Average No. of Orphans	Death rate (percent)
1923	12,800	1.6
1924	7,500	0.7
1925	4,400	0.4

SOURCE: C. Luther Fry, Frank A. Ross, and Elbridge Sibley, *The Near East and American Philanthropy* (New York: Columbia Univ. Press, 1929), 137.

to offer the standard public school education of Greece. Within a short time the orphans, many of whom spoke only Turkish, were able to speak, read, and write in Greek. The care of each child involved the dispensing of twenty-five specialized services. For the last six months of 1923 the cost of this work averaged $7.53 per child per month.[32] Boys over the age of ten attended vocational schools where manual and industrial skills were taught, while girls were given training in domestic skills and home economics. At all times the ultimate goal was self-sufficiency. During an inspection tour of these schools, Plastiras was so touched by the reception he received and by the progress he witnessed that he adopted five orphans as his own. Special institutions were created to aid handicapped children, some of whom were blind or deaf-mutes. A Braille code was developed especially to help the Armenian orphans for whom the language was a serious problem. Scholarships were awarded to selected Greek teachers so that they might attend the Perkins Institute in Boston for training in the teaching of the deaf and blind.[33]

It was evident that education and training would have minimal value unless efforts were made to facilitate the assimilation of these young people into Greek society by providing them with jobs and a wholesome environment. A special department was created for the placing of children with relatives, in foster homes, or on farms where they could establish normal social relationships and put to use the skills they had learned in the orphanage schools. By 1 January 1927, 5,428 children were under the care of this division. In order to meet the needs of those children who could not be placed in proper surroundings, the NER established working boys' homes under the direction of C. C. Thurber.[34] For a small sum, a boy could obtain clean lodgings under safe and wholesome conditions.

Though the NER's chief responsibility was the care of orphans, it was inevitable that, after its arrival in Greece, it should have become involved in adult relief and rehabilitation as well. The NER provided assistance by organizing Near East Industries, an adaptation of the Goodwill Industries' workshops. Some refugees were hired to restore used clothing shipped from the United States, while refugee women were engaged to produce needle work which was sold to tourists and in NER offices in the United States. At one point, the income from these activities reached $100,000 per year and was used to further additional relief work.[35]

Finally, the NER worked in close cooperation with smaller organizations by providing them with organizational assistance, information, buildings and equipment, and financial aid. The organization's expenditures are illustrative of the magnitude of its contribution. From 1915 to 31 December 1923, $85,774,269 were spent in the Near East to cover a wide variety of relief, philanthropic, and educational services. Of this amount $9,489,515 were spent in 1923.[36] By 31 December 1924 the total reached the sum of $90,337,821.[37] The amount for general and individual relief in Greece to the end of 1922 was only $35,914.[38] For 1923 the NER's appropriations jumped to $866,626.[39]

Such expenditures would have been impossible without the full support of the American people and the American press. Large metropolitan newspapers did an effective job in advertising the plight of the refugees and arousing an interest in their behalf. Advisory committees sprang up throughout the United States, representing various religious, social, and philanthropic organizations. The nationwide interest in America is illustrated by the fact that in a single month (December 1923) 76,735 separate, numbered receipts were issued by the NER to individual contributors. Of greater significance, perhaps, is the fact that 73 percent of this number were issued to persons who had never contributed to an NER fund-raising drive. The most important role was played by American educational leaders, both religious and secular, who contributed not only to the salvation of children in the Near East, but to the development of character in American youngsters by teaching them the lesson of personal sacrifice. One NER official testified that without the assistance of such organizations as public and private schools, the Boy Scouts, and Girl Scouts in America, the NER's achievements would have been virtually impossible.[40]

The influence of the NER often extended beyond the realm of relief work. By request of the Turkish and Greek governments, for example, the organization served with the International Commission as a neutral intermediary in the exchange of Turkish and Greek populations following the signing of the Treaty of Lausanne. For its monumental service to humanity the NER earned the praise of President Coolidge who wrote that the contribution of the Near East Relief "is a story of philanthropic achievement which may well be a satisfaction to all our people."[41]

The American Women's Hospitals

The overall relief effort was given additional impetus by the work of the American Women's Hospitals of New York (AWH). The group was founded in 1911 by women doctors desiring a share in the "glory" of overseas medical relief work. Accordingly, they adopted "a naive resolution calling upon the War Department for a square deal regardless of sex, color, or previous condition of servitude."[42] The idealism of this resolution was perhaps an anachronism in relation to the temper of the times, but the sense of devotion which it inspired in those women, who accepted it as an article of faith, was real.

The AWH worked closely with the ARC and NER in a cooperative effort which was exemplary. When the fire in Smyrna broke out, Dr. Esther Lovejoy went directly to the city, without papers or a military permit, and joined other Americans in arranging immediate relief for the destitute.[43] Other personnel of the AWH were posted in islands of the Aegean and in Greece to help with the medical needs of the fleeing refugees. A "Quarantine island" (Macronissi) was used for the care of those with communicable diseases. In October, Dr. Lovejoy left for the United States to raise funds for medical relief. Within a few months the AWH's headquarters in New York had succeeded in raising $500,000—certainly, no mean accomplishment for a group prone to "naive resolutions."

The AWH was, in effect, the medical arm of the NER. It assumed full responsibility for the medical care of all orphans and NER medical relief work in Greece. The organization paid the salaries of medical personnel and provided large sums for the purchase of medicines and medical supplies. A total of 1,500 beds was provided in NER hospitals under the administration of the AWH. Every effort was made to heal, comfort, and reduce the trauma of uprooting. If there is any common denominator applicable to those women, it surely must be heroism, for heroism

American Minister Robert P. Skinner addressing the 1930 graduating class at the American Women's Hospitals School of Nursing at Kokinia (near Piraeus). (Photo courtesy of American Women's Hospitals Service Committee of the American Medical Women's Association.)

was the common denominator among AWH physicians and nurses in the field who braved the elements, death, and the loneliness of desolate posts throughout Greece. For their dedication, the women of the AWH earned the gratitude and devotion of the Greek people. Dr. Lovejoy summarized the influence of the AWH as follows: "There isn't anything on these islands we can't have. [The Greeks] watch our every move, and so long as we take orders from no man (especially from an Englishman, the highest authority) we can give orders to almost anybody."[44]

The Y.M.C.A. and the Y.W.C.A.

The presence of the Y.M.C.A. was not new in Greece. In 1892 a chapter was established in Athens, but before 1914 its work was terminated, partly because of hostility from the Greek Orthodox Church. In 1918, by an invitation to the War Council from Venizelos, the organization was reestablished in Salonika where twenty-five Americans arrived to form a staff that served returning men in uniform.[45] In several towns and cities, "homes" for soldiers and sailors were established in which reading material, entertainment, recreational activities, and meals were provided to ease the pain of loneliness and battle fatigue. Schools were opened to raise the literacy level of many destitute children and adults. S. S. Papadakes, the Director of the Y.M.C.A. in Greece, has estimated that by 1926 the Y.M.C.A. had spent approximately £200,000 sterling in Asia Minor and Greece. The credibility and integrity of the Y.M.C.A. prompted the League of Nations to ask for its assistance in the investigation of Turkey's allegations that Turkish prisoners in Greece were interned under inhuman conditions.[46]

When Smyrna burned, the Y.M.C.A. was there to help. Its activities actually began as soon as the mass retreat of Greek troops gave evidence of an impending catastrophe. The organization worked closely with the American Disaster Committee to feed and shelter the refugees. When evacuation plans were completed, the energies of Y.M.C.A. personnel were turned to the securing of ships and to the protection and feeding of refugees during the actual process of evacuation. Representatives of the Y.M.C.A. escorted the refugees across the Aegean Sea to Greece. They cooperated closely with various American agencies in the distribution of food, milk for infants, blankets, and medicine. They also arranged for suitable housing, provided recreational facilities, and helped to reunite families whose members had been separated in the panic which attended the burning of Smyrna.[47]

The Y.W.C.A. complemented the work of the Y.M.C.A. by concentrating on the care and welfare of females. Among its accomplishments was the establishment of a home for girls and young women; the teaching of Greek, English, shorthand, and typing; and the establishment of a small clinic.

The Role of Private Committees

Another important aspect of American relief was the initiative of committees of various sizes and longevity whose cumulative contribution was substantial. The outstanding examples were the Anglo-American Committee of Salonika, which represented a cooperative effort by British and American private citizens, and the Athens American Relief Committee, headed by Dr. Capps. The Salonika committee worked with the Y.M.C.A. to provide a large array of social, medical, and educational services. Its activities ranged from the saving of lives to the procurement of films and film projectors.[48]

The Athens American Relief Committee was created immediately after the destruction of Smyrna and was composed of influential Americans who made important contributions to emergency relief work. Tons of food, clothing, and medical supplies were distributed through its headquarters. It also exerted a strong political influence in the matter of refugee settlement because its members were representatives and heads of American commercial and relief organizations, educational institutions, and several former members of the American diplomatic corps in Greece. Consequently, the committee played a vital and, at times, controversial role in the relations between the Greek government and the Refugee Settlement Commission. The most important contribution of this group was undoubtedly its catalytic role in the matter of refugee assistance. In late September 1922 the committee issued a report which formed the basis for the urgent appeal that sent American relief agencies to Greece and provided them with a preliminary basis of operation. The British government made an official request for a copy of the report which it promptly passed on to its own relief agencies.[49]

The Role of the Greek Government and the Greek People

The impact of American philanthropy would have been minimal had it not been for the support of the Greek authorities. It is impossible to estimate accurately the magnitude of the Greek government's contribution in dollars, since no accurate figures are available. It is obvious, however, that the expenditures were great. When the Turkish authorities gave permission for Greek ships to enter Smyrna harbor to evacuate the refugees, the Revolutionary government placed vessels of every kind and size at the disposal of Admiral Bristol and the American Navy. There was complete remission of all custom duties on ships carrying relief supplies. This policy was in contrast to the action of Turkish authorities in Constantinople where full duty was levied on all supplies received by the NER. Every available public and private building under the jurisdiction of the government was used to house the refugees—from rehabilitated stables to the National Theater. Wheat was milled and bread was baked at government expense. Transportation and communication services were given free to relief workers. Warehouse and office space, light and heat, private vehicles for relief workers in the field, and living quarters were also furnished at the expense of the government. To expedite its relief work, the government established an elaborate organization in which foreign and domestic relief agencies were brought together for the common good (see Table 6). Cooperation with relief agencies was exemplary. Independent of the expenses incurred in the rendering of these services was the payment to the Red Cross of 530,000,000 drachmas ($9,084,676) to carry on its work. Every effort was also made to facilitate the task for NER in its work with orphans. The American chargé, Ray Atherton, who was conservative in the matter of giving praise to Greek officials, recognized the Greek government's contribution when he wrote: "I venture to point out the . . . efficacious handling and disposition on the part of the Greek authorities of a Greek problem."[50]

In addition to the efforts of the government, the Greek people themselves immediately undertook to help in the solution of the refugee problem. In October 1922 a group of private citizens—under the direction of a leading industrialist, Epaminondas Charilaos—created a nongovernmental organization to render emergency relief assistance. With the cooperation of the authorities and the Greek Red Cross, the group established the Refugee Treasury Fund for the purpose of collecting money to purchase food, medical supplies, and building materials. The governing board of the fund directed the distribution of 200,000 blankets, 2,000 beds, thousands of mattresses, about 2,000 bundles of clothing, as well as many thousand cases of milk and flour. Practically all these supplies came from the American government and private groups in the United States. Parallel with these emergency relief operations, the fund had to execute the difficult task of urban refugee settlement. The erection of permanent communities was begun, and soon several suburbs began to appear around Athens. In a very real sense, therefore, the fund was the precursor to the Refugee Settlement Commission.[51]

European Relief Agencies

Although an account of the work of European relief agencies and international organizations is beyond the scope of this work, the role of these agencies from about October 1922 to 30 June 1923 deserves to be noted in order that the American contribution might be viewed in its

TABLE 6

Organizational Structure of the Greek Government's Relief Program

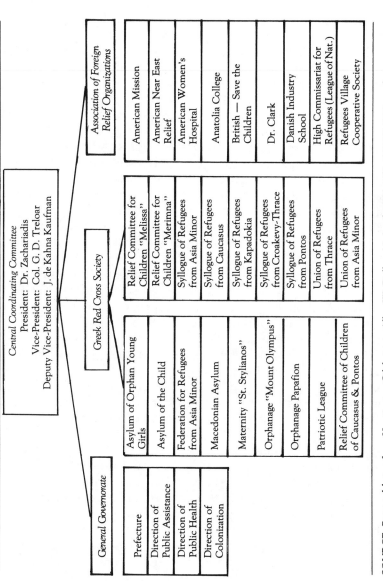

Central Coordinating Committee
President: Dr. Zachariadis
Vice-President: Col. G. D. Treloar
Deputy Vice-President: J. de Kahna Kaufman

General Governorate

- Prefecture
- Direction of Public Assistance
- Direction of Public Health
- Direction of Colonization
- Asylum of Orphan Young Girls
- Asylum of the Child
- Federation for Refugees from Asia Minor
- Macedonian Asylum
- Maternity "St. Stylianos"
- Orphanage "Mount Olympus"
- Orphanage Papafion
- Patriotic League
- Relief Committee of Children of Caucasus & Pontos

Greek Red Cross Society

- Relief Committee for Children "Melissa"
- Relief Committee for Children "Merimna"
- Syllogue of Refugees from Asia Minor
- Syllogue of Refugees from Caucasus
- Syllogue of Refugees from Kapadokia
- Syllogue of Refugees from Croakevy-Thrace
- Syllogue of Refugees from Pontos
- Union of Refugees from Thrace
- Union of Refugees from Asia Minor

Association of Foreign Relief Organizations

- American Mission
- American Near East Relief
- American Women's Hospital
- Anatolia College
- British — Save the Children
- Dr. Clark
- Danish Industry School
- High Commissariat for Refugees (League of Nat.)
- Refugees Village Cooperative Society

SOURCE: Personal letter from Huntington Gilchrist to Allen W. Dulles, 11 April 1924, 868. 51RSC/185, enclosure.

proper perspective. The British Red Cross spent 1,589,011 drachmas ($27,237). The British Relief Committee and the Save the Children Fund spent 12,500 pounds ($57,185) and 10,177,192 drachmas ($174,446), respectively. The contributions of the Action Suisse amounted to 407,268 drachmas ($6,987). Those of the Action Hollandaise reached a total of 300,000 drachmas ($5,142), while the International Red Cross gave 203,354 drachmas ($3,486).[52] There were many other groups involved in emergency relief, but their true impact is difficult to ascertain, since reliable figures regarding the size of their membership and the magnitude of their expenditures are not available.

The massive nature of the relief effort soon began to put a serious strain on the financial resources of all American relief organizations. It was clear that emergency relief could not be continued indefinitely and that a realistic solution to the refugee problem must be found quickly. Despite the initial enthusiasm of the American people, the president's coordinating committee was not able to reach the initial goal of $20,000,000. One factor was the policy of the ARC. Because November was usually the month for the ARC's annual fund-raising drive, it seemed unwise to make a separate and distinct effort to obtain relief funds. Accordingly, Red Cross chapters were requested to offer an opportunity for subscriptions to the Emergency Relief Fund, but not to urge the matter to the prejudice of the annual fund-raising drive. As a direct result of this policy the returns from the appeal fell short of the original goal. There also was the inevitable intrusion of politics into an area ostensibly nonpolitical. Will Hays complained to President Harding that the effort to stir up a greater sympathetic interest in the United States was often diverted into discussions of international politics.[53]

Financial considerations were only one part of the problem. Important, too, was the fundamental aspect of the relief organizations. These groups existed specifically for the purpose of meeting the first shocks of the disaster and for easing the pain of uprooting until local agencies and institutions could reorganize themselves to undertake the task of refugee settlement. It could be expected that by June, Greece would be at the highest point of productiveness and would have available a maximum amount of grains, fruits, and vegetables. There was also the social aspect to consider. It was evident that self-sufficiency and the assimilation of the refugees into Greek society would have to be the basis of any permanent settlement scheme. To continue indefinitely the mass relief work in segregate refugee camps would have been self-defeating.

Greek authorities were aware of the probability of a speedy withdrawal by American relief agencies. Anticipating this eventuality, government officials began to plead with American representatives against a hasty termination of emergency assistance. Plastiras delivered a public plea in which he explained that "Greece would be happy and proud if she were able alone to accomplish this work of relief; but this is materially impossible." He warned against "a terrible tragedy" if the "Governments of Europe and America do not hasten to her assistance. In the name of human solidarity," he pleaded, "I ask for the help of the Governments of the Christian nations."[54]

American officials were sympathetic, but they were also adamant in their determination that no class of "professional refugees" should be created. On 29 January, Colonel William H. Haskell, ARC commissioner for Greece, advised the president of the ARC, John Barton Payne, that the ARC conclude its work in June at the latest. The problem was going to continue for years and unless there was a speedy cutoff, the difficulty of withdrawal would increase with the passing of time. Payne agreed. On 1 March he officially informed the State Department of the ARC's decision to terminate its work on 30 June. The ensuing months witnessed a spirited correspondence among the Foreign Ministry, the American legation, the State Department, and the central offices of the various relief agencies in the United States. All efforts to postpone the withdrawal, however, proved futile. On 30 June, American emergency relief work came to an end.[55]

There followed a series of banquets, religious ceremonies, and social functions to honor and express the gratitude of the Greek people to the departing Americans. These affairs were often very moving, especially those in which small refugee children took part. On the evening of 27 June, thirty-seven ARC workers and officials were decorated by the Greek government in an elaborate ceremony. The highest decoration of the Greek nation, the Grand Cross of the Savior, was awarded to the ARC. In order to add drama to the event, the king attached the medal at the top of the ARC flag.[56]

The attention of the Greek government now focused on the problem of filling the vacuum left by the departing Americans. At this crucial point in time the League of Nations came to the rescue and, with the cooperation of the American and British governments, established the Refugee Settlement Commission, the agency destined to play the most important role in the permanent settlement of the refugees.

American Influence in Greece

The importance of American aid to Greece rests not merely on the fact that it served certain specific and short-term needs. More significant are the lasting, beneficial effects this aid had on Greek-American relations during the next four decades. To the popular mind, all past impressions and expectations in regard to American altruism were amply justified by the response of the American people to the Greeks' call for help, when they had reached the lowest point in their history since their liberation from Ottoman-Turkish domination.

8

The United States and the Establishment of the Refugee Settlement Commission

In July 1923 peace between Turkey and the Allies was concluded with the signing of the Treaty of Lausanne.[1] A separate part of the Treaty was the *Convention Concerning the Exchange of Greek and Turkish Populations* signed at Lausanne on 30 January 1923. By the terms of this *convention* a compulsory exchange would take place between Turkish nationals of the Greek Orthodox faith living in Turkey and Greek nationals of the Moslem religion living in Greece. Article I reads:

> As from 1st May 1923, there shall take place a compulsory exchange of Turkish nationals of the Greek Orthodox religion established in Turkish territory and of Greek nationals of the Moslem religion established in Greek territory. These persons shall not return to live in Turkey or Greece respectively without the authorization of the Turkish Government or Greek Government respectively.[2]

With these words the fate of approximately 1,800,000 people was sealed, and their uprooting was given a semblance of legitimacy by the exigencies of international politics.[3]

To exchange so many people was one thing; to provide for their permanent settlement was quite another. The response of the Great Powers to this need was the creation of the Refugee Settlement Commission under the auspices of the League of Nations. The initiative of the State Department and the American Red Cross was a significant factor in the conception of the commission, though in the final analysis, international politics intervened to prevent active American participation in the creation of a permanent settlement scheme.

The Withdrawal of American Relief Agencies

The Treaty of Lausanne simply formalized a status quo whose inevitability had become self-evident months before the conclusion of the Lausanne Conference. At the same time, American relief agencies were anxious to terminate their work in Greece as soon as possible. The Greek government was left with no alternative but to seek a permanent solution to its refugee problem. This burden loomed large because the technical and financial resources of the country were insufficient to cope with such a monumental task. It was clear that foreign agencies would again be called upon to provide most of the necessary assistance.

The Division of Near Eastern Affairs was reluctant to attach itself to any refugee settlement scheme for fear that such an involvement would compound the complications surrounding the issues of recognition and the settlement of war credits. But neither could the attitude of the United States government be one of complete aloofness. American Red Cross officials wanted to withdraw with the official approval of Washington in order to blunt the criticism which would surely follow the official announcement of their intentions.[4] Dulles explained to a delegation of ARC officials the State Department's reluctance to become involved in the matter of the ARC's departure. He pointed out, however, that although the desirability of withdrawing from Greece was recognized by the Division of Near Eastern Affairs, the Greek government would undoubtedly require continued assistance.

On 28 February the ARC was informed that, if it were willing to aid Greek officials in devising a program for permanent refugee settlement, the State Department would be willing to consult with officials of the ARC in regards to the method of carrying it out. The Red Cross was receptive to this proposal on condition that the State Department invite the participation of other governments and other agencies willing to assist in the formulation of a permanent program of reconstruction. If such a plan could be worked out, the ARC was prepared to place all its facilities at the service of the Greek government and would also contribute financially. Red Cross officials expected the transitional process to last four to six weeks. The State Department expected from the beginning, and made it a condition of its cooperation, that the ARC would assist in the formulation of a plan of permanent refugee settlement, while the ARC clearly acquiesced.[5] This understanding was destined to become the crux of the problem insofar as American involvement in the Refugee Settlement Commission (RSC) was concerned.

The Initial Response of the State Department

On 31 March 1923 Secretary of State Hughes sent similar notes to the British, French, and Italian ambassadors in Washington in which he made an appeal on behalf of the refugees. He outlined the salient points of the problem and stressed the need for international cooperation. He informed the British ambassador that if a constructive program could be worked out for the apportionment of the task and for the gradual solution of the refugee problem, American relief agencies would be ready to cooperate. Such cooperation would continue after the termination of the emergency relief work of the American Red Cross. If the British government were "disposed to concur as to the desirability of coordinated action to liquidate the relief emergency in the Near East, an early exchange of views would be desirable."[6] Reaction to the note was favorable, but lukewarm, for in one way or another all three powers made clear their intention to wait for America to take the initiative.[7]

The British ambassador in Washington replied that the British government welcomed the proposal. It would be glad to cooperate with the United States as far as possible, but would wait the receipt of definite proposals from Washington. The French government's response was sympathetic, but hardly encouraging. Pointing to the great loss in manpower and to the heavy financial burden the war had imposed on his country the French ambassador in Washington intimated that rather than giving refugee aid, France could use some assistance. Furthermore, French officials in Paris made it clear to the Greek ambassador that, in the final analysis, the solution to the refugee problem rested on the ability of the Greek government to secure an international loan. France was hardly in the position to participate in such a project.[8] The Italians were ready to consider the American proposal, but they said little else.[9] These replies resolved themselves to a single tacit proposition: The British, French, and Italian governments would agree to cooperate in the formulation of a refugee settlement plan if America would provide a substantial portion of the needed manpower and financial aid to make the plan work.

In the meantime, the proposal for an international refugee loan under the auspices of the League of Nations was in its formative stages. On 25 May the British embassy informed the State Department that the matter would be taken up at a meeting of the Finance Committee of the League of Nations on 15 June and should the United States government be willing to cooperate, the presence of an American representative would be welcomed by the British government.[10] The State Department was receptive to the idea of American participation in these dicussions, but only in an unofficial capacity. In fact, the British proposal had been anticipated for some time in the discussions among officials in the Division of Near Eastern Affairs.

The most significant result from those discussions was the genesis of the idea that an international organization should be created to oversee the settlement of the Greek refugees. On 23 May, Dulles suggested the establishment of an international commission at Athens, which would be representative of those governments willing to give relief and would assist in the formulation of a plan for permanent refugee settlement. He added that if it were agreeable to the participating nations, the president of the commission should be an American. Finally, he suggested the allotment of $500,000 per month in the following six months of the year for the functioning of the commission and for relief work. Of this sum, half should be contributed by American relief agencies.[11] It was emphasized, however, that no American commitment could take place unless the State Department made a "clear definition" of its position relative to the Tripartite Loan of 1918 and unless the Greek government was willing "to meet any obligation, which as a result of the proposed conference . . . may be found to exist."[12]

An additional element of concern was the increasing friction between British and American commercial interests. Contrary to Henry Morgenthau's assertion that Greece was a "fine, broad highway, on which the United States was traveling to and from, in pleasant competition with Great Britain," the facts of the situation were very different. The British were anxious that the United States would exploit the refugee situation to its own benefit. Bentinck, the British chargé in Athens, reported that Greek-American trade threatened to exceed that of Great Britain and Greece and that American financial interests in the country were increasing rapidly. There was also friction between the two governments over the issue of American influence in the RSC and within the relief agencies of the Greek government. Somewhat prophetically, the chargé wrote: "It was sometimes asked whether this great display of charity on the part of America was entirely altruistic, and whether, in return for American assistance in one of the darkest hours of Greece's history, the Greek Government might not later be called to grant all sorts of commercial and economic concessions which, in the circumstances, they hardly would be in a position to refuse." Atherton informed the State Department that Bentinck bluntly stated that the investigation on the part of the League of Nations of possible refugee relief in Greece was virtually a British proposal.[13] This attitude was a significant departure from the original British reaction to Hughes' note of 31 March. From the point of view of American policy it became imperative that the United States government remain outside any settlement scheme which would be directed by the League of Nations. There were two reasons for this attitude: one was the fact that the United States was not a member of the League; the other was the virtual certainty that official American participation in such a plan would serve to embroil the United States government in Greece politically, and it would precipitate a confrontation with Great Britain.

Therefore, it was with certain reservations that Secretary of State Hughes brought to the attention of President Harding the seriousness of the refugee situation. He expressed confidence in the willingness of American agencies to offer their assistance. It was clear, however, that no viable settlement scheme was possible without the support and cooperation of the United States and its wartime allies. In view of American interests in the Near East and the concern of the American public for the fate of the refugees it was difficult for the United States government to remain aloof. American participation in the negotiations at Geneva was desirable, if not absolutely necessary. Hughes also suggested the appointment of an ARC official to serve as a member of an American delegation to attend the meetings of the Finance Committee of the League of Nations, but only insofar as those meetings related to the question of permanent refugee settlement. The secretary cautioned that because of concurrent negotiations with regard to an international refugee loan, American representatives should not appear to assume a commitment which might be interpreted as an involvement by the United States government in the business of the Financial Committee of the League. Finally, no opportunity should be given to the Greek government to connect the American participation in the refugee problem with the issues still separating the State Department and the Greek Foreign Ministry. On the basis of these recommendations and with the approval of the president,[14] the State Department agreed to authorize Frederic R. Dolbeare, a member of the American Special Mission at Lausanne and first secretary of the American embassy in London, to attend the meetings of the Finance Committee in a consultative capacity.[15] It was agreed that Dolbeare would serve as an unofficial spokesman for the ARC until a Red Cross representative could be appointed.

The meetings at Geneva were held during 22–24 June. Dolbeare immediately set out to dispel any misunderstandings regarding America's involvement in Greece. In a lengthy statement he stressed the keen interest of the United States government in the refugee situation, but also noted that the ultimate responsibility for the settlement of the refugees lay with the Greek government. He made no reference to the willingness of the Red Cross to assist in the formative stages of a refugee settlement plan, nor of its offer to contribute supplies towards this purpose. Instead, he painted as dark a picture as possible lest the Greek representatives be induced to entertain exaggerated hopes of American assistance. At the same time, it was recognized that the situation must not be described as hopeless, for such an impression would have had a depressing effect and would not have stimulated the Greeks to help themselves. Dolbeare assured the Financial Committee that, if a definite plan of relief were formulated, the State Department was prepared to recommend the formation of a commission in Athens which would oversee the permanent settlement of the refugees. Such a commission would be comprised of representatives from those governments and agencies that wished to participate.[16]

Although refugee settlement was discussed within the framework of the Financial Committee of the League, as late as 22 June American officials continued to labor under the assumption that any refugee settlement commission would be separate from the League of Nations. Hence, Dolbeare's concluding statement: Such a commission could assist the Greek authorities in continuing the emergency relief work after the departure of the ARC. But in order to make this transition financially feasible, "it would be appropriate that interested Governments or agencies should contribute. The American Red Cross is disposed to appoint a representative and to contribute a fair share to the expenses of the Commission."[17]

The American Red Cross Reverses Itself

Up to this point, it appears to have been expected by everyone concerned—and certainly the State Department had proceeded on this understanding—that the ARC would attempt to enlist the support of other organizations, while its own contributions would continue on a reduced scale.[18] It was with considerable surprise, therefore, that the State Department watched as the Red Cross suddenly stiffened its attitude. The primary factor behind this change of attitude was Colonel Haskell, ARC Commissioner for Greece.

Haskell was a critical factor because the ARC's refugee policy in Greece was formulated on the basis of his recommendations. He appears to have had a strong antipathy for the League, particularly insofar as the refugee question was concerned. He was especially critical of the decision to have Macedonia as the main location for the establishment of the refugees. In a conversation with Atherton, Haskell recommened no affiliation with the League and no announcement of possible American help to Greece until after a thorough investigation of the country's needs had been determined by an international commission. In his opinion, supplies left over by the Red Cross, the improvement of the exchange, and the excellent crop prospects would enable the Greek authorities to support the refugees until November. The time had come for foreign nations to force the Greek government to seek solutions within the limits of its own resources. Irresponsible promises of loans and relief by foreigners, especially Americans, perpetuated the lethargy with which Greek officials seemed to be afflicted.[19]

Despite these developments, the State Department maintained the impression that the ARC would be an integral part of any settlement scheme which might emerge from Geneva. On 29 June the State Department telegraphed instructions to Colonel James A. Logan, Jr.,[20] who was present in Paris as an unofficial assistant delegate to the Reparations Commission, requesting him to attend the meetings of the Greek subcommittee of the League scheduled for the first week in July. He was instructed to reiterate the department's willingness to arrange, through an appropriate agency, for American representation in a refugee settlement commission. As the chief of the Division of Near Eastern Affairs, H. D. Dwight, stated later: "The Department would hardly have given such instructions if it had not supposed that the Red Cross intended to take an interest in the situation and to continue contributions."[21]

The meetings of the finance committee were held on 3 and 4 July, when it was formally proposed that a Refugee Settlement Society be incorporated to provide the organizational basis for refugee settlement. The society would consist of two representatives of the Greek government, one representative of the relief agencies, and an American chairman. The Greek government was to assign suitable land and arrange with Greek banks for a loan of not less that £1,000,000 sterling. It also was stipulated that an earnest effort would be made to secure a loan in the European and American markets. These proposals were communicated to the Greek government on 5 July, and were promptly accepted by the Foreign Ministry.[22]

The Problem of American Participation in the RSC

Colonel Logan did not participate officially in the formulation of the Refugee Settlement Commission, but he took an active part in the meetings and often served as a tempering influence in the deliberations. He cautioned the delegates that a careful reading of Secretary Hughes' note of 31 March would appear to preclude the continuation of charitable relief from American sources on a large scale. He was careful not to suggest that American assistance would be withdrawn entirely; nor did he have any reason to suppose that such a decision was imminent. After the RSC was officially established in September, Colonel Logan reiterated his misgivings regarding the continuation of aid at the levels of the preceding twelve months. He pointed out that, until the RSC could begin its work in earnest and the League could secure a loan for reconstruction purposes, somebody would have to support the refugees. He inquired how the Greek subcommittee proposed to handle the situation.[23]

It was in these circumstances that a committee headed by the famous explorer, Dr. Fridtjof Nansen, was established by the League to deal precisely with the issues raised by Colonel Logan. American agencies were urged to appoint a delegate, while the remaining members of the committee were to be representatives of European relief agencies and the Greek government. There is no doubt that the formation of the Nansen Committee was the fatal blow to all hopes of American participation in the RSC.

The State Department and officials of American agencies became increasingly resentful of the arrogant attitude which was manifested by Dr. Nansen and some representatives of the League. By September the American initiative in the matter of refugee settlement had become more or less passé as Nansen and his committee extolled the success of the League in establishing the RSC and in taking the lead for the reconstruction of Greece. Dr. Nansen contributed to the controversy by his anti-American sentiments. In January 1924 he wrote: "It is not my purpose here to remind the United States of the [Tripartite] agreement of 1917–1918 . . . only fifteen million were actually paid. . . . I only call attention to the fact that in one sense the United States has saved more than you planned in Greece."[24] Such statements served to aggravate the situation and alienate American relief agencies. Petty rivalries and personal quarrels developed which helped to poison the atmosphere to the point where negotiations for the refugee loan became difficult.

After consultations with the State Department, the ARC issued a statement in which it expressed the opinion that the formation of the Nansen Committee would probably encourage Greek authorities to hope that others would solve the refugee problem for them. Furthermore, the scope of the operations contemplated by the RSC appeared to fall outside the emergency activities of the Red Cross. Consequently, Hughes instructed Colonel Logan to state that, while the State Department would not oppose the formation of the Nansen Committee, the American Red Cross did not wish to be represented. The ARC also refused to appoint or recommend a representative lest the Red Cross be made responsible for the success of the RSC.[25]

These explanations tended to gloss over two major problems which had evolved during the preceding months. One was the prevailing antipathy between American and European officials deliberating in Geneva and Lausanne. The former stressed their contributions of the preceding year, while the latter emphasized the need for additional American relief assistance. The State Department refused to involve itself in matters that could be interpreted as a tacit approval of the League of Nations, while private American agencies believed they had done enough.[26] The second problem concerned the motives of the British government. Colonel

Haskell reflected the uncertainty of State Department officials when he wrote: "Personally, I believe the whole proposition [the creation of the RSC and the granting of the refugee loan] is another scheme to secure American finance for Greece and have it administered by European financiers, notably British, under the cloak of the League of Nations."[27]

Greek officials tried to convince the State Department to take a more direct hand in the matter of refugee settlement and to convince American agencies that the need for emergency relief was far from over.[28] On 18 August, Michael Tsamados, the Greek chargé in Washington, addressed a long communication to the Division of Near Eastern Affairs requesting American participation in the Nansen Committee and the RSC. Dulles replied that the department was anxious to place no obstacles to the solution of the refugee problem and had not failed to bring to the attention of the ARC and NER the Greek government's urgent appeals. However, it was the responsibility of these organizations to indicate directly to the appropriate European officials what policy they intended to pursue. Tsamados interpreted Dulles' response as a sign of official indifference, and concluded that it was the State Department which prevented American relief agencies from active participation in the Nansen committee.[29] This impression was strengthened by Secretary Hughes. He instructed Atherton to prod Greek authorities relative to the transfer of those refugees who had not yet been transported to Greece. The State Department felt that, in view of the conclusion of the Lausanne Treaty, Greece and Turkey should be compelled to see their own obligations in the matter.[30]

The withdrawal of the State Department and the ARC from the affairs of the RSC became final in August 1923. As in the case of the League of Nations, it is ironic that the RSC, whose establishment was in no small measure the result of American encouragement, should find itself under the exclusive control of European governments. In retrospect one can see that the repudiation of the RSC by the United States government was inevitable. A persistent theme in the diplomatic correspondence is the firm conviction that, except for emergency relief, no American cooperation should be given which did not provide for appropriate American supervision.[31] With the formation of the Nansen Committee the opportunity for suitable American supervision was eliminated. Insofar as the United States government was concerned, the central obstacle to an American participation in the organization and management of the RSC was the disavowal of the League of Nations by the United States Senate.

In the ensuing months the State Department did its best to follow a neutral course, though not without difficulty. A variety of groups in Greece and the United States emerged. They polarized themselves into two hostile camps—one pressing for more American relief; the other emphasizing the need for the Greek government to assume the responsibility for the refugees. The former had Henry Morgenthau as its unofficial spokesman, while the latter was led by officials of the ARC and the United States government. In the controversies which resulted, the State Department often found itself in the role of a reluctant and unofficial arbitrator. A study of the documents, however, reveals a marked tendency on the part of department officials to be sympathetic to the latter group.[32] Regarding the RSC, three areas remain to be examined: its administrative structures, the selection of its first president, and its accomplishments.

The Organization of the RSC

The formal proposal for the creation of a refugee settlement commission was made in early July 1923; however, almost three months passed before a definite settlement scheme was finally presented to the Council of the League of Nations for official approval. The plan for the RSC was drafted by the Greek subcommittee and presented to the council in the form of two agreements: the *Protocol Relating to the Settlement of Refugees in Greece and the Creation for this Purpose of a Refugees Settlement Commission* and an appendix to it defining the *Organic Statutes of the Greek Refugees Settlement Commission* (see appendixes B and C). The council approved the plan on 29 September 1923, and the Greek representative signed it on the same day.[33]

Under the conditions in these agreements the Greek government undertook to establish a Refugee Settlement Commission which would possess the legal authority and independence of action outlined in the *Organic Statutes*. The commission could make appropriate changes in the domestic laws of the country for the purpose of facilitating the work of refugee settlement. From the point of view of Greek officials this was an onerous provision that bordered on extraterritoriality. Frequently, it served to inflame relations between the RSC and the Greek government.

It also helps to explain Morgenthau's assertion that, in practical terms, he had dictatorial political powers. The Greek government agreed to assign to the RSC 500,000 hectares (1,235,500 acres) of land in which the refugees would be settled and to raise a loan of not less than £3,000,000 or more than £6,000,000 sterling. The proceeds from this loan were to be placed at the disposal of the RSC, while the service of the loan would be guaranteed by the International Financial Commission. The Greek government also agreed to stabilize the economy and to refrain from pledging any new revenues as loan security without the consent of the IFC. Finally, the RSC was to be exempted from all taxes, and taxes paid by the refugees were to be turned over to the commission.

The Organic Statutes defined the legal status, composition and functions of the RSC. The Commission was an independent entity, capable of initiating or being the subject of litigation. There were to be four members: two appointed by the Greek government, one selected by the Council of the League of Nations, and a chairman with a casting vote.

Henry Morgenthau (*center, front, wearing bow tie*) with members and staff of the Refugee Settlement Commission. (Benaki Museum)

The Chairman was to be an American citizen representing those relief organizations which possessed the official sanction of the council. Articles XII and XV stipulated that all property and funds assigned to the commission, as well as income from its own resources, were to be used for the establishment of refugees in productive work. The commission, then, was not a substitute for private relief, but an organization with the task of effecting a long-range program for the permanent settlement of the refugees.

The work of the RSC was organized along three lines: financial, urban, and agricultural. Though the first two departments were integral parts of the total scheme, it was the agricultural phase which touched the people in the most direct way. Most of the refugees were settled on lands where a knowledge of farming and vocational skills were indispensable to survival; therefore, every attempt was made to make the refugees directly responsible for their own fate in order to instill in them a sense of self-accomplishment, independence, and hope. An administrative structure was created by the Greek government in which all the positions that could be filled by refugees were assigned to them. In 1929 Henry Morgenthau reported that 70 percent of the people who had done this work of reconstruction had been refugees.[34]

The RSC's First President

One of the ironies to emerge from these events was the stipulation that the chairman of the RSC be a citizen of the United States—the nation whose government and philanthropic agencies had chosen to remain officially aloof. Dulles had suggested such an appointment in the spring of 1923, but it was the League of Nations which insisted on an American chairman. One reason for this stipulation was the desirability to have the RSC headed by an eminent person whose country enjoyed the unqualified trust and confidence of the Greek people. On a more practical level, Morgenthau was a member of the executive committee of the NER and could not very easily be ignored. Barclay Acheson, associate general secretary of the NER, confessed to Dulles that a genuinely embarrasing situation would have arisen if Morgenthau's availability had been ignored.[35]

American diplomats in Europe and representatives of the ARC and NER were approached repeatedly by delegates of the League and the Greek government with requests for assistance in the selection of a

147

commission chairman. The ARC refused to consider the idea, fearing an entanglement which would make it impossible to divorce itself from future responsibility. The State Department remained uncommitted and made no effort to interfere. The NER, on the other hand, "welcomed an invitation to nominate [and] if the United States Government made no objection, [it] would like to propose ex-Ambassador Morgenthau."[36] The American government made no objection, and thus Henry Morgenthau became the RSC's first chairman (see appendix D).

Morgenthau was eminently qualified to serve in his post. He was a member of the executive committee of the NER. He had many years experience in the affairs of the Near East as ambassador to Turkey and as a representative of several European nations' interests there. After the Russo-Polish war in 1920 he served in the American Commission to Investigate Conditions in Poland. He had been active in refugee affairs in the Near East long before the burning of Smyrna. He was also a successful businessman with contacts in the highest financial and government circles in the United States and Europe. To these qualifications can be added an overdose of self-confidence, which often served as the tonic that enabled the RSC to carry on its work during the first years of its turbulent history.

Morgenthau's candidacy, however, was not popular in some government and private circles in the United States and Europe; and, although it was the NER which gave final approval to his appointment, it appears that his name was first introduced by European sources. Morganthau suffered from a Messianic complex which left little room for dissenting opinions. He arrived in Athens on 16 November 1923 with considerable pomp and ceremony, and immediately proceeded to proclaim loudly his faith in the willingness of the American people to take part in the salvation of Greece by participating in the forthcoming refugee loan.[37] His human frailties notwithstanding, Morgenthau played a vital role in the rehabilitation of Greece by his tireless devotion to a commitment which others saw fit to avoid.

The RSC would be officially dissolved on 31 December 1930. In the seven years of its existence, hundreds of thousands of refugees found permanent homes, primarily because of the unceasing and unselfish dedication of the commission's officials and the Greek people. Towns rose where animals had grazed, farms were cultivated where malaria-ridden swamps had plagued the countryside, and industry developed to a degree unprecedented in modern Greek history. A monumental transformation began to take place. These accomplishments, however, would not have been possible had it not been for the willingness of the United States and Great Britain to make possible the refugee loans that ultimately helped to pay for this progress.

The role of the United States in the formation of the RSC might appear negligible in view of the eventual American withdrawal. The important fact to note is not that active American participation in the RSC did not materialize, but that it was the catalytic role of the State Department and the ARC which helped to conceive the idea of a commission for the refugees. When viewed in these terms, the American contribution was no mean achievement.

9

Financing the Settlement of the Refugees: The Refugee Loan of 1924

In December 1924 the Greek government signed contracts with Hambros Bank, Ltd. in London, Speyer & Company's Bank of New York, and the National Bank of Greece for a loan of £12,300,000, which was intended to produce a net sum of £10,000,000. The proceeds from the loan were put at the disposal of the Refugee Settlement Commission with the stipulation that all money was to be used for refugee settlement, not for relief. Thus fortified, the RSC was able to make considerable progress in the gradual solution of the refugee problem and, in the long run, toward the salvation of an entire people.

Background to the Refugee Loan

The consummation of the Refugee Loan of 1924 was no small achievement, considering the magnitude of the financial and political ills confronting Greece. It required the intervention of the League of Nations and the cooperation of Great Britain and the United States to make the loan a reality.[1]

The first meeting of the RSC took place on 11 November 1923 in Salonika amidst high hopes and expectations. Its members were Henry

Morgenthau, Chairman, Sir John Campbell, and the Greek representatives, Etienne Delta and Pericles Argyropoulos. The commission was able to report that £1,000,000 had been placed at its disposal by the British government with which to begin its work.[2] This amount represented a fraction of the funds necessary for the completion of the commission's task. A crucial part of the RSC's responsibility was the procurement of a large loan that would make possible the settlement of the refugees on a solid, permanent basis.

The inevitability of a refugee loan was a topic of discussion in the Division of Near Eastern Affairs as early as November 1922. American officials expected that in the event an international loan was approved for Greece the United States would be asked to participate. However, the conservative attitude of Congress relative to new foreign loans was a formidable obstacle to overcome. There also was much doubt whether the semibankrupt condition of the Greek government would enable it to offer adequate security and whether the proceeds might be diverted toward nonproductive purposes. Finally, there was the problem of separating a theoretical refugee loan from the controversy surrounding the remaining 1918 credits. Dulles advised a favorable attitude on the condition that Greece renounce her claims to the remaining credits under the terms of the Tripartite Loan.[3]

In November 1922 Ambassadors Richard Washburn Child and Joseph C. Grew, representing the United States at Lausanne, reported that British and Greek officials had reached the conclusion that relief had the tendency to keep the refugees in a continuing state of helplessness by depriving them of incentive. To circumvent this problem some League officials urged the granting of a refugee settlement loan to the Greek government with a commission in charge of its expenditures.[4] The State Department, however, remained uncommitted because the Lausanne Conference had just begun, and it was difficult to predict what the results of the deliberations would be.

The refugee situation was in a state of flux. Refugees were still entering Greece in large numbers, and their status remained uncertain. Strenuous efforts were under way to arrange a compromise with the Turkish government which would permit Greek and Turkish refugees to return to their homes. The refugees contributed to the uncertainty. They made no secret of their antipathy for their new surroundings and for their desire to return to their homes. They were reluctant to be put to work away from the coastal areas, and preferred to hang about the ports to be ready to take the first boat back to Asia Minor should the fortunes of diplomacy make this possible.[5] American Chargé Atherton developed serious misgivings about the willingness of the refugees to participate in a permanent settlement scheme. He questioned their initiative and their ability to engage in productive pursuits that would help support a foreign loan.

Another obstacle was the quixotic nature of Greek politics. At a time when the burning issue was whether Greece should have a monarchy or a republic, European and American financiers were reluctant to enter into long-range agreements with a regime whose existence was extremely tenuous. Morgenthau reflected the American attitude when he wrote laconically: "The formula we had constantly to keep in mind was 'No political stability, no money.' " The mood of the large European powers did little to inspire confidence. Atherton was informed that the French and Italian governments had no intention of participating in any Greek refugee loan, while the British government adopted a very conservative attitude in the matter. As far as the State Department was concerned it made little sense to permit American funds to be administered by the League of Nations when the Council of the League was dominated by the same governments which were reluctant to assume the initiative. Finally, there was the matter of determining what portion of the loan was to be derived from American capital. It was an open secret that America would be asked to lend the largest amount. League officials stated openly that the League's scheme for refugee settlement contemplated raising about 70 percent in the United States, while the American Red Cross would agree to continue its work after 30 June 1923.[6]

Greek Foreign Minister Nicholas Politis appealed to the Greek Sub-Committee of the League of Nations and declared his government's willingness to submit to almost any conditions the League wished to impose on the service and amortization of the refugee loan. Without League support, Greece would be unable to borrow money in the international market at reasonable interest rates. He estimated that the amount required for refugee settlement was £10,000,000 sterling. The Greek government was prepared to accept stringent controls and supervision regarding the issue of repayment. The foreign minister offered his government's assurances that all money raised abroad would be used specifically for the refugee settlement and would never be diverted from that purpose.[7] This promise was reassuring, though the State Department remained officially uncommitted.

The Lausanne Conference and the Role of the United States

With the opening of the second phase of the Lausanne Conference in April 1923 the attitude of the United States government underwent a significant change.[8] The experience of the preceding five months had enabled American negotiators to arrive at a more clear definition of what American interests in the Near East should be. Then, too, the permanent nature of the refugee situation was no longer academic, but a compelling problem with which the large European countries had to come to terms. In the meantime, discussions for a refugee loan under the auspices of the League of Nations had already begun and appeared to be progressing rapidly. The Bank of England assumed the leading role in the negotiations. The Division of Near Eastern Affairs took an active interest in the proceedings, not because the loan represented an attractive investment, but because the State and Commerce Departments were determined to protect the interests of American businessmen and financiers in the new markets emerging in postwar Europe and the Near East.

A closely related problem was the Turko-American peace treaty under negotiation. Since no peace agreement had been signed between the two countries, technically, the United States was still at war with Turkey. The destruction of the old Ottoman dynasty saw the rise of a Turkish national consciousness which rejected the remnants of a colonial past with its legacy of political and economic subservience to the Western European Powers. The United States did not suffer from historical handicaps, a fact which provoked concern and resentment from British officials.[9] An integral part of the U.S. government's Near East policy was the expansion of American influence in Turkey. The work of American educational institutions, philanthropic organizations, and relief agencies had done much to create the impression that America was the most altruistic country in the world. Consequently, Kemal's Nationalist government was inclined to accept the inroads of American capital. American financiers competed aggressively with their British and French counterparts to fill the commercial vacuum in those territories of the Ottoman Empire which before World War I had been the domain of German bankers and businessmen, and to capture, wherever possible, even those enclaves which were spheres of influence of Great Britain and France.

One catalyst in the more active role of the United States government was the attitude of the Allied Powers. During the first phase of the Lausanne Conference (20 November to 5 February) the weight of the American delegation was thrown behind the Allies on most issues, including those involving the Straits and the maintenance of the Capitulations. When it came to the Open Door policy, however, the liberal position taken by the United States greatly strengthened the hand of the Turkish delegation in opposing Allied attempts to retain what they could of the economic privileges under the Treaty of Sèvres.

The conference broke down on 5 February over certain juridical and economic clauses which the Turkish delegation found unacceptable. The State Department protested that it had not been given adequate opportunity to state its attitude on these provisions. After making its position on the treaty clear to the British government, the State Department declared that the United States government would oppose any effort by the Allied Powers to insert in the treaty "any provision designed to confer upon Allied nationals . . . rights which were more extensive than those which were acquired under or by virtue of the conventions, contracts, agreements, or decisions in question."[10] The Allied response was an attempt to exclude the United States from participation in the conference when it reopened in April. Repeated requests by the State Department for information regarding the resumption of talks were met by complete silence.

British officials concluded eventually that the United States should be informed formally of the resumption of talks because the "United States representatives might do more harm outside the conference, especially if they know invitation had been deliberately withheld from them."[11] When the invitation arrived, American officials had already determined that the United States government should not be reduced to the role of a bystander. The State Department took the position that the conference merely had been postponed in February, and instructed Ambassador Grew to attend the meeting as an observer in the same capacity and on the same basis as he and Ambassador Child had participated in the earlier discussions. American participation in the Refugee Loan of 1924, then, was inspired by humanitarian sentiments, but it also was a manifestation of overall United States policy in the Near East.

The Issues Surrounding the Loan Negotiations

When the Finance Committee met at Lausanne in June to consider the financing of refugee settlement, the State Department assigned

Colonel Logan, the assistant unofficial delegate to the Reparations Commission, to attend the meetings unofficially in view of the technical character of the financial questions which were likely to come up for discussion.[12] From the point of view of Greek-American relations, there were five main obstacles hindering the loan negotiations: 1) the status of the Tripartite Loan, 2) the recognition of George II, 3) the question of suitable securities for the refugee loan, 4) the interconnected issues of war credits and war debts, and 5) certain technical questions regarding Greek-American commercial relations.[13]

The three lending governments were anxious to end the Tripartite Agreement, not only for the purpose of ridding themselves of an irksome obligation whose legitimacy had become debatable, but also for the purpose of facilitating the refugee loan negotiations. Secretary Hughes was willing to employ diplomatic coercion to induce the Greek government to renounce its claims to the 1918 credits in exchange for American permission to float a new foreign loan. Colonel Logan was instructed to work discreetly in applying pressure toward the creation of a formula for the termination of the agreement. At the same time, the secretary could not ignore the fact that a rigid, noncompromising policy could prove detrimental to American financial interests in Greece. Logan was instructed to say that, if a loan were contemplated for relief work and refugee settlement in Greece and if American bankers were willing to share in the financing, there would be no objection from the State Department to raising a portion of the loan in the United States. It was essential, however, that the Lausanne Conference should give a reasonable assurance of peace in the Near East. If peace could be assured, "the Department would not object to your cooperating with the [League Finance] committee to whom a share in the relief loan might be offered." The secretary was reassured when four days later Grew reported that the delegates at Lausanne did not consider the problem of the Tripartite Loan to be an insurmountable obstacle.[14]

The issue of recognition was more serious because it presented the State Department with a difficult situation. To be sure, America's policy was tied closely to the refusal of France and Great Britain to grant their recognition. But beyond that, the United States government could not recognize George II and simultaneously refuse to turn over the remaining credits it had granted the Greek government five years earlier. The State Department's dilemma was summarized succinctly by the British chargé in Washington who wrote to Curzon that American recognition would place the United States government in a somewhat embarrassing position. The United States did not have the same grounds as the British and French governments for withholding recognition, while at the same time it was anxious to do nothing which might embarrass these governments in their policy vis-à-vis Greece. This contradiction was a source of concern for Secretary Hughes who concluded that British financial houses would accomplish a financial coup at the expense of American financiers.[15] In June, Hughes intimated that despite the "Pandora's Box" which the recognition issue presented, he was ready to give his approval to a refugee loan, if the Allied representatives were ready to proceed without regard to recognition.[16]

The problem of suitable security was troublesome. Despite the financial plight of the country, the crux of the problem was not whether Greece would have the necessary drachmas to repay the loan, but whether the Greek government could obtain the foreign exchange needed for this purpose. This was the crucial point which Great Britain and the United States disregarded. This short-sighted approach contributed to the fiscal deterioration of the Greek treasury. In 1927 the Greek government was forced to undertake a general reform of the country's finances and to raise a second refugee and stabilization loan.

Nevertheless, the profit motive, the moral support of the League of Nations and the IFC, and persistent lobbying by Greek officials at Geneva,[17] Lausanne, and in Washington combined to tip the scales in favor of the Greek loan request.[18] To these factors must be added the fact that the American Red Cross had virtually ceased its relief work, and Near East Relief had reduced its services drastically. It was obvious that something had to be done quickly to fill the vacuum created by the curtailment of American emergency assistance. The Bank of England responded to the challenge in August 1923 by advancing Greece £1,000,000 sterling with the stipulation that this advance would be paid off from the proceeds of the foreign loan. The funds were to be used exclusively for the purpose of refugee settlement by the Refugee Settlement Commission.[19]

The action by the Bank of England was reassuring, for it affirmed the British government's determination to contribute to the solution of the refugee problem. The British advance, however, was a source of concern for the State Department because the £1,000,000 were already at the disposal of the RSC, while not a single dollar had yet been invested. With the Tripartite Loan in mind, Hughes instructed the American ambassador to Great Britain to inform the British government that the United States would not object to the pledging of security by Greece if the governments of Great Britain and France would agree to raise no objection.[20] Two months later Great Britain and France officially agreed to waive their vetoes on the assignment of new security for a foreign loan.

The removal of Allied opposition did not simplify matters appreciably. The outstanding differences between the Greek Foreign Ministry and the State Department were inextricably related to the overall postwar policy of the United States in Europe and the Near East. This was especially true in the case of war debts owed to the United States by foreign governments. As of 1 March 1935 these debts totaled $1,350,479,075.[21] The vast literature on the subject and the turbulent debates in Congress bear eloquent testimony to the task with which the State Department was confronted in its efforts to form a comprehensive, coherent policy on the issue of war debts. It was evident that before the Treasury Department and the Congress should be drawn too deeply into the war debts controversy the diplomatic aspects of the problem must be resolved.

Dr. Young, economic adviser to the Department of State, was especially adamant on this point. He recognized the legitimacy of Constantine's successor and that the United States was not free from obligation under the Tripartite Agreement. This opinion was shared by the acting secretary of state, Norman H. Davis, who admitted to the British chargé in Washington that the United States had no grounds for cancelling the loan. Diplomatically, Greece came to represent a serious problem, not because of the size of its debts, but by virtue of the embarrassment the recognition issue would create if all the facts were made known to the Treasury Department, to "argumentative members of Congress," and to the American public.[22]

American public opinion was an additional thorn in the side of the Division of Near Eastern Affairs. Many informed persons were at a loss to understand the attitude of the United States government. The State Department received many inquiries demanding an explanation for the American procrastination in granting financial assistance to Greece. The general secretary of the Federal Council of Churches of Christ in America, Samuel McCrea Calvert, reflected the general public attitude when he wrote to the chief of the Division of Near Eastern Affairs: "The matter looks to me a simple as this—either the United States Government does or does not owe a substantial amount of money to Greece."[23] The necessity to return vague and evasive replies did little to enhance the credibility of the State Department. Dulles also recognized the contradiction inherent in the American position, but could find no acceptable alternative. He reflected Dr. Young's concern when he wrote: "The more I puzzle over this [Calvert's] letter the more I am inclined to believe that until we are prepared to tell the whole story it will be better to remain silent rather than attempt to involve the Treasury and possibly Congress."[24] In the year that followed, silence was precisely the policy of the State Department. There is considerable material available for this period, but it contains hardly more than an exchange of platitudes, proposals, and counter proposals. The most important activities of the State Department during this period were repeated reminders to American representatives in London, Lausanne, Geneva, and Athens to report regularly on the loan negotiations and on the attitudes of the French and British governments.

The Role of Henry Morgenthau

It is ironic that, in view of this American inactivity, the most important figure in the negotiations during the same period was an American, Henry Morgenthau. It will be recalled that when the first £1,000,000 advance was granted by the Bank of England in August it was understood that the money would be repaid from the refugee loan which, League officials believed, would soon be granted. The negotiations moved slowly, however, so that by the end of the year the money was spent and the Greek government was at the end of its resources.[25]

Morgenthau's first major act as chairman of the RSC was to gather all the responsible editors of Athens' newspapers and make clear to them that, if they expected foreigners to have faith in the resiliency of the Greek people, the Greek people must have faith in their own ability to save themselves. It would be futile to attempt to solve the entire refugee problem with £1,000,000. If, however, 125,000 refugees could be restored to productive independence with this sum, then it would not be difficult to convince international bankers that £10,000,000 would be required to do the same thing for a million and a quarter refugees.[26] Only then, could the Greek government expect to get the necessary foreign credit to complete the task of refugee settlement. In the meantime, the funds of the RSC were exhausted. Since the floating of the loan required protracted negotiations, a second advance from the Bank of England was the most realistic short-term solution.

There followed intense activity on Morgenthau's part. He employed all his diplomatic and negotiating skills to convince British and American leaders that a loan to Greece was not only an investment in humanity, but a sound financial investment for any lending institution willing to participate in such a noble experiment. He went to England, and after considerable difficulty, he was able to negotiate a second advance in May for £1,000,000 which, together with advances from the Greek government, enabled the RSC to continue its work until the end of the year.

By the summer of 1924 two things had become clear. One was that foreign loans on a piecemeal basis were not the solution to the refugee problem. The other was the fact that the loan of three to six million pounds sterling specified in Article IV of the *Protocol* would be insufficient to develop a permanent plan of settlement. The consensus among financial experts was that £10,000,000 would be required. Improvements in the domestic political situation enabled the Greek government to appear before the Council of the League and appeal for an amendment to Article IV that would permit Greece to float a loan of £10,000,000. The Greek subcommittee took the request under consideration, but gave no immediate reply.

Morgenthau made little effort to hide his diappointment at the procrastination of the League. In September, he appeared before the council and delivered an address in which he gave his full approval to the Greek request. He implored his listeners to investigate the present economic conditions in Greece through the Financial Commission and to give their approval to the loan.[27] The matter was submitted to the Greek subcommittee and to the Financial Commission to which the Greek government submitted a memorandum offering additional securities (i.e., in addition to those specified in Article V of the *Protocol*). These securities guaranteed full payment of the loan.

The Role of the League of Nations

The council agreed that the sum of the securities was adequate. However, since the *Protocol* of 27 September 1923 and the *Organic Statutes* of the RSC had not anticipated the magnitude of the refugee problem, it became necessary that these documents be amended to lend greater flexibility to the entire process of refugee settlement. Action to this end was taken at a meeting held by the Council of the League on 19 September 1924. Some of the amendments are very technical and do not need to be discussed here. Article IV was amended to permit the Greek government to borrow a sum not to exceed £10,000,000. Of this amount £2,000,000 were to be subscribed by Greek bankers or other Greek financial groups. The modifications to Article V related to the additional guarantees mentioned above. These securities can be divided into four categories: 1) a first charge on certain revenues under the control of the International Financial Commission. (These revenues consisted of the proceeds from monopolies in New Greece.); 2) a charge upon the surplus of the revenues assigned to the IFC which exceeded the sums needed for the service of existing foreign loans; 3) land assigned for settlement, as well as the buildings erected on it; 4) mortgages and taxes payable by the refugees.[28]

The sum from the first two categories equaled 1,213,974,936 drachmas ($20,826,621), five times the amount necessary for the service of the loan of £10,000,000.[29] Furthermore, the land assigned for the settlement was estimated by the Greek subcommittee to be worth about £10,400,000[30] ($47,577,920). Finally, the taxes that would be paid by the refugees would be an additional source of revenue.

Article VI was amended in order to give the Greek government greater latitude with respect to the procurement of further loans. This point proved to be a source of apprehension for the State Department. Article XV of the *Organic Statutes* had specified that the RSC's revenues were to be expended exclusively for productive work, not for relief. The experience of the preceding year, however, had proven this provision to be too narrow and impractical in its application. The article, therefore, was amended to allow the RSC to render such relief assistance as might be necessary to facilitate the settlement of the refugees. This arrangement was important because it enabled the commission to broaden its activities and accelerate its work.

American Consent for the Refugee Loan

In view of these developments, the Greek government believed that repayment of the proposed loan was amply guaranteed and that the amendments to the *Protocol* and to the *Organic Statutes* were a clear indication of the confidence the new republic had earned from the League of Nations. On 9 October, Constantine D. Xanthopoulos, the Greek minister in Washington, was instructed to notify the State Department officially of the amendments to the Geneva *Protocol*. He also was instructed to ask for American consent that would enable Greece to provide the securities required under the terms of the proposed agreement. Xanthopoulos complemented his official instructions with repeated appeals to the State Department for a speedy and favorable reply. He implored Hughes and Dulles not to jeopardize "this eminently humanitarian loan."[31]

Hughes' reply was prompt and direct. The State Department was still smarting from a recent revelation that the Greek government had been less than ethical regarding its obligations to the United States government under the Tripartite Loan of 1918. On 27 December 1923 the Greek and Canadian governments signed a loan agreement for $8,000,000, which was not ratified until 7 August 1924. Under the terms of Article VI, Greece had pledged new securities without the consent of the United States government. When the agreement was published in the Official Gazette, officials in the State and Treasury Departments became irritated at what they considered to be a clear act of duplicity on the part of the Greek government. The secretary of state, therefore, informed Xanthopoulos that the Department of State was "in entire sympathy" with the humanitarian purpose of the refugee loan and would place no impediment in the way of the Greek government's furnishing new security for the loan. But the Greek minister was implicitly and informally warned that the United States government would never again overlook or tolerate a transgression like the one inherent in the Greek-Canadian loan agreement.[32]

The State Department understood American consent to apply only to the pledging of the security specifically mentioned in the note of 9 October. It was not to be assumed by the Greek government that the United States acquiesced in the view set forth in the amendment to Article VI of the Geneva *Protocol*, which allowed the Greek government to retain the right to mortgage any surplus from the revenues or the loan, in excess of the amount necessary for its service. In other words, the United States government would resist all efforts to dilute its authority inherent in Article IV of the Tripartite Loan. Hughes informed Xanthopoulos that the consent was given "with full reservation of all questions with respect to the Tripartite agreement of 1918."[33]

The Problem of Financing

The State Department next turned its attention to the problem of ascertaining which financial institutions would participate in the American portion of the loan. This issue was sensitive, since the Division of Near Eastern Affairs wished to keep abreast of all negotiations between the Greek government and American banks, while simultaneously preserving its impartiality in the matter. At the end of November, Dulles was informed by Raleigh S. Rife, a representative of the Guaranty Trust Company of New York, that Hambros Bank, Ltd. of London had offered his firm a $15,000,000 share in the loan. Guaranty Trust felt disposed to go along with the offer, but the volatile nature of Greek politics and the fact that, since late 1921, Greece had made no interest payment on the $15,000,000 borrowed from the United States was of great concern.

Dulles tried to be reassuring. He described the folly of trying to measure Near East politics by Western standards. He expressed his belief that the problem of the Greek indebtedness to the United States would soon be resolved. When Dulles was pressed to commit himself to a definite policy regarding the extent to which the State Department was prepared to support American bankers, Rife received no satisfactory reply.[34] As a result of the uncertainties surrounding Greece's political and economic stability and the State Department's reluctance to clarify its position, the Guaranty Trust Company soon lost interest in the project, and turned over the negotiations to Speyer & Company's Bank of New York which promptly reached an agreement with the Greek government.

In a letter to Hughes, Speyer & Company outlined the main points of the loan agreement and expressed the hope that the participation of American bankers and the American public in this venture would prompt the United States government to encourage Americans to participate in the rehabilitation of European countries.[35] One week later the assistant secretary of state, Leland Harrison, informed Speyer & Company of the State Department's decision to give its final approval to participation in the Refugee Loan by an American firm. This consent was not given free of any qualification.

Hughes instructed the American minister, Irwin Laughlin, to inform the Greek Foreign Ministry that the humanitarian gesture of the United States government imposed upon the Greek government the moral obligation to initiate negotiations relative to the settlement of major issues separating the United States and Greece. Furthermore, the agreement between Greece and Canada appeared to have violated the agreement of 1918, so that the government of the United States was under no obligation to make further advances.[36] The attitude inherent in this statement is significant, because it embodied the single most important theme in Greek-American relations from 1925 to 1929.

Terms of the Loan

The Greek government signed contracts with three banks in London, Athens, and New York. The breakdown of the Refugee Loan of 1924 is as follows:

Hambros Bank, Ltd.	£ 7,500,000
National Bank of Greece	£ 2,500,000
Speyer & Company's Bank of New York	£ 2,300,000
TOTAL	£12,300,000

The dollar issue of the loan was floated in two parts—$5,000,000 in London and $6,000,000 in the United States. The face amount of £12,300,000 was granted at 7 percent. The issue took place at the rate of 88 percent. However, if one deducts the British stamp duty of 2 percent, the expenses which attended the issue, and the commission of the banks at the rate of 5 percent, the net produce was 81 percent. Thus, the nominal interest of 7 percent rose to 8.71 percent. The net proceeds of the loan were £9,970,016 6s. 9d ($45,610.829).[38] The loan was covered twenty times in London, five and one-half times in Athens, and was entirely subscribed by Speyer & Company in New York.

The terms of the loan created heated debate in Greece. One Greek expert in refugee matters wrote bitterly: "This is a tragic-comic commentary on high-sounding discussion of the Refugee Loan as a humanitarian and philanthropic work!"[39] Andreas Andreades, an eminent Greek economist and expert on international loans, offered a concurring view. These indictments, though far too sweeping to be taken literally, were not without foundation. Even the conservative Atherton was impressed by the successful efforts of the Greek government to establish a sound budgetary and fiscal policy and to improve the credit of Greece in the world's money markets. The American minister expressed the opinion that a review of the Greek government's achievements in 1923 gave every reason to be optimistic for the future. He cited as primary examples the doubling of the value, in pounds sterling, of the national bonds and the improvement by 50 percent of the drachma.[40]

The debate was not confined to Greece. In the United States, Greeks and Greek-Americans chose sides generally along Venizelist-Royalist lines, and often with little regard for the facts. Adamantios Th. Polyzoides, editor of the Royalist-oriented *Atlantis*, asserted that "the terms . . . are such, indeed, that not even Venizelos dared support [them]." Former Prime Minister Gonatas, however, declared in the Chamber of Deputies that Venizelos sent him the following telegram: "I wish to warmly recommend that you accept . . . with enthusiasm the proposed terms."[41] The general attitude of the government was perhaps the most realistic. Political leaders agreed that the terms were unfavorable, but so were the circumstances.

Not the least significant element in these circumstances was the size of the public debt of Greece, a subject which had the closest scrutiny from the United States government. At the end of 1923 the total public debt averaged seventy-seven dollars per capita.[42] In absolute terms this figure does not appear excessive. However, since the poorer classes were overwhelmingly in the majority, the purchasing power of the Greek people was extremely low. If examined from this point of view, the seventy-seven dollar figure assumes a magnitude which reflected a serious social and economic problem that even a multimillion dollar loan could not solve entirely.

The seriousness of Greece's economic situation, along with the subsequent turbulent course of the Greek Republic and repeated financial crises over the next two decades, lead the detached observer to the conclusion that the terms of the loan were indeed strict, though hardly Draconian. The Refugee Loan of 1924 was an integral part in the plan to settle one and a half million refugees. It was unique, because never before had a Greek loan of any kind been brought to the American market. As R. O. Hall, the acting American commercial attaché, aptly put it: "The loan is the first truly important departure from the 'soup-kitchen' refugee policy of the Greek government during the past two years."[43] America's participation in that enterprise was a humanitarian gesture, the profit motive notwithstanding, which the United States government encouraged, despite the serious financial and commercial differences that remained unresolved in the relations between Greece and the United States.

10
Public Works in Greece and the Role of American Capital

The inroads of American capital in Greece from 1918 to 1940 constitute an important phase in Greek-American relations. Before 1914 Greece traded mostly with Europe. After 1918 trade with America increased rapidly. Eventually, American exports to Greece ran the gamut from sewing needles and movie-house concessions to tractors and the financing of public works. By 1929 the United States had risen to first place as a source of Greek imports and as a market for Greek products (see Figures 1–4). This situation prevailed until the world-wide depression in the 1930s when Germany outstripped all other countries in both the export and import trade. These standings are cited as one indication of a trend that evolved in the Near East during the first third of the twentieth century. It is not to suggest that Greece was of intrinsic importance to the United States. Greece, both politically and economically, was inconsequential in American calculations. But to the degree that Greece was located on the periphery of an area in which the United States was attempting to make inroads, the commercial and financial relations between the two countries are important. This chapter will be limited to an analysis of the construction of the Marathon waterworks

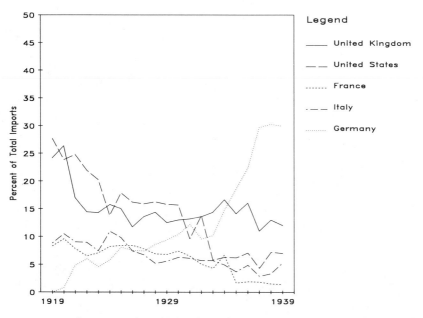

Fig. 1. Greek Imports by Principal Countries. *Source:* U.S. Department of Commerce, Bureau of Foreign and Domestic Commerce, *Commerce Reports,* 1921; *Commerce Yearbook,* 1922–1932; and *Foreign Commerce Yearbook,* 1933–1939.

and to land reclamation in northern Greece. These projects deserve special attention because they are illustrative of the scope of America's influence in Greece during the interwar period. These enterprises also had a profound impact on the social and economic history of the country after 1930.

The Emergence of American Commercial Influence

Greek-American commercial relations go back to the 1830s. In 1919 the Department of Commerce gave tacit recognition to the commercial importance of Greece by appointing Elliot Grinnel Mears as the first American resident trade commissioner to that country. In the 1920s there were large American interests in Greece, particularly around Cavalla, where Americans virtually controlled the tobacco

167

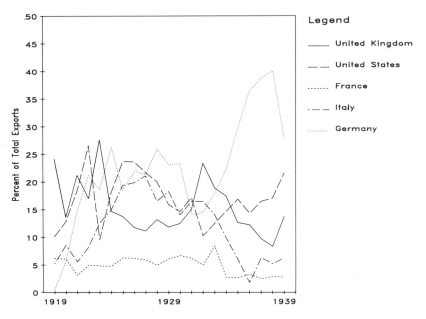

Fig. 2. Greek Exports by Principal Countries. *Source:* U.S. Department of Commerce, Bureau of Foreign and Domestic Commerce, *Commerce Reports,* 1921; *Commerce Yearbook,* 1922–1932; and *Foreign Commerce Yearbook,* 1933–1939.

market. In some respects, trade between the two countries exceeded that between Greece and Great Britain.[1] By 1921 Greece was importing as much from the United States as from all the Balkan countries combined.[2] In 1922 there were more American firms (243) doing business in Greece, through branches established there and through local representatives, than from any other single country.[3] From 1924 to 1929 American governmental and private financing totaled $95,000,000.[4]

The American trade commissioner to Greece wrote in 1929 that the most remarkable foreign influence to emerge in Greece from 1918 to 1929 was that of the United States of America. After the influx of the refugees, Greece turned principally to the United States for material assistance and general guidance in practically all matters except those relating to politics and the military. In reference to these developments,

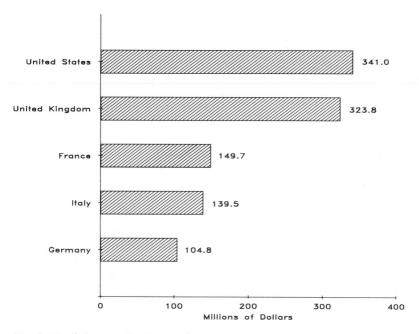

Fig. 3. Greek Imports by Principal Countries (1919–30). *Source:* U.S. Department of Commerce, Bureau of Foreign and Domestic Commerce, *Commerce Reports,* 1921; *Commerce Yearbook,* 1922–1932; and *Foreign Commerce Yearbook,* 1933–1939.

one authority on the Balkans has written that "the period between the World Wars marked a high point in American influence in Greece."[5]

Despite the steady improvement in the position of American business in Greece, American officials saw little reason for complacency. British competition, in particular, was a source of concern to those within the Commerce Department who believed that the United States was not sufficiently aggressive. They were supported by Americans who had the opportunity to observe the struggle for concessions first hand. One expert on waterworks admonished American capitalists for their conservatism. After giving his assessment of British competition, he concluded that in spite of the negative connotations conjured up by the phrase "dollar diplomacy," it would require precisely this kind of diplomacy

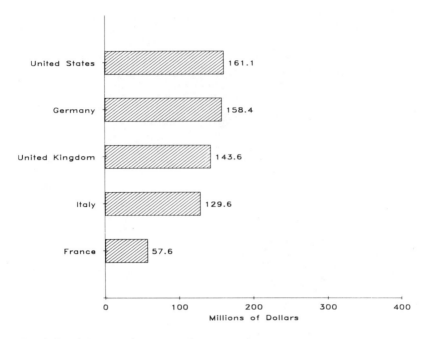

Fig. 4. Greek Exports by Principal Countries (1919–30). *Source:* U.S. Department of Commerce, Bureau of Foreign and Domestic Commerce, *Commerce Reports,* 1921; *Commerce Yearbook,* 1922–1932; and *Foreign Commerce Yearbook,* 1933–1939.

"if American financiers and American engineers and contractors are going to have their share of the business in underdeveloped foreign countries."[6] After 1922 dollar diplomacy would assume a prominent place in the Greek policy of the Departments of State and Commerce. Dollar diplomacy and political involvement went hand-in-hand, and while the American role in Greek politics was passive and minimal, it was hardly nonexistent. A case in point is the reclamation of the Struma Valley in Macedonia.

Although the British firms of Henry Boot and Helbert Wagg underbid all competitors for these projects, the contract was granted to American firms "owing to political pressure" exercised by the United States minister, Robert P. Skinner, who gave the Greek government to understand that the War Debt Funding Agreement would not be ratified by Congress unless the Struma reclamation works were entrusted to American contractors. Indeed, throughout the 1920s the American legation employed similar techniques to coerce the Greek government.[7] In their anxiety to reassure Washington that American interests were not being overlooked and American capital not disdained, the Ministry of Finance made concessions which were often prejudicial and detrimental to British interests. The British minister, Percy Loraine, admonished British contractors and financiers for allowing the quixotic nature of Greek politics (which he considered normal for that part of the world) to act as a deterrent to investment. He reminded the Foreign Office that

> Greece and the United States of America meet almost exclusively on the ground of finance, and the principal function of the American representative at Athens appears to be that of pushing American industrial and financial interests and obtaining for the United States as many as possible of the large contracts for public works on which the Greek Government are at present embarking—an aim which he appears to pursue at times with a definite anti-British bias, and without any very scrupulous choice of the arguments which he uses with the Greek Government.[8]

Twenty years later Skinner defended America's aggressive policy. It was unrealistic, he asserted, for the United States to help bolster the Greek national economy with hydraulic projects and large public works, while taking only a casual interest in Greek political life.[9]

The American military attaché in Athens, Colonel Edward Davis, summarized the rise of American influence in Greece as follows:

> Just at present [1929] the United States appears easily to be "top dog" in Greece in almost every way. Our tourists outnumber all others and spend more money per capita . . . our engineers and other technicians engaged in large water-supply irrigation projects and similar activities have shown themselves far superior to their European competitors, and our bids, loans, and other bases for large projects have been found more generous and straightforward than [those] of our competitors. Much of the foregoing is due to the present American Minister to Greece whose ability to see our opportunities and to develop and defend them is rather striking.[10]

With an eye to American political and economic penetration in the Balkans, Colonel Davis expressed the conviction that the attention of the State Department should be devoted, at least in part, "to observing

171

whether the achievement of Balkan peace may not be in the ratio of American economic penetration" (see appendix E).[11]

Thus, the construction of public works in Greece was often accompanied by virulent international intrigues and high-level political corruption. The intensity of the competition often pitted one American firm against another, while on one occasion, the fall of a ministry (that of Alexander Zaïmis, 3 February 1928) was precipitated, in part, by official underhandedness in the granting of road contracts.[12]

The Marathon Waterworks

Throughout their history, Athens and its environs were never free from serious difficulty in securing an adequate water supply. As early as the sixth century B.C., rigid laws were passed by Solon to conserve the city's meager resources. Not until A.D. 140, when the Roman Emperors Hadrian and Antonius Pius completed the Hadrian aqueduct, was any reliable supply of water provided. This aqueduct served the city until the Middle Ages when the invading Goths and Vandals inflicted serious damage to key sections of its construction. For centuries it lay forgotten and not until 1847 were its possibilities rediscovered. It was then repaired and used.[13]

Athens, however, continued to suffer from perennial thirst.[14] As the city grew rapidly during the nineteenth century the problem became critical. Incidents were reported by the police which ranged from hairpulling by irate housewives to involuntary manslaughter, as Athenians struggled to tap the last drops of water from a trickling spring or a dry communal well. Even in the larger towns, piped water was virtually unknown. Every householder carried his daily supply from whatever source he could find. "Often," wrote one American observer, "the container is a 5-gallon can provided by the Standard Oil Company."[15] So serious was the problem that it supplied abundant material for poets, satirists, and playwrights. Two Greek historians have written: "The word 'water,' in those days, had become practically synonymous with the word 'hunger.' "[16]

In 1922 the American chargé, Jefferson Caffery, told one American observer that he "urgently desired a transfer," because the city water pressure was so low that it left the only bathroom, located on the second floor of the legation, dry. He laid the fact to "royalist mismanagement or possibly deliberate discrimination [because of the United States' failure

172

to recognize Constantine]." Three years later the American minister, Irwin Laughlin, expressed his annoyance at this sad state of affairs by resorting to dry humor. In a conversation with Andreas Michalakopoulos, he quipped: "You must understand, Mr. Prime Minister, that it is impossible for me to bathe and have tea on the same day. One day I must do the one and the following day the other." Laughlin pursued the matter further. When he returned to the United States, he wrote a letter to a member of Congress complaining that during his two-year tenure as American minister in Athens, he had never been able to take a complete bath. The editor of the Athenian newspaper, *Hestia*, was more direct in expressing the Greeks' own frustrations when he wrote: " 'A place disappearing in clouds of dust cannot be qualified a city.' "[17] When refugees flooded the country the problem was magnified considerably.

The first serious effort to alleviate the problem was made by Venizelos in the period between 1912 and 1914. Bids were opened and the United States government was requested to notify any American contractors who might be interested. Domestic politics and the First World War intervened and the project was dropped. Venizelos made a second attempt in 1919. During a visit to Paris he met with George H. Davis of Ford, Bacon and Davis, Engineers of New York City, and discussed the feasibility of constructing a water supply and sewerage system for Piraeus. The cost was estimated at $100,000,000. A portion of the project was begun, and in December 1920 the work was completed.[18] This happy event, however, occurred hardly a month after the electoral defeat of Venizelos. The resulting furor raised serious doubts in the minds of the contractors about the willingness of the Royalists to pursue the public works policies of their predecessors. When neither their financial backers in Piraeus nor the American legation could be reassuring relative to the political stability of the new government, the contractors lost interest.[19]

The events of the next three years were not conducive to the negotiation of public works contracts. However, the influx of refugees forced the Revolutionary government to turn its attention to the physical rehabilitation of their country. In September 1923 bids were opened for the building of an artificial lake near the historic plain of Marathon to give Athens and Piraeus an adequate water supply for the first time in their history. The reservoir was designed to collect the flowing waters from Mount Parnes and from the Charadros and Varnavas rivers whose primary source was also Mount Parnes. After some intense competition by

173

"practically every contractor in the United States," the firm of Ulen & Company of Lebanon, Indiana emerged as the only serious American challenger to European contractors. The fact that the Greek government was anxious to alleviate the water shortage of the Athens-Piraeus area had been brought frequently to the attention of Ulen & Company by the Greek legation and by private sources during the period from 1919 to 1923. Consequently, it is fairly clear that, despite international bidding, the Greek government favored the Indiana firm from the beginning. The company possessed an impressive list of credentials and had an imposing record as a reliable builder of large waterworks in the United States and Latin America.[20] In view of this record, its vice-president, C. M. Bounel, felt disposed to ask the State Department for assistance in recommending his firm to the Greek government. The sources for the next eight months are fragmentary, and consequently the course of the negotiations is not entirely clear, though it is certain that the department complied with the request. On 6 November Bounel wrote to Hughes to express "special thanks" for the assistance rendered by the American legation, especially by Laughlin and the commercial attaché, Barton Hall. One Greek historian had written simply: "Bids were opened on an international scale, but not one of those [financial] Houses that appeared had the necessary capital to build the project."[21]

This is probably what happened. In order to eliminate bidders with a record of questionable business practices and to reduce the strain on the country's financial resources, in 1920 the government adopted a policy of requiring foreign contractors to supply half of the capital necessary to build a public project. This requirement appears to have been a decisive factor in the process of elimination. The records do not mention any other firm which made an offer that equaled or surpassed that of Ulen & Company. Nevertheless, it is important to note that after all bids were rejected by the Greek government, including Ulen's, only Ulen & Company was invited to make new proposals. The result was a contract between the American firm and the Greek government based on noncompetitive bids.[22] This detail is significant, since it set the tone for much of the subsequent public works bidding in the 1920s. The contract was signed on 22 December 1924 and was ratified by the Chamber of Deputies on 3 April 1925. The work was begun immediately. The story of the eight-month period following the signing of the agreement is a sordid tale of intrigue and heated debate that embroiled four governments, two American contracting firms, and four banks. The controversy will be summarized briefly here because it reflects a theme which manifested itself repeatedly and with many variations throughout the 1920s.

The ink was hardly dry on the contract when John R. McArthur, formerly of McArthur, Perks, & Company, New York Contractors, appeared in Athens and attempted to undermine the waterworks agreement. McArthur had placed several proposals before the Greek government during the competition, but they were rejected outright.[23] The biggest problem was the fact that no reliable evidence could be found to identify the organizations he represented or the nature of his financial backers. Nevertheless, McArthur proceeded virtually to copy Ulen's contract, at slightly better terms, and endeavored to present a counterproposal. When the Greek government refused to be swayed, McArthur sent a copy of his offer to every member of the Chamber of Deputies in an effort to defeat ratification. With the cooperation of the political opposition, he distributed a pamphlet in which he unleashed an attack upon the Greek government for what he claimed were restrictive policies in the granting of public works contracts. When all else failed there was still bribery as an alternative. Major James F. Case, Ulen's representative in Greece, reported that McArthur's agent in Athens "repeatedly suggests to me that we buy them off."[24]

The State Department found itself in the middle, as both Ulen and McArthur pressed the American legation with requests for assistance. The State Department and the American legation were scrupulous in their efforts to protect American interests, while simultaneously maintaining strict impartiality. When it became obvious that a legitimate agreement was before the Chamber of Deputies for ratification and that the obstructive tactics of McArthur were detrimental to the American "image," the secretary of state, Frank B. Kellogg, instructed Laughlin to lend his support to Ulen & Company. On 3 April the contract was ratified unanimously by the Greek Parliament.

Under different circumstances, McArthur's activities could be dismissed as the intervention of an adventurer with unknown backing. But the problem was more complicated. There is circumstantial evidence to suggest that McArthur was a tool of the British firm of Speyer & Company, of Hambros Bank, Ltd. and, perhaps, of the French government. Indeed, McArthur claimed to be associated closely with Speyer & Company.[25] When it became obvious that ratification was inevitable, Speyer and Hambros, with the apparent approval of the British legation, entered the controversy by protesting directly to the Greek government.

They claimed that the issue of bonds for the waterworks would injure the market of their refugee loan. Ulen & Company tried unsuccessfully to give assurances that they had no intention to offer their bonds for several years, if at all, and that they would use their good offices to convince the Bank of Athens, which held half the bonds, to do the same.[26] Speyer and Hambros remained unconvinced, and decided to strike at the "Achilles heel" of the Greek Ministry of Finance—the perennial problem of Allied consent to the floating of new foreign loans.

When the Greek government formally asked for the consent of the Allies on 23 April, Great Britain and France demurred. The British government did so at the request of Speyer and Hambros. The French government insisted that the floating of another foreign loan would prevent Greece from fulfilling the heavy financial obligations already incurred. The United States gave its consent with full reservation of all questions with respect to the Tripartite Loan of 1918.[27] Despite repeated appeals by Ulen & Company and the Greek government, the French and the British remained adamant in their determination to withhold their consent. The result of this uncompromising attitude was two months of difficult diplomacy in which the State Department found itself as the unofficial liaison between Ulen and the Greek government on one hand and the French and British governments on the other. The American ambassadors in Paris and London made tactful and informal representations which ultimately contributed to the elimination of French and British opposition. Official consent by France and Great Britain was given in July 1925. Ulen & Company acknowledged their debt to the State Department. "We beg to thank you," they wrote, "for your very efficient assistance in this instance."[28]

The financing of the waterworks offered an interesting innovation which became a point of interest within banking circles in the United States. The entire project, including the emergency work, totaled about £13,000,000. Financing was derived from several sources, including a bond issue of $10,000,000—half of which was taken by Ulen & Company and half by the Bank of Athens. All phases of the design, construction, and financing were coordinated under a three-way agreement between the contractor, the bank, and the Greek government. The government could terminate the operations of Ulen and the bank by taking up the bonds. This significant arrangement meant that a public body could purchase its utilities on an installment loan without resorting to a public bond issue.[29]

The waterworks were put into use on 25 October 1929, though the project was not completed until 3 June 1931. All eyewitnesses agree that the inaugural ceremonies were an emotional experience which evoked tears of joy from grateful Athenians. At the appropriate moment the waters were turned on while a military band played the Greek national anthem and the "Star Spangled Banner." "The Athenians," wrote Skinner, "had never seen or dreamed of such a spectacle. It was too wonderful. I expected to hear roars of applause, but there was no applause, only emotion. The Athenians were too astonished at their good fortune to cheer. Many were weeping." The press, government officials, and all who had lived a lifetime in Athens were at a loss to find the appropriate words with which to extol the American achievement. Perhaps the most important benefit accruing to the United States government and to American businessmen was the reinforcement of the perception in people's minds that, unlike most other governments and foreign contractors, Americans had a prominent place in their lexicon for the words "integrity" and "reliability." "Ulen & Company," wrote Robert Skinner, "are looked upon as being in a category by themselves, as an honorable company who set out to accomplish an important piece of engineering and made every effort within their power to satisfy their clients."[30]

From an engineering point of view the Marathon dam is one of the structural wonders of the early twentieth century. It is also one of the most beautiful dams in the world. The dam's surface is faced with Pentelicon marble, such as that used in the ancient temples surrounding the Acropolis. The width at the base is 154 feet; width at the crest, 15 feet; height, 180 feet; and the length of the crest and spillway, 1,200 feet. A total of 233,000 cubic yards of concrete was used, while the reservoir is capable of containing a maximum of 1,500,000,000 cubic feet of water.[31] The visitor at Marathon is still impressed by the engineering and artistic skill that went into the construction of the water supply system. Marathon remains a vivid reminder of a positive period in the formative stages of Greek-American relations.

Land Reclamation

Concurrent with the problem of water supply was the need to reclaim large tracts of land for the settlement of over a million refugees. According to the Geneva Protocol, the Greek government had agreed to provide the Refugee Settlement Commission with 500,000 hectares (1,235,000 acres) of land for this purpose. By the end of 1924, 479,487 hectares were at the disposal of the RSC of which only 284,999 hectares (704,233 acres) were arable.[32] The remaining lands had considerable potential for farming, but an assortment of topographical and climatic irregularities prevented their cultivation. Wide fluctuations in precipitation and temperatures, large areas of malaria-infested swamplands, untamed rivers and streams, and primitive methods of farming presented serious obstacles. Land reclamation on a massive scale was imperative, if the rural phase of the RSC's refugee settlement plan was to be successful. From the technical point of view the task was fourfold: drainage of swamplands, adjusting the size and shape of river banks, building irrigation canals, and diverting the mouths and courses of rivers to prevent the accumulation of silt in commercial harbors. Most of the lands under the control of the RSC were in three large valleys stretching from east to west in Macedonia. The last two are often referred to as the Struma Valley,[33] after the river Strymon and its tributaries which run through both of them.

As the necessary technical staff was not available in Greece, the contracts for the reclamation projects were given to three American firms: The Foundation Company of New York for the Salonika Valley, John Monks and Sons for the Serres Valley, and Ulen & Company for the Drama Valley. The last two projects, in effect, constituted a single enterprise, since Monks and Ulen agreed to pool their proposals and to undertake the work under a single contract. The history of the contract negotiations, the financial arrangements, and the construction of these public works is a long (1924–1939) and complicated story in which the commercial interests of Great Britain and the United States were at stake. The British minister's succinct summation of the competition for concessions is revealing. In 1929, he wrote: "The inception of this programme [of reclamation] resolved itself into a struggle between British and American contractors . . . and British and American financial houses . . . a contest in which honours were approximately divided."[34]

Reclaiming the Salonika Plain

West of Salonika lay an area of approximately 347,000 acres of fertile, though swampy and malaria-infested land, much of which was subject to inundation by the Axios and Aliakmon rivers and their tributaries. It was expected that of this total, 95,478 acres could be reclaimed and put at the disposal of the RSC.[35] On 23 June 1925 the Greek government signed a contract for $25,000,000 with the Foundation Company of New York to undertake the reclamation project, though after careful investigation it was concluded that a loan of $17,330,730 would be sufficient. For reasons which are not entirely clear, the Foundation Company had no American competition. Consequently, the contract with the Greek government was, as in the case of the Marathon waterworks, the result of noncompetitive bidding.[36] The work was to be done by the British branch of the Foundation Company of New York, using chiefly British engineering and technical personnel. Closely related to this agreement were the issues of government ratification and financing. These problems require some attention because they are central to the thesis of this chapter—that dollar diplomacy was an integral part of United States policy in Greece during the interwar period.

The reclamation contract was signed two days before the coup d'état of General Pangalos on 25 June 1925. The general refused to ratify the agreement because he was determined that none of the credit for the project should go to his predecessor, Andreas Michalakopoulos. There is also evidence that his procrastination was fortified by the Foundation Company's consistent refusal to offer any bribe to various government officials. But if bribery of government officials was against the policy of the company, no such scruples seemed to manifest themselves where the private sector was concerned. The company's vice-president, Franklin Remington, went to several leading Athenian newspapers and put the question squarely up to them. He insisted, somewhat hypocritically, that he did not seek to buy support for his firm, but they could study the contract, and if it were found to be "a good thing for Greece" he was willing to pay them to carry out a campaign to force the Greek government to ratify it. With such an offer as an inducement, it was not difficult for any editor to conclude that the contract was a good thing for Greece. "Unceasing propaganda" was undertaken which finally forced the Pangalos government to give its ratification.[37]

These activities were carried out with the tacit approval of the State Department whose primary concern was that no American firms should compete unfairly against one another. Dulles frankly admitted that the Foundation's tactics "could often be justified in business" as long as the

State Department itself was not guilty of illegal or questionable activities. Thus reassured, the American legation undertook an aggressive policy in support of the Foundation Company's proposal. Ultimately, the legation's cooperation and assistance proved to be a decisive factor in the negotiations, which earned the gratitude of the company's officials.[38] It soon became clear, however, that the financing of these works would become entangled with the issue of war debts and British opposition.

To the chagrin of the State Department it was learned that the contract for the Salonika Plain provided for financing through Speyer Company's Bank of New York and Hambros, the bankers who had undertaken the Refugee Loan of 1924. Consequently, the loan was, in effect, a British loan. The State Department protested against the virtual exclusion of American capital. The vice-president of the Foundation Company made an effort to placate the Division of Near Eastern Affairs. He pointed out to Dulles that any loan to a government in the Near East in which British bankers participated was bound to be more sound and desirable, since the impregnable position of the British navy in the Eastern Mediterranean offered ample "security." State Department officials were assured, moreover, that American business would benefit, since most of the material and heavy machinery could be obtained only in the United States. It was this assurance that finally helped to secure American support for the loan. Subsequent expenditures show that American business was, indeed, a major beneficiary. By 1 March 1932, $10,818,044.71 (or 62 percent) from the face amount of the contract ($17,330,730) had been spent. Of this amount approximately 33 percent was spent in the United States.[39]

In the meantime, the British had begun to have second thoughts. They were apprehensive about the rapid rise of American commercial influence in Greece. The need for Allied consent for new security gave Great Britain the opportunity to undermine the entire reclamation project. The new business that would accrue to American companies and the virtual exclusion of British contracting firms from the bidding were troublesome.[40] Although British capital and technology were to be used almost exclusively, this advantage seemed hardly enough. When the Foundation Company, apparently in ignorance of the technical issues surrounding the Tripartite Loan, made certain advances to the Greek government without securing Allied consent, the British took the opportunity to suggest British-American representation to the Greek government. The acting secretary of state, Joseph C. Grew, retorted that

Greece had taken action in violation of the 1918 Tripartite Loan on several occasions and in each case, the United States, France, and Great Britain had overlooked the transgression. In view of this record of leniency, it was not clear why the British government was now anxious to make a joint protest. After a lengthy and evasive reply from the British embassy, the State Department ended the matter by stating that in view of the humanitarian nature of the Foundation Company's project, no useful purpose would be served by the application of additional pressure on the Greek government.[41]

The loan was issued in 1928 bearing an interest rate of 6 percent, and payable in forty years. Steady progress in construction continued until 1932. At that time the chaotic state of Greek finances, resulting to a large extent from the effects of the world-wide economic depression, brought to a virtual standstill the procurement of additional cash advances under existing public works agreements. The Greek government was forced to progress on a piecemeal basis and to rely partly on funds from the second Refugee and Stabilization Loan of 1927 and partly from its own resources. The work was completed in 1938, with inestimable benefits to Greece and her refugees. The American ambassador, Lincoln Mac-Veagh, provided a fitting epilogue when he wrote: "Thus a chapter of American participation in Greece's economic development, and one of which Americans may well be proud for its quiet efficiency as well as its magnificent results, has been brought . . . to a close."[42]

Reclaiming the Struma Valley

The third major contract in which American firms participated was the reclamation of large tracts of land in the Struma Valley. The issues surrounding contract negotiations and the financing of these works were not appreciably different from those which dominated the discussions for the Marathon waterworks and the reclamation of the Salonika plains. There are some technical variations to the established pattern, and the figures are different, but the diplomatic setting remains essentially the same.

East of Salonika lie the plains of Serres and Drama, drained by the Struma and Angiti rivers, respectively. These valleys were once the highways of oriental conquerors and barbarians who chose to venture into the Greek peninsula. The land is fertile, though it suffered from the same drawbacks as the plains of Salonika. It differed, perhaps, only in the greater degree to which it served as a breeding ground for malaria-carrying mosquitos. It was estimated that through drainage, irrigation, and artificial barriers to control the depth and course of rivers, 107,939 additional acres could be put at the disposal of the RSC.[43] The cost was set at $23,000,000.

Early in 1928 the Greek government announced its intention to undertake the reclamation of the Struma Valley. Apparently, the announcement was anticipated because agents of John Monks & Sons of New York appeared immediately on the scene, and in cooperation with representatives of Ulen & Company proceeded to open negotiations with the Greek government. To the consternation of the British, no other firms were seriously considered. According to the American minister, the British firm of Boot and Company, financed by Helbert Wagg and Company, made certain vague offers, but with no clear indication as to the source and nature of its financial backers. Monks and Ulen, on the other hand, were able to satisfy the Greek government's requirement for joint technical and financial bids.[44] Thus, for the third time in three years, a major public contract was about to be granted to American firms on a noncompetitive basis.

The British minister's account on this point differs significantly. The bid of Boot and Company was a bona fide offer and appreciably lower than that of any of its rivals. Early in the year, however, a road contract for £6,000,000 sterling was awarded to British firms, "a decision . . . [which] was not well received in Washington." In an effort to convince the State Department that American capital was not being overlooked, the Greek government gave in to pressure from the American legation and granted the Struma Valley contract to Monks and Ulen.[45] On the basis of the sources it is evident that this version is closer to the truth, while that of Robert Skinner is considerably "sanitized."

The State Department was reluctant to grant its support. A tentative settlement had been reached the previous December for the funding of Greece's indebtedness to the United States. Immediately thereafter, the Greek ministry of finance began to lend new interpretations to the terms of the agreement (see chapter 11). The Greek attitude was unexpected. Officials within the State and Treasury Departments questioned whether the Greek government could be trusted to honor its agreements with American contracting firms. The secretary of commerce, Herbert Hoover, urged the State Department not to allow the squabble over Greek indebtedness to the United States to intervene in the participation of American business in a "profitable and eminently humanitarian venture." Former chargé to Greece, Dr. Edward Capps, expressed similar sentiments. On the basis of conversations with Robert Monks, he felt certain that, if the contract was awarded to Monks and Ulen, the work would be carried out according to the best American tradition. In view of the fact that no other American firms were competing for the contract, Secretary of State Kellogg instructed Skinner to give his full support to the Monks-Ulen proposal with the provision that financing was to take place after the debt settlement had been finalized. Skinner was to remind the minister of foreign affairs of a promise by the Greek minister in Washington that the Struma Valley contract would be given to an American concern.[46]

Throughout the period of the negotiations, the British legation made concerted attempts to undermine the American proposals through an assortment of allegations regarding the integrity of American firms in dealing with each other. Skinner made every effort to protect American interests "to the fullest possible extent . . . that they might present a fairly united front . . . and avoid being led into disastrous competition among themselves."[47] Despite these obstructive tactics by the British, a contract was signed on 20 October 1928 between Monks and Ulen and the Greek government. The financing was to be provided by Seligman and Company of New York, though for certain technical and political reasons, the loan contract that was to accompany the Monks-Ulen agreement was not immediately forthcoming.

The financial arrangements are extremely technical, but to the extent that they throw additional light on the character of Greek-American relations, they are important. Since the days of Garrett Droppers (1914-1920), the various Greek governments had attempted repeatedly, if unsuccessfully, to use the United States government as an instrument with which to elicit certain actions from the Western Powers. The financing of the Struma Valley project offered Venizelos an opportunity to try one more time. On 19 October an offer was made by Hambros to finance the project "in order to preserve Greece as territory for their exclusive operations."[48] It was obvious that Hambros was prepared to offer conditions hard for competitors to meet. The result was a series of devious maneuvers designed to pit Seligman against Hambros and to reap whatever benefits this competition might produce. The fact that this policy was a complete contradiction of his government's call for joint technical and financial bids was a detail which the premier chose to ignore. Eventually, a public works loan of $75,000,000 was negotiated—$50,000,000 more than the original $25,000,000 deemed necessary for the reclamation works. The remaining money was to be used for a wide variety of public works programs. Seligman and Hambros were to share in the loan equally.

Seligman & Company naturally felt that they had not been treated fairly and that, in effect, they had been coerced into a much larger loan than they had anticipated. Skinner had a frank conversation with Venizelos on the subject. The premier agreed that the situation was unfortunate, but the propositions from Hambros Bank presented certain advantages which he could not ignore. Evidently, the British used their membership in the International Financial Commission to enable the loan to be floated free of IFC control. The price for this convenience was higher terms than would have been the case had the loan been put under international supervision. "There are not wanting plenty of thoughtful people," wrote Skinner, "who feel that this will prove to be a costly mistake to the Hellenic Government in the future."[49] The negotiations with Hambros were pressed to completion, and the contract was ratified by Parliament on 11 December 1928. The first issue was for only £4,000. Additional amounts were to be placed on the market at an undetermined date. The bonds were floated at 89, bearing an interest rate of 6 percent and a maturity period of 40 years.

In the meantime, Seligman & Company continued to negotiate for their half of the loan. However, the 1929 depression and the fiscal crises of the 1930s intervened, and the American portion of the loan was never floated. After 1932 the Greek government was forced to rely on its own resources to complete the work. Despite the loss of the American portion of the loan, it is fairly clear that in terms of purchases generated by the Struma Valley project, the United States and, to a certain extent, Germany were the main beneficiaries. Throughout the 1930s many technical obstacles and petty controversies plagued the construction. The work was completed in 1939. In the words of Lincoln MacVeagh, "another brilliant chapter in Greco-American cooperation has thus, after many headaches for all concerned, come to a successful conclusion." The Greek government expressed its "complete satisfaction to the Companies for the workmanlike, complete, economical and entirely successful execution of these extensive works."[50]

The rise of American influence in Greece after the First World War was not the product of a conscious effort in a political way. The American aloofness from Greek political affairs, the absence of a propaganda machine, and the refusal to cater to local sentiments perpetuated the traditional belief that America could be trusted. To the popular mind, the successful construction of vital public works by firms from the United States was visible proof that the faith in American integrity and workmanship was not misplaced. The significance of waterworks, reclamation projects, and loans went beyond the fact that through these enterprises the rehabilitation of an entire nation was made possible. Equally important for the future would be the establishment of a continuity in Greek-American relations which was maintained up to the outbreak of the Second World War.

11
The United States and the Refugee and Stabilization Loan of 1928

The most complex and persistent problem confronting the governments of Greece and the United States from 1918 to 1929 was the two-facet issue of war credits and war debts. Almost every aspect of Greek-American relations revolved around the controversy regarding the remaining credits owed to Greece under the Tripartite Loan of 1918 and the funding of Greece's indebtedness to the United States. In the interest of brevity and clarity, this chapter is confined to the four basic aspects of the problem: the nature of the controversy, the legal standpoint, the role of moral considerations, and a summary of the negotiations leading to the final settlement.[1]

The Status of the Tripartite Loan, 1920–1925

Article 3 of the Tripartite Loan provided that cash could be advanced under two conditions: 1) if the foreign balances of the Bank of Greece and of the Greek treasury should fall below 100,000,000 francs, or 2) Greece in any event could claim all of the cash six months after the termination of the war. In a supplementary agreement on 25 November 1919, the second provision of Article 3 was waived to enable Greece to make immediate withdrawals. This revision enabled Greece to comply with Article 1 of the original agreement. Greek authorities promptly spent the full amount of the loan in the belief that cash advances would automatically follow the establishment of credits. The National Bank of Greece, on the strength of the credits opened by the three lending governments and with those credits as security, issued an equivalent amount of its own bank notes. The effects of this misplaced optimism on Greek currency were disastrous. The drachma depreciated from 19.27 cents in 1919 to 1.23 cents in December 1922, a decline of almost 94 percent.[2]

As a result of the unexpected defeat of Venizelos in November 1920 and the subsequent return of Constantine, France and Great Britain refused to recognize the king and to make any additional advances. The United States, following the Allied example, did the same. There was, however, a fundamental difference between the Allied and the American positions inherent in this change of policy. Whereas the French and British made their position clear regarding the remaining credits vis-à-vis the return of Constantine, the United States never gave any warning.[3] It was not until December 1924 that the State Department, for the first time and through informal conversations, informed the Greek government that the agreement with Canada in December 1923 released the United States from any obligation to make further advances.[4] The warning was informal, and no record of a written, official communication on this specific point has ever been found.

The sources make it clear that, from the beginning, practically every top official in the departments of the Treasury, State, and Commerce believed the Tripartite Agreement to be three separate loans, independent of each other. The obligation of the United States was clear and binding. Legally, there was no reason to connect any political action on the part of the French and British to American policy in this regard. President Wilson and his Administration left no doubt about this legal point. On 31 December 1920 Wilson's assistant secretary of the treasury, Nicholas Kelly, informed the Division of Near Eastern Affairs that the president was in agreement with the State Department's assessment of the Greek situation. The credit obligations negotiated with the Venizelos government were still binding on the United States and that the Greek chargé d'affaires, on proper application, should be recognized as representing the government of King Constantine. The undersecretary of state, Norman H. Davis, concurred. If the United States government were to extend its recognition or establish relations with the Greek government, the Treasury could not legally or morally cancel its financial obligation to Greece.[5]

There was also a practical side to the matter. Major James F. Case, Ulen & Company's representative in Greece, informed the American commercial attaché, R. O. Hall, that he had the assurances of unimpeachable sources that the Greek government was prepared to apply one half of whatever money it could extract from the United States government to public works, principally highways. Hall emphasized that by making the further advances under the Tripartite Agreement the United States government would escape all charges of bad faith or sharp dealing and open the way to greater opportunities for American capital. If it appeared that the United States was eager to aid the Greeks in the face of French and British displeasure, the interests of American companies in general would be enhanced considerably. "In other words," wrote one State Department official, "we might keep this matter in such shape that it could be used for trading purposes. We have a healthy commerce with Greece, with a favorable trade of balance."[6] Thus, there was ample justification for the United States to advance the additional credits, but the realities of international politics were a serious obstacle.

The United States government recognized that there was a point beyond which it could not proceed independently when it came to matters affecting the domestic politics of Greece. Consequently, it broke diplomatic relations with Constantine, and refused to admit that a legitimate government was in power in Athens. It followed, then, that if there was no legitimate government ruling the country, there was no government to receive any additional cash advance. The State Department clung to this interpretation for almost three and a half years in its efforts to justify its refusal to advance additional credits.

The shaky grounds upon which the American position rested can best be illustrated by the attitude of the Treasury Department. In late autumn 1921, Stamos Papafrangos, solicitor of the National Bank of Greece, arrived in the United States, hoping to gain recognition for Constantine's government and to receive additional cash installments. The Treasury accepted from Papafrangos payments for all accrued interest (up to 15 November 1921), but refused to release further credits. The question which this procedure raises is obvious: How can one government participate in a business transaction with another government whose existence it refuses to recognize. The Treasury Department was also inconsistent in its statements sent to the Greek government regard-

ing the sums of interest falling due. Before November 1920 this procedure was an established practice. After the resumption of diplomatic
relations in 1924 no further statements were sent. With this omission,
the United States seems to have admitted, or at least had given the impression, that nothing was due from Greece.[7] Application of logic, however, was generally subordinated to expediency, so that self-serving
statements and spurious arguments, by both sides, were allowed to assume the stature of axioms.

Legal Considerations

By August 1925 Greek-American relations had stabilized to the
point where the Greek government felt confident enough to accept an
invitation from the United States government to come forth and settle
its indebtedness. A Greek delegation met with the World War Foreign
Debt Commission in January 1926 and proceeded to state its case in the
most direct terms. The Greek government would be glad to consider
settling its debt, if the United States would consider releasing the remaining credits. The commission's reply was a veritable legalistic litany.
Resorting to every legal and technical argument it could muster, the
American delegation presented an impressive array of objections to the
Greek claims.[8] The American position reduced itself to three fundamental points: 1) the failure of Great Britain and France to comply with all
the terms of the Tripartite Agreement; 2) the fact that Greece had
stopped paying interest on the advances of $15,000,000; and 3) the
floating of a loan in Canada without American consent.[9]

The commission's first major contention was that the Tripartite Loan
was essentially a wartime agreement to promote the Allied cause. It differed from the financial agreements under which the United States made
loans to the Allied governments, other than Greece, in that it was a joint
undertaking with France and Great Britain to make advances by equal
shares. France had made no advances,[10] while Greece released Great Britain from any claim to further advances under the agreement signed in
London on 22 December 1921.[11] The United States agreed to participate in the Tripartite Agreement on the understanding that none of the
participating governments would be expected to assume the responsibility alone. "It is a silly and dangerous argument—a boomerang," commented Hall. Altogether, "unjust and . . . unworthy of the American
people," insisted Congressman Theodore E. Burton of Ohio.[12] These

comments are illustrative of the criticisms which were directed at the commission from persons in and out of government.

The Greek delegation was eager to adopt this "joint undertaking" theory. They questioned, however, whether the United States government was prepared to make itself liable as the obligor for the obligations of all three lending nations and thus be placed in the position of having to pay what France and Great Britain might fail to pay (see appendix F).[13] The debt commission remained undaunted and persisted in its determination to hold to its own interpretation of the provisions of the 1918 Tripartite Loan.

The commission pointed next to the failure of Greece to make interest payments after October 1921 on the $15,000,000 advances. At this point the Greeks decided to resort to some legal technicalities of their own. They put forward the argument that there was no neglect or default on the part of Greece, since the United States still owed the Greek government $33,236,629. The back interest could be regarded merely as a partial offset against the amounts payable to Greece by the United States.

The commission's conclusions generated considerable interest in Congress and in the executive branch. Since the debate in Congress tended to follow party lines, there were many Republicans who were eager to espouse the Greek cause as a matter of principle and as a matter of practical politics. Democrats were generally opposed to further foreign loans or credits of any kind. The war debt issue enabled the former to appear as the defenders of American honesty, justice, and fair dealing with foreign nations, while the latter wished to appear as the champions of fiscal responsibility.

The Greeks also found many supporters within the Departments of State, Commerce, and the Treasury whose intimate knowledge of the problem made them more sympathetic to the Greek point of view. Ogden L. Mills, the undersecretary of the treasury, argued that if there was a breach of faith, it was the United States which set the example first. The facts were clear. When Great Britain and France became disturbed at the sequence of events following the defeat of Venizelos in 1920, they maintained relations with Greece and conducted business with the ministry representing the parliamentary majority. They withheld from Constantine all the courtesies prescribed by diplomatic etiquette. The United States maintained diplomatic relations until the inauguration of the Harding administration on 4 March 1921, when it ceased to maintain a minister in Athens and to recognize a diplomatic representative of Greece. Greece continued to pay interest on the $15,000,000 for six more months. It was contrary to all reason to expect that the Greek government would continue to uphold its part of the bargain when the United States withheld its recognition and refused to make further advances. The American commercial attaché was direct on this point. In view of the nonrecognition policy of the State Department the United States government had no reason to demand or to expect interest payments from Greece. "How can a non-recognized government pay the debts of a recognized government?" Congressman Burton, a member of the debt commission, simply said: "I never was proud of the answer the commission made to the Greek Government."[14]

The third major objection raised by the debt commission was the nature of the pledged security Greece offered to Canada in December 1923 for a loan of $8,000,000. The entire proposition is extremely technical; however, it is an inseparable part of the debt negotiations. At the center of the controversy was the confusion arising from the effort to translate Article 4 of the original French text into English.[15] According to the article, no new security could be pledged by Greece without the consent of the three lending governments. But what precisely was "new pledged security?" No one seemed to know for certain. The debt commission insisted on interpreting Article 4 in the broadest possible terms to include security of any kind. The Greek delegation argued that the original agreement concerned itself with new security from revenues only insofar as those revenues were under the control of the International Financial Commission. The fact is that the security assigned for the Canadian loan came from surplus revenues turned over to the Greek government by the IFC after the servicing of all existing loans under its control. The American position, the Greeks charged, enlarged the prohibition contained in the 1918 agreement far beyond its true intent.

The debt commission replied that it was Greece which was guilty of broad interpretations. Article 6 of the Greek-Canadian contract concludes with the following sentence: "In the event of the above-mentioned surplus [under the control of the IFC] being insufficient, the service of the Bonds will be completed out of the other receipts of the Hellenic State."[16] In the minds of the American delegation, this was the crux of the problem. It was not clear how Greece could offer "other receipts of the Hellenic State" without infringing on the security of loans under the control of the IFC.

The Greek line of reasoning, however, had the greater merit, if subsequent events (i.e., after December 1923) can be used as a standard of measurement. When the negotiations for the Refugee Loan of 1924 were in the last phase, the Greeks approached the State Department officially and asked permission to float part of the loan in the United States. Permission was given, thereby admitting tacitly that the Tripartite Agreement was still in force, and that the Canadian loan, despite its controversial character, had no effect on the continuity of the 1918 Loan. When the discussion reached an impasse, the Greeks offered to submit the matter to binding arbitration, perhaps at The Hague. This offer was refused, and the discussions were terminated.

Considerations of Morality

By April 1927 conditions had changed sufficiently to justify the resumption of discussions. The differences separating the two governments were then reduced to a question of morality and to the compelling necessity to complete the work of the Refugee Settlement Commission. The dissolution of the World War Foreign Debt Commission on 9 February 1927 helped to shift the emphasis from strict interpretation of contract law to the principle of equity as a basis for settlement. American officials and legislators gradually came around to the view that it was wrong to hide behind a mass of legalities in the face of what was clearly a moral obligation. In fact, every government official and congressman who had served on the debt commission eventually reversed himself and promoted a settlement based on equity rather than on the narrow interpretation of contractual law.[17] When expressed in its basic terms, the question becomes disarmingly simple. Undersecretary of the Treasury Mills put it succinctly as follows: ". . . we said to Greece, put in the field nine divisions to help us, and spend 750,000,000 francs, and we will stand back of the 750,000,000 francs by a credit on our books."[18] Whatever legal grounds the United States government had in support of its position, the fact remained that Greece performed its work: Greeks fought valiantly on the side of the Allies, the Greek government financed what it agreed to finance, and, in general, the country completed the expected tasks. Whatever Greece's tansgressions, they occurred *after* its contractual obligation had been satisfied under the terms of the Tripartite Loan. Considerations of morality, then, contributed heavily to the creation of an atmosphere in which negotiations could be resumed. There was also the practical side to the matter.

When the £10,000,000 refugee loan was floated in December 1924 more than £3,000,000 had already been spent. By 1927 the remaining sum had been exhausted, and the task of refugee settlement was far from complete. By 1926, 622,685 refugees had been settled and had become economically self-supporting.[19] This number represented only about half of the total refugee population, which was still living under deplorable conditions. The Refugee Settlement Commission estimated that an additional £5,000,000 were needed for the completion of its work. In its "Tenth Quarterly Report," RSC suggested the floating of a second refugee loan on basically the same terms as the first. The Financial Committee of the League of Nations agreed to create a committee of experts to investigate the economic condition of Greece and to decide accordingly. The committee concluded that a loan was necessary, though not solely for the purpose of refugee settlement. Closely related to this problem was the need to end a series of budgetary deficits and the restoration of fiscal responsibility through the stabilization of the drachma. Accordingly, the committee recommended the floating of a £9,000,000 loan: £3,000,000 for the continuation of the work of establishing the refugees, £3,000,000 to cover the deficits generated by the 1927 budget, and £3,000,000 for the stabilization of the drachma on a gold basis. Finally, the loan was to be an integral part of reorganizing and strengthening the National Bank of Greece.

The Final Settlement

While Greece was endeavoring to improve her economic position through additional financial assistance from the League of Nations, negotiations were under way to settle the differences which had arisen under the terms of the Tripartite Loan. Great Britain had advanced approximately £6,540,000 ($31,826,910). The agreement was signed in London on 9 April 1927. The Greek government agreed to repay the loan over a period of sixty-two years at an interest rate of 6 percent. The terms were favorable to Greece. Essentially, the Greek government escaped 67 percent of its obligation. This generosity was prompted by a sense of guilt within the Foreign Office which viewed Greece's financial plight partly as the result of Britain's encouragement and, later, its lack of support of the Greek campaign in Asia Minor. The British also were concerned that the Ecumenical Cabinet of Alexander Zaïmis would not be able to survive a political crisis unless there was an infusion of money to stabilize the currency. In return, Greece was to relinquish all claims to the remaining 1918 credits and to certain other obligations of the British government.[20]

Immediately, the State Department notified the Foreign Ministry that it expected as favorable treatment as that received by Great Britain. To the surprise of American officials, the Greeks insisted on holding on to a dead issue. They argued that the Greek-British settlement was entirely separate from the problem of Greece's indebtedness to the United States. The minister of finance, George Caphandares, informed Skinner that the Greek government was under no obligation to settle with the United States unless and until Greece received the balance of credits alleged to be due under the 1918 contract.[21] However, with the cooperation of the British government, the State Department was able to apply pressure on the Greek government, which reluctantly came around to the American point of view. In June, Caphandares informed Skinner that Charalambos Simopoulos, the Greek minister in Washington, would soon have new instructions relative to the resumption of negotiations.

The Treasury and State Departments were apprehensive lest the impending Greek proposal should press for binding arbitration. The foreign minister, Andreas Michalakopoulos, already had announced that Greece would be ready to propose binding arbitration in case the negotiations should encounter insurmountable difficulties. The chief of the Near Eastern Division, G. Howland Shaw, had serious misgivings over this point, and suggested to Undersecretary of the Treasury Mills that it would be a mistake to fall into the bottomless pit of technicalities inherent in the process of arbitration. He advised a simple and direct approach. American negotiators should insist that the United States was entitled to as favorable a settlement as that accorded to Great Britain. Mills agreed, and he replied reassuringly that Montagu C. Norman, Governor of the Bank of England, was in agreement with the American position.[22]

Apparently, Simopoulos was instructed to make a last effort to salvage anything he could of the remaining credits and in general to remain as unconciliatory as he dared under the circumstances. The minister did his best to comply, though he saw clearly that conciliation would have to be an integral part of any settlement—a realistic appraisal of the situation which his superiors obviously did not fully appreciate.[23] Simopoulos, made a feeble effort to convince the secretary of state to see the problem from the Greek point of view and to connect the debt negotiation to the 1918 credits. Secretary of State Kellogg, however, insisted on treatment equal to that accorded to Great Britain. The Greek Minister eventually conceded the correctness of the American position, whereupon Mills seized the opportunity to make a counterproposal.

Why not, the undersecretary asked, set aside the past and consider the problem from the standpoint of contemporary realities. The finances of Greece were in shambles, the refugee question was far from over, and the need for additional funds was critical. Furthermore, the League was in the process of approving a loan for the purpose of fiscal stabilization and refugee work. If Greece would renounce her claims to the 1918 credits a debt settlement could be arranged and the United States government could participate in the League loan. Because the League of Nations was on the verge of unveiling the final form of the proposed agreement, no immediate reply was given to Mills' suggestion.

On 15 September 1927 the League of Nations adopted a Protocol which stated in part: "The Council . . . approves in particular the scheme drawn up to enable Greece to continue the settlement of the refugees, to finally balance its budget, and to stabilize its currency."[24] On the basis of this resolution a £9,000,000 refugee and stabilization loan was floated on the British and American markets.[25]

As far as Greek-American negotiations were concerned, the State Department and the Foreign Ministry soon found the elusive formula for the settlement of Greece's indebtedness to the United States. A tentative agreement was reached on 5 December. Greece agreed to renounce her claim to the remaining credits and to fund its $15,000,000 debt over a period of sixty-two years. In return, the United States agreed to join Great Britain and to participate in the League's refugee and stabilization loan.[26] Contracts were signed on 30 January 1928 in London with the firms of Hambros Bank, Ltd. and Enlangers, and in the United States with Speyer & Company and the National City Company of New York. The British portion of the loan was £6,000,000. It was issued at 91, at 6 percent interest, though the net yield was 86 and the real interest, after service fees and stamp duties, amounted to 7.05 percent—a considerable improvement over the 8.71 percent real interest rate of the 1924

Refugee Loan. The balance, £2,500,000 ($12,167,000), was granted by the United States government at an annual interest rate of 4 percent in forty semiannual installments.

Throughout the negotiations Simopoulos insisted that if the United States deserved to be treated on an equal basis with Great Britain, so did Greece. The United States agreed, and the difference in the sums advanced by Great Britain and the United States became the face value of the new American loan.[27] The entire sum was to be used solely for refugee settlement. Because the American loan fell £500,000 short of the Protocol's requirements, half a million pounds were subtracted from the British portion of the loan and turned over to the RSC.

The lenient terms of the loan generated much favorable comment and a discernible sigh of relief that this difficult problem was resolved. One of the most severe critics of the 1924 Refugee Loan wrote: "This loan at par and at 4 percent could indeed properly be considered a refugee settlement loan."[28] The sense of relief in Greece was considerable. Enlarged photographs of Robert Skinner, many interviews, and florid editorials were published in Athenian newspapers. Almost everyone predicted a new era of improved Greek-American relations which would bring the two countries closer together.

What some Greek officials did not seem to realize was the need for congressional approval. The debate in Congress was heated.[29] For the next seventeen months the debate went on unabated to the surprise of both Greeks and Americans. The debt settlement was finally approved by the House of Representatives on 10 December 1928, passed by the Senate on 9 February 1929, and signed by President Hoover on 10 May 1929.[30] The settlement, however, was achieved on the "capacity-to-pay" theory which was commonly applied to the financial settlements of the period. The efforts of the Foreign Ministry to apply the theory to Greek-American financial relations would give rise to many disputes throughout the 1930s.

The Refugee and Stabilization Loan of 1928 and the settlement of the financial controversies which preceded it represent the culmination of a formative period in Greek-American diplomatic relations. The problems generated by the Tripartite Loan of 1918 were at the center of almost everything that transpired between the State Department and the Greek Foreign Ministry from 1918 to 1929. Consequently, the issues of war loans, credits, and debts provided many of the opportunities for the United States and Greek governments to discover each other in the diplomatic sense. By 1929, a process of diplomatic orientation had reached a fair degree of maturity, so that future relations between Greece and the United States were conducted with a greater awareness of one another's needs and aspirations.

The diplomacy between Greece and the United States after 1929 assumed a different character.[31] Relations between the two countries continued as an extension of the issues that were generated during the preceding decade. But they were also more in the nature of historical footnotes and historical commentary than a conscious effort by either government to explore new diplomatic initiatives. The events of the 1920s, which had brought Greece under the scrutiny of the United States government and the American public, had run their course or were greatly altered by the international realities of the 1930s.

By 1929 a semblance of economic and political stability had been restored to Greece. The refugee problem was on its way toward an acceptable solution, and the controversy surrounding the terms of the Tripartite Loan was essentially resolved.[32] Greek-American political relations gave rise to no serious controversy, despite the turbulent course of the Greek Republic. Finally, the coming of the Great Depression and the rise of fascism in Europe and the Far East served to focus the attention of the United States on the solution of problems with world-wide implications.

Greece was also compelled to direct her attention to problems affecting Europe and the Balkan peninsula, in particular. The social, political, and economic issues of the 1920s continued to influence Greek domestic politics, but the international ramifications which those issues inspired were no longer overriding considerations in the formulation of overall American foreign policy.

For these reasons, Greek-American diplomacy in the 1930s was more passive. Relations between the United States and Greece were generally friendly, and the issues which did separate the two countries assumed a more technical character. Disputes surrounding the financial agreements of the 1920s and the completion of public works projects; Greek monetary policy and its effect on Americans living in Greece; the status of American citizens during the dictatorship of John Metaxas; the formulation of commercial agreements; and efforts to sign a reciprocal immigration treaty dominated the diplomatic relations between the two countries. Nevertheless, American interest in the Balkans did not decline. The specter of another global war served to heighten the interest of the State Department in the politics of southeastern Europe. Greece, therefore, remained under the close scrutiny of the United States government and, consequently, a large amount of information flowed from the American legation to the State Department.[33] This information, however, is more in the nature of diplomatic intelligence than diplomatic dialogue. By way of summing up this study, the present section will touch briefly on the problems raised by the Refugee and Stabilization Loan of 1928 in the 1930s, since the two-facet problem of war loans and war debts remained the most pervasive issue that provided a sense of continuity to Greek-American relations from 1917 to 1940.

The consequences of the 1929 depression did not reach Greece until the autumn of 1931. From 1928 to 1931 Greece was able to reduce her public debt by 11 percent, while simultaneously stabilizing her currency.[34] Nevertheless, it became virtually impossible for the Greek government to obtain foreign exchange because the agricultural products of Greece, despite their depressed prices, found few markets abroad. Furthermore, remittances from emigrants to the United States and from sailors in the Greek Merchant Marine, foreign loans, and reparations were sources of revenue that disappeared quickly. The Hoover Moratorium, which postponed foreign payments due to the United States during the fiscal year 1932, did little to alleviate the problem. Still, the economy continued to expand, at a very slow rate perhaps, but without a catastrophic breakdown. The turning point came in September 1931 when Great Britain abandoned the gold standard. The British action posed a threat to the country's trade, and was responsible directly for the depreciation of the sterling assets of the Bank of Greece. Investors became alarmed, and there were signs of a flight from the drachma.

In January 1932 Venizelos traveled to Rome, Paris, and London in search of a loan that would enable the Greek government to continue its foreign debt payments and the reclamation works in northern Greece. But Italy had little to spare, while France and Great Britain were beset with problems of their own. In April, the council of the League of Nations took up the question of financial aid to Greece, but given the uncertain state of affairs in Europe, the major powers were reluctant to take financial risks. By the end of April, with its gold reserves down to $2,350,000, Greece abandoned the gold standard, and declared a unilateral moratorium on the payment of her foreign debts. By 10 November the interest owed to the United States had reached the sum of $444,000.[35]

The American chargé d'affaires, Leland B. Morris, protested to the Foreign Ministry that the Greek foreign debt default was a breach of faith.[36] Foreign Minister Andreas Michalakopoulos responded by recounting the financial ills afflicting the Greek Treasury and by describing the disastrous consequences the collapse of the drachma would have upon the internal order and social peace of the country. The result, he predicted, would be a financial, economic, and social catastrophe such as was seen in Germany in 1922–23. Michalakopoulos asked for the cooperation and patience of the United States government. He implored Morris to recommend to the American bondholders that they not adopt an unreasonable attitude which might be diametrically opposed to their own interests.[37] The State Department did not press the matter, pending the outcome of an investigation by the League loans committee on Greece's "capacity to pay," as well as the outcome of negotiations between the Greek government and the representatives of foreign bondholders in London. Eventually, the Greek government came forth with a proposal. It was prepared to make payments amounting to 30 percent of the total annual interest service on each of the respective loans affecting the bondholders. After careful examination it was agreed that the Greek offer was fair, and that the bondholders would do well to accept these arrangements.[38]

In view of this tentative settlement, the State Department expected the Greek government to make a similar proposal to the United States government relative to the Refugee and Stabilization Loan of 1928. To the surprise of American officials the Greek minister in Washington requested a two and a half year postponement of all payments due to the United States Treasury. The Greek government contended that the refugee and stabilization loan was an integral part of the war debts settlement (a position held until 1940). Therefore, it should be included among intergovernmental war debts and be subject to any further moratorium or scaling down of war debts. The secretary of the treasury disagreed. The 1928 loan, he insisted, was purely commercial and had nothing to do with war debts. He protested against any possibility of holders of the Greek stabilization and refugee loan receiving more favorable treatment than the United States government in respect to its loan of 10 May 1929.[39]

After three and a half years of difficult negotiations, and with the support of the French and British governments, a compromise was reached on 30 January 1936. The Greek government would pay 36 percent of the interest due in semiannual installments under a schedule of payments to be established by mutual consent. Despite this agreement, the loan controversy continued to be immersed in a quagmire of technicalities up to the outbreak of the Second World War. The matter was formally settled in 1964.[40]

Epilogue

The enunciation of the Truman Doctrine on 12 March 1947 was a unique and comprehensive statement relative to the political and military role that the United States was prepared to play in the Eastern Mediterranean. It was also a departure from a historical tradition that went back two hundred years. In the eighteenth and nineteenth centuries American interest in Greece was humanitarian, cultural, commercial, and sentimental. The classical heritage of Greece and the struggle for national independence in 1821 inspired romantic and philhellenic sentiments among many Americans. Greek immigration to the United States after 1900 strengthened the ties between the two countries, though they remained of a non-political character.

In the Paris Peace Conference following the First World War, the United States became involved in the negotiations concerning the delineation of Greek frontiers and in Greece's military venture in Asia Minor. The Greek landing at Smyrna on 14 May 1919 was accomplished, in part, with the approval of President Wilson. However, this political involvement was temporary because domestic politics prevented an American participation in the final settlements of the Near East.

The interwar period witnessed a great increase in American economic and cultural influence in Greece. The outbreak of hostilities in Europe in 1939 brought to an end a chapter in Greek-American diplomacy whose significance is generally underestimated. After giving credit to the preeminence of the French and British presence, the fact remains that American influence permeated all levels of Greek society. When Greece was on the verge of social and economic collapse after the Asia Minor debacle, it was primarily America which intervened to mitigate the pernicious effects of that catastrophe. The preceding pages have documented the benevolence which prompted American private agencies and citizens to undertake a humanitarian task of Herculean proportions. And while the official policy of the United States government followed typical rules of expediency which sought to promote American commercial and financial interests, it cannot be said that Washington's official policy was devoid of altruism.

American cultural organizations also increased their activities after 1922. With the exodus of the Greek and Armenian populations from Turkey, a number of American mission schools moved their facilities to Greece and continued to operate there. The most prominent American educational institutions were Athens College (founded in 1925) and Anatolia College, which was moved from Asia Minor to Salonika. These institutions compared favorably to the other American colleges in Constantinople, Beirut, Smyrna, and Sofia. The American School of Classical Studies, founded in 1881, conducted important excavations in various parts of the country, including Corinth and the Agora in Athens.[1]

In addition to these cultural activities, Greek-American commercial relations from 1919 to 1930 increased rapidly to the point where the United States assumed top place in the overall trade of Greece. The participation of American investment capital in the construction of public works contributed heavily to the physical and social rehabilitation of the country.

To be sure, America's record is not beyond reproach, but neither is that of any other power. The obvious example on the debit side is the United States government's position on the issues of recognition, war credits and war debts. But these problems were inextricably connected with complex international considerations so that an independent course and a totally objective policy were impossible. State Department officials often saw the contradictions inherent in America's Greek policy and privately expressed regret for their inability "to tell the whole story," as Allen W. Dulles pointed out. Nor can the United States be chastised for pursuing its own self-interests; so did everyone else. The significant point is that long before the United States became the dominant foreign influence in Greece, an American presence in that country was already established, though from the political and strategic viewpoint Greece remained outside the range of American special interests.

With the outbreak of World War II the American role in Greece was destined to undergo a basic change, largely as part of America's fundamentally changed position toward world issues. The United States gradually abandoned its traditional aloofness from Greek internal political affairs and adopted a policy which soon became one of direct intervention. At the center of this transition were Britain's Greek policy and the need of the United States government, first to react to that policy, and ultimately to make it its own.[2]

Britain's attitude towards Greece during the war was essentially the result of two considerations. One was the pressing need to consolidate the resistance movements within the country in a struggle of liberation from Axis occupation. The other was the desire to protect British interests in the Balkans, the Eastern Mediterranean, and the routes to the Middle East oil fields. The incompatibility inherent in these goals was often at the center of the difficulties in which the British Foreign Office found itself. A close corollary to British policy was the future of the Greek monarchy. From the British viewpoint, therefore, it was imperative that Greece not become communist and that it become a parliamentary democracy within the framework of a constitutional monarchy. The British hoped to find the necessary leadership within the ranks of Greek politicians. By 1944, however, it had become apparent that the political environment in the country offered no viable candidates for the task; hence, Britain's direct intervention in Greek internal affairs.

Initially, the exigencies of war forced the Foreign Office to offer its support to virtually all Greek left-wing resistance groups without much attention to the ideologies upon which they were based. As the end of the war drew near, the British began to think in terms of postwar Europe. By the spring of 1944, their concerns were heightened by the penetration of Soviet influence in Eastern Europe and by the decline of their own influence in the Balkans.

In these circumstances Britain's prime minister, Winston Churchill was prompted to search for some accommodation with the Soviet Union vis-à-vis Eastern Europe, the Balkans, and Greece in particular. Acting unilaterally and without the knowledge of U.S. President Franklin Delano Roosevelt, Churchill reached a tentative agreement (the "percentages agreement") with Joseph Stalin in the spring of 1944 for the division of the Balkans into Anglo and Soviet spheres of influence. The agreement was formalized in Moscow on 9 October at a meeting between Stalin and Churchill. Greece was to remain within the British sphere.

American officials, led by Secretary of State Cordell Hull, initially objected to any American approval for an agreement that promised dangerous, long-term political consequences. A major concern was the probable entanglement of the United States in the politics of the Balkans and the Middle East. It was also essential to avoid the perception that British policy in Greece was, in effect, an Anglo-American policy. These admonitions notwithstanding and despite serious philosophical reservations on the subject of spheres of influence, Roosevelt yielded to pressure from Churchill and on 13 June gave his conditional approval to the plan in the interest of allied solidarity.[3] Roosevelt's approval rested on his understanding that the percentages agreement would be a provisional wartime arrangement.

The issue of the Greek monarchy was also vital to British foreign policy. The turbulent history of the Greek Republic during the interwar years inspired no confidence and offered no assurances that a republican form of government was a viable alternative to monarchy. Consequently, Churchill planned for the return of George II at the head of a liberating army that would free the country from Axis occupation and restore the monarchy to its rightful place in Greek life. He saw the Greek monarch as a stabilizing, anticommunist influence in the country's political arena and he made several attempts to elicit American support. Churchill's policy, however, was not without its critics. Public opinion in England and political pressure from the Labor Party were important sources of opposition. Furthermore, the British War Office and especially the Special Operations Executive (SOE), through their Greek contacts, generally were better informed about the trend of public opinion within Greece than was the Foreign Office. They tended to see the political situation in more realistic and pragmatic terms, acknowledging widespread opposition to the return of the monarchy among Greeks. Consequently, they offered advice that was often ignored by Churchill.[4]

The attitude within the State Department was entirely negative, if not hostile. In an intraservice memorandum on June 1942, the State Department left no doubt about its position relative to the restoration of

George II. The king's sympathies for the Metaxas dictatorship were well-known, while his recent efforts to pass himself off as a democrat and libertarian were viewed in Greece with cynicism. Such a hypocritical about-face was the result of pressure from the British and from the Greek people who were becoming increasingly hostile. Furthermore, Britain's support of the monarchy's restoration was interpreted by many Greeks as a blatant incursion into their nation's internal affairs and as an effort to impose upon them a monarch for whom they had little sympathy. Finally, American officials rejected Churchill's contention that the king would serve as a stabilizing influence.[5] In a memorandum to the Secretary of State on 16 March 1943, the adviser on political relations, Wallace Murray, reflected the prevailing sentiment within the State Department. It was important for the United States government to distance itself from any British machinations on this issue because, "There is reason to believe that the Greeks are aware of Britain's plans to restore the monarchy; that they are looking to the United States to see that they get the promised opportunity to express their own will; and that if we fail them, they will turn to Soviet Russia." American policy, therefore, should strive for Anglo-American cooperation in convincing the king to remain outside the country until the people had been given the opportunity "to express their will freely under the auspices of an impartial Allied occupation."[6]

Opposition to George II extended to the military and to the Office of Strategic Services (OSS). For certain political and tactical reasons American military officials were adamant in their determination to remain wholly aloof on the issue of the King's restoration. For example, when George II requested assistance from the American minister in Cairo in obtaining a station wagon for his personal use, the War Department refused.[7] Within the OSS the mood was equally hostile. It appears that many OSS agents were Greek-Americans whose familiarity with the republican and democratic institutions of the United States prompted a proclivity for liberal, even left-wing sympathies. In an OSS report (dated 18 August 1944) an American observer viewed the Greek political situation as "a social revolution extending over wide areas. A large percentage of the people are working for the success of this revolution." Consequently, the OSS was generally critical of British efforts to impose George II upon the Greek people, though it seems that no high-ranking OSS official was in favor of a major postwar role for the left in Greek politics.[8]

Epilogue

Yet, hardly three years were to pass before the United States government would adopt the very policy for which it had always expressed the greatest disapproval. Central to this change in attitude were the rise of the Greek left, the pernicious and unpredictable consequences of the Greek civil war, and the fear of Soviet communist ideology with the attendant need to "contain" it. The death of Roosevelt and Churchill's fall from power in 1945 also were important factors in facilitating the search for new solutions to the Greek dilemma.

From national liberation in October 1944 to the enunciation of the Truman Doctrine on 12 March 1947, Great Britain had bolstered the various governments in Athens with an army stationed in Greece and with large amounts of economic aid. While this policy assured "friendly" governments in office, none of these governments succeeded in establishing its viability, and the national economy failed to show any significant improvement. Military aid also did not prevent the outbreak of a fratricidal civil war which left a legacy of bitterness that has yet to run its course.

The first stage in this national catastrophe occurred in the fall and winter of 1943–44. A series of clashes among rival resistance groups contributed to the collapse of a precarious balance which hitherto had forestalled outbreak of civil war. In February a cease-fire was arranged, but an ominous precedent had been established.

In December 1944, a "Second Round" erupted. The most pressing problem facing the government was the need to replace the existing guerrilla formations with a national army that would be acceptable to the left. Premier George Papandreou insisted that all guerrilla forces be disbanded. EAM (the National Liberation Front), the most influential Greek resistance group, agreed but only on condition that certain government-backed forces also be disbanded. Papandreou was receptive to this offer, but under pressure from the British he reversed his decision and rejected EAM's proposal. During the political impasse that followed, feelings ran high. Underestimating British resolve to keep Greece free of Soviet influence and apparently unaware of the percentages agreement of 9 October, the Greek communists prepared to force the issue. In an atmosphere of mounting crisis, EAM called for demonstrations in Athens on 3 December as a prelude to a general strike. Thousands of demonstrators converged in the center of the city. Panic-stricken police fired on the demonstrators, inflicting a considerable number of casualties. This act of repression was met with resistance which escalated into an armed confrontation with the British. There is no conclusive evidence, however, that EAM aimed for a complete takeover of the government. Rather, it appears that their immediate goal was the removal of their principal political opponent, George Papandreou. This episode led to a brief, though violent, phase in the Greek civil war, which ended with the signing of the Varkiza Agreement on 12 February 1945. Sixty thousand people were involved in this confrontation, and any semblance of reason and restraint that remained was then given a fatal blow. This stage in the Greek civil war is unique because it was the only instance where a wartime resistance force engaged Western troops in battle. More important for the future, however, was the creation of a virulent political climate that would contribute to the outbreak of the final phase in the civil war—the so-called "Third Round" (1946–49). For four years the very fabric of the Greek nation was threatened by a fratricide unprecedented in the history of modern Greece.

As postwar relations between the Western Powers and the Soviet Union began to deteriorate, the position of Greece in the international diplomatic arena underwent a fundamental change. Great Britain attempted to supersede the "percentages agreement" with the Yalta Declaration on Liberated Europe, and sought to exert its influence in Eastern Europe. The Soviet Union countered by protesting British policy in Greece. American officials understood the Soviet action to be a response to British forays in Eastern Europe. But when Yugoslavia intervened in the Greek civil war the American perception of the Soviet role began to change. It was assumed that Yugoslavia's intervention was a corollary to the role that the Soviet Union was prepared to play in Greece and elsewhere in the Eastern Mediterranean. In these circumstances it seemed natural that the United States would lend its support to an old friend in an effort to prevent the expansion of Soviet influence.

At the various international conferences in 1945 and 1946 and as the conflict between East and West became more acute, the policy of the United States shifted from a position of political aloofness to one of strong political support for Great Britain. In February 1946, when Britain's presence in Greece came under attack from the Soviet Union in the Security Council of the United Nations, the United States rose to Britain's defense.[9] Another illustration of this shift in diplomatic emphasis is the participation of the United States in the American-British-Franco mission that observed the controversial Greek national elections on 31 March 1946. The personnel of the mission was predominantly American. On 1 September a plebiscite was held, which decided by a margin of 69 percent in favor of the return of the monarchy, and on 28 September George II returned to the throne in Athens. Prime Minister Constantine Tsaldaris wanted Allied officials to observe the plebiscite, but it proved impossible for the United States to provide sufficient personnel for the task. Nevertheless, British and American officials did examine the electoral registers.[11] These episodes are significant because they are the first tangible indications of the political role that the United States would soon play in Greece.

The election resulted in an overwhelming majority for the Royalist Populist Party, primarily because the left and a good part of the center abstained. The Royalists lost no time in establishing a reactionary regime under the premiership of Constantine Tsaldaris. Whatever the guise in which the right cloaked itself, wrote the American ambassador, the program of the government " 'actually approximates Fascism.' "[12] The acute fear of Soviet expansionism in Europe, however, was an overriding consideration. The Department of State thus was forced to deal with the Tsaldaris government despite serious reservations with the election results. In the thinking of American officials the specter of the left loomed much larger than the specter of the right. This association with a reactionary regime was a critical precedent that would have profound implications for Greek-American relations in the ensuing four decades. In October 1946 the U.S. representative at the Paris Peace Conference, Jefferson Caffery, publicly pledged American aid to Greece in the event of foreign aggression.[13] This announcement is significant because it is indicative of the abandonment of the Yalta policy of tripartite accord in favor of a policy of cooperation with Great Britain.

By the summer of 1946 the impotence of the Greek government and the apparent futility of Britain's efforts in Greece led to growing demands from the Labor Party for a reexamination of Britain's Greek policy. In August, an All-Party Parliamentary Mission investigated the situation in Greece and in a very critical report concluded that "the opportunity given by the return of . . . King [George II] should be used to initiate an entirely new policy in and towards Greece."[14] Thus, when the Foreign Office announced Britain's inability to continue its financial commitment to Greece after 31 March 1947, the stage was set for the United States to take the logical and final steps. These steps included the sending of an economic mission to Greece in October, the sponsoring of a United Nations investigation of Greek border disputes in December,[15] and finally, the enunciation of the Truman Doctrine.

While the American economic mission and the United Nations border commission were still in Greece, the Truman administration decided to act immediately and unilaterally. On 24 February 1947 Great Britain announced that she would be unable to continue economic aid to Greece and Turkey beyond 31 March. Faced with the imminent withdrawal of the British, President Harry S. Truman and his advisers concluded that American assumption of Britain's responsibilities in the Eastern Mediterranean could no longer be avoided. In a message to Congress on 12 March, the president requested economic aid to Greece and Turkey in the amounts of $300,000,000 and $100,000,000, respectively. The emphasis was on the preservation of free institutions from the threat of totalitarianism. The Soviet Union was never mentioned. With the enunciation of the Truman Doctrine new chapters in American foreign policy, in general, and Greek-American relations, specifically, had begun.

Since the end of the Second World War, American policy in Greece has varied in form, but it never has wavered from the fundamental aim of controlling and circumscribing the influence of the left. Towards this end, the United States shifted from earlier criticism of the monarchy to support for George II and his successors, while manipulating the Greek political scene to deprive the left of cabinet and parliamentary representation. American economic and military assistance has been put consistently at the disposal of the right. From 1946 to 1964, for example, American foreign aid to Greece totaled 2,810.3 million dollars.[16]

Greece emerged from the tragic decade of the 1940s with her economy, political institutions, and social fiber in ruin. In these circumstances, it was natural that Greek political leaders should look to the West, in general, and after 1952 to the North Atlantic Treaty Organization (NATO), in particular, for internal security and for the preservation of their nation's territorial integrity.[17] Consequently, the Greek conservative governments of the early postwar years adopted an anticommunist posture in their domestic policy and a pro-American, pro-NATO orientation in their foreign policy. The most visible manifestation of this attitude was the bilateral agreement in 1953 with the United States for the establishment of American bases in Greece. A significant provision in that agreement, which helped to set the tone for the American presence, was the implicit understanding that American military and civilian personnel would enjoy the right of extraterritoriality.[18] The diplomatic setting appeared clear-cut: Soviet communism was the enemy, and NATO solidarity appeared to be the only realistic defense of Greece's security.

This simplistic view began to change after 1955 in response to the advent of the Cyprus controversy. Opposition parties, and even those allied with the government, began to ask whether the policy of the United States towards Greece was even-handed and benign. Most alarming, from the Greek viewpoint, was Washington's apparent "tilting" in favor of Turkey on the issues of Cyprus and related problems in the Eastern Mediterranean. The political opposition began to press for issues generally associated with the left. These included the pursuit of detente with the Eastern Bloc, denuclearization, and the demilitarization of the Balkans. This explosive situation was defused temporarily by the Zurich and London agreements (1959–60) from which Cyprus emerged as an independent state. The new constitution, however, gave the Turkish minority disproportionate political power through the exercise of the veto in the formulation of foreign and domestic policy. Efforts by Cyprus' president, Archbishop Makarios, to revise the constitution in 1963 inflamed the political atmosphere and produced a continuing crisis.

The Soviet-American detente during the Nixon Administration and the political and economic stability that was emerging in Greece combined to produce a national self-assurance and to create the impression that the communist threat had diminished. But the issue of Cyprus remained unresolved and served to heighten the frustrations of Greeks and Cypriots alike. From these circumstances arose a vocal movement which called for an end to American interference in Greek internal affairs and an end to the subservient role that Greece was compelled to play vis-à-vis American interests in the Eastern Mediterranean. The most articulate exponent of this viewpoint after 1965 was Andreas Papandreou, a member of the Center Union Party which was led by his father, George Papandreou.

In 1967 a coup d'état by a group of army officers established a right-wing military dictatorship which ruled the country for seven years. During this period the United States, by not opposing the dictatorship's existence, helped keep it in power. The American association with such an oppressive regime reinforced the growing perception that the United

States was abandoning the principles that had guided Greek-American relations and was now adopting a Greek policy which was purely Machiavellian.

Another serious setback to American influence in Greece occurred in July 1974 when the military junta carried out an ill-conceived coup d'état in Cyprus that sought the overthrow of President (Archbishop) Makarios. This tragic mistake played into the hands of the Turkish government which promptly invaded the island under the guise of protecting the Turkish minority. The Cyprus debacle thoroughly discredited the junta and brought about its demise. A civilian government was established immediately under former Prime Minister Constantine Karamanlis. The junta period, therefore, was crucial to the future of Greek-American diplomacy.

American buttressing of the military dictatorship reinforced the impression that Greece had become dependent, once again, on the support and goodwill of another powerful "ally" for whom the national interests of the country were, at best, secondary. This assessment of Greek-American relations added impetus to those forces calling for a reexamination of Greece's close affiliation with NATO and the United States government. Whereas, before 1967, the clarion call for an independent Greek foreign policy came mainly from the left, after 1974 the center and the right would add their voices in support of the same principle. After 1974 a variety of internal problems and regional issues, of which neighboring Turkey is an integral part, emerged to intensify and complicate the relations between Athens and Washington.

In the present diplomatic setting, the United States finds itself the embattled mediator between two of NATO's vital southern flank members. This difficult role is fundamental to the continuing Greek perception that when "push comes to shove," the United States will sacrifice Greece's interests and will favor those of Turkey. The most articulate exponent of this view continues to be Andreas Papandreou, prime minister since 1981. His anti-American, anti-NATO posture has galvanized public opinion and has raised the national consciousness of the Greek populace. But even the voluble prime minister has had to yield to harsh international realities. A falling out with the United States can only improve Turkey's position in the Aegean and in Cyprus, while adversely affecting the interests of Greece by altering the balance of power in the Eastern Mediterranean. Furthermore, it is unlikely that the present level of economic and military support can be found from other sources. Thus, inflammatory rhetoric is being replaced by a sense of sober realism and a conciliatory attitude. "Accommodation" and "cooperation" have a prominent place in the lexicon of government officials. At the same time, these officials emphasize that conciliation or the improvement in diplomatic relations is each a process with reciprocal obligations. The prevailing patron-client relationship, which even the American ambassador, Robert V. Keeley, has acknowledged,[19] must give way to something more positive. Dependence must be replaced by interdependence, and a true diplomatic partnership must be established. To continue the policies of the postwar years would be to cling to a dangerous anachronism.

It would be inaccurate to attribute all the ills of present-day Greece to a single nation, government, or political party. All who participated in the events of the 1940s and after must assume a part of the responsibility for the excesses which have contributed to the prevailing political mood in the country. With the wisdom of hindsight, however, one can see that the unqualified American support for the political right facilitated the domination of Greece by conservative and reactionary regimes for three decades after 1946. Greeks across the political spectrum now demand the opportunity to shed this postwar heritage—a heritage which, in the Greek view, amounted to nothing less than complete subservience to the interests of the United States. This perception has contributed to a dramatic decline of pro-American sentiment in Greece. It is to be hoped that enlightened counsels will prevail and that the exigencies of international politics will not prove an insurmountable obstacle to the restoration of the ties that have bound the two peoples together since the inception of the modern Greek state.

Appendix A
The Tripartite Loan
of 1918

The financial delegates of the United States of America, Great Britain, and France, as a consequence of the decision of the Supreme War Council, dated December 1, 1917, the American delegates, ad referendum, have approved the following agreement with the Greek Government:[1]

ARTICLE 1.

The Governments of the United States of America, France and Great Britain agree to make advances to the Greek Government by equal shares during the year 1918 in order to allow them to get in their own country the credits necessary to provide:

1. For the settlement of arrears.
2. For the expenses during 1918 of the Greek Army and Navy, the strength of which having been increased as delineated in the military arrangements.

The latter expenses, including navy expenses, to be made in Greece, apply to the following items:

(a) Pay and indemnities of the army.
(b) Separation allowances.
(c) Utilization of local resources.
(d) Requisition of the animals and carts of the country.
(e) Transports by sea and rail.

The advances mentioned in this article will be liable to come up to the amount of francs 750,000,000 including the 50,000,000 about which the arrangement of November 30, 1917, was made.

ARTICLE 2.

These advances will be dealt out to the Greek Government according to their needs from time to time upon their asking and subject to the agreement of an interallied financial commission which will be created in Athens. This commission will include delegates of the United States, France, Great Britain, and Greece.

The employment of these credits will be controlled by the aforesaid commission as far as the arrears are concerned and by a similarly composed interallied military commission, also meeting in Athens, which commission, previous to the grant of advances meant for the organization and keeping of the army and navy, will have given its advice to the financial commission.

ARTICLE 3.

These advances granted in dollars, francs, and sterling, intended to be security for issues of the National Bank of Greece to the same amount, will be available during the war within the scope of needs by means of drafts on one or the other of the lending countries in case the foreign balances of the Greek treasury and the National Bank should fall below 100,000,000 francs.

Six months after the conclusion of peace the balance of these advances will be available without the restrictions of the first paragraph.

ARTICLE 4.

The advances will be represented by obligations of the Greek Government.

For each draft, and from the day on which it will have been made, these obligations will yield interest at a rate determined with each of the Governments concerned, and, save the right reserved by the Greek Government of beginning the amortization in advance, will be redeemable by the end of the fifteenth year following the cessation of hostilities.

Until the redemption of the aforesaid obligations, no new security may be used for an exterior loan without the assent of the Governments of the United States of America, France, and Great Britain.

ARTICLE 5.

In consideration of the advances granted to them, the Greek Government pledge themselves to take immediately the necessary steps to prevent in the future the granting in Greece of remittances upon foreign countries, unless it be for legitimate needs, and upon production of documentary evidence.

Done in Paris, 1918, in four copies.

A. BONAR LAW.

Lu et approuvé:

L. L. KLOTZ.

Approved ad referendum:

OSCAR T. CROSBY.

GENNADIUS.

The above contract has been approved by the Government of the United States of America with the following reservation:

The obligations given to the Government of the United States of America may be redeemed within a lapse of time which will not exceed the maximum limit allowed by the laws of the United States, but will never be longer than 15 years from the date of the cessation of hostilities.

OSCAR T. CROSBY.

February 13, 1918.

Appendix B
Protocol Relating to the Settlement of Refugees in Greece and the Creation for this Purpose of a Refugees Settlement Commission

The undersigned, acting in the name of the Hellenic Government and duly authorized for the purpose, accepts on behalf of the Hellenic Government the following plan which has been approved by the Council of the League of Nations for the establishment of a Refugees Settlement Commission and the settlement in Greece of refugees upon lands to be assigned to the Commission or otherwise in productive work.[1]

I. The Hellenic Government undertakes to establish a Refugees Settlement Commission to possess the constitution, capacity and functions set out in the Organic Statutes which form an Annex to the present Protocol and are considered as being an integral part thereof. The ratification of this Protocol and of the Annex by Greece shall constitute an assurance that the Hellenic Government has taken the measures required by the internal law of the country to establish the Commission and ensure to it during the period of its existence the prescribed capacity and powers. Particulars concerning these measures shall forthwith be communicated to the Council of the League and no alteration in them shall be made without the Council's consent.

II. The Hellenic Government undertakes to assign to the Refugees Settlement Commission to be held by it as its absolute property for the purpose contemplated by its Statutes, an amount of land of not less than 500,000 hectares approved by the Commission as suitable for the said purposes in regard to both its character and situation.

III. The Hellenic Government will secure that any advances which have been obtained by the National Bank of Greece, in connection with the Refugees Settlement Commission's foundation, for the purpose of the establishment of refugees in productive work in Greece, shall be forthwith placed at the disposal of the Commission.

IV. The Hellenic Government will as soon as possible raise a loan, or loans, to an amount not falling below the equivalent of three million pounds sterling, nor exceeding the equivalent of six million pounds sterling, and will arrange for the subscription of Greek Banks or financial groups of not less than the equivalent of one million pounds sterling of such loan or loans. The issuing houses shall place the whole proceeds of the loan or loans directly under the disposal of the Refugees Settlement Commission for the purpose specified in its Organic Statutes, and for the repayment, if necessary, of any advances.

V. The service of the loans to be raised in pursuance of Article IV shall be assured in the first instance by the International Financial Commission established by the Law on the International Control of February 26th, 1898 (in accordance with the consent given by the Governments at present represented on that Commission by the Declaration annexed to this Protocol) out of certain public Greek revenues in accordance with the following provisions:

(1) Such revenue and surplus revenues as may be agreed upon between prospective lenders and the Hellenic Government (for example, those indicated in Schedule I) shall be assigned to and placed under the control of the International Financial Commission, and shall be collected and paid to that Commission.

(2) The revenues and surplus revenues above-mentioned shall so far as is considered necessary, be held and applied by the International Financial Commission for the purpose of meeting the service of loans raised in accordance with Article IV.

The service of the loans shall also be a first charge upon the property and income of the Refugees Settlement Commission.

VI. The Hellenic Government undertakes not to create any charges by way of security, without the consent of the International Financial Commission, upon its other revenues, and, in particular, those specified in Schedule II, except for the purpose of meeting its external obligations or of obtaining loans destined exclusively to improve the financial position of Greece, so as to prevent depreciation to the exchange value of Greek currency and a consequent depreciation of the value of the revenues assigned under Article V. It further undertakes to make immediately and to persist in making every effort to secure as soon as possible a complete equilibrium between the ordinary receipts and the expenses of the State.

VII. The Hellenic Government undertakes to exempt the Refugees Settlement Commission from all taxes and charges, whether general or local, in particular, of the lands assigned to it or any financial year to the Commission (or to the Financial Commission if the Refugees Settlement Commission is dissolved) the total sum at which the occupiers of land originally assigned to the Refugees Settlement Commission and still continuing to be its property (or, if the Refugees Settlement Commission is dissolved, held at the disposal of the International Financial Commission pursuant to arrangements made in connection with such dissolution) are assessed for taxation upon such lands for such year, until the loans raised in pursuance of Article IV are completely refunded.

VIII. The reimbursement of advances made to refugees by the Refugees Settlement Commission shall have priority over taxation or any other claim.

IX. The Hellenic Government, accepting the provisions contained in the Organic Statutes of the Refugees Settlement Commission under which the Council of the League of Nations may enquire into and exercise a supervision over the activities of the Commission, undertakes to facilitate any enquiries which the Council may direct, and to accept and give effect to the Council's decisions taken thereupon in so far as they require action by the Hellenic Government.

X. Nothing in this Protocol or the Organic Statutes thereto annexed shall change in any way the obligations of the Hellenic Government under the Greco-Turkish Exchange of Populations Convention signed at Lausanne on January 30th, 1923, or under the Greco-Bulgarian Reciprocal Emigration Convention signed at Neuilly-sur-Seine, on November 27th, 1919.

XI. The obligations assumed by the Hellenic Government under this Protocol shall cease as soon as the Refugees Settlement Commission shall have been dissolved and the loans raised in accordance with Article IV of this Protocol have been repaid in full.

XII. In the event of any difference as to the interpretation of this Protocol, the opinion of the Council of the League of Nations will be accepted.

XIII. In the event of any difference between the French and English texts of this Protocol, the English shall be considered to be authentic text.

XIV. This Protocol shall be ratified and the ratification shall be deposited at the Secretariat of the League of Nations as soon as possible and in any case not later than October 15th, 1923. It shall enter into force on the date of deposit of ratification.

In faith whereof, the undersigned, duly authorized for this purpose, has signed the present Protocol.

Done at Geneva on the twenty-ninth day of September 1923, in a single copy which shall be deposited with the Secretariat of the League of Nations, and shall be registered by it without delay.

(Signed) A. Michalakopoulos.

Schedule I

The revenues referred to in Article V of the Protocol under the number (1) are the following:

(1) The monopolies of New Greece, i.e., salt, matches, cards and cigarette-paper.
(2) The customs receipts received at the customs of:
    Canea,
    Candia,
    Samos,
    Chios,
    Mitylene,
    Syra.

Schedule II

The revenues referred to in Article VI of the Protocol are the following:

(1) The surplus revenues already assigned to the International Financial Commission.
(2) The tobacco duty in New Greece.
(3) The stamp duty in New Greece.
(4) The duty on alcohol in the whole of Greece.
(5) Any of the revenues or any surplus of the revenues mentioned in Schedule I not utilized for the service of loans under the terms of Article V of the Protocol.

Appendix C
Organic Statutes of the Greek Refugees Settlement Commission

I. There is established in Greece, domiciled at such place as it shall select after its constitution, a Refugees Settlement Commission invested with the capacity and powers and entrusted with the duties specified hereinafter.[1]

II. The Refugees Settlement Commission is established as a legal person competent to sue and be sued in its own name, to hold and alienate property of all kinds, and generally to perform any acts which can be performed by a corporation possessing full legal personality under the law of Greece.

III. The Refugees Settlement Commission shall not be dependant upon any Greek executive or administrative authority, but shall be completely autonomous in the exercise of its functions.

IV. The Refugees Settlement Commission shall be composed of four members. Two members shall be appointed by the Hellenic Government, with the approval of the Council of the League of Nations; one member shall be appointed by the Council of the League of Nations; the fourth member shall be the Chairman of the Commission, shall be a national of the United States of America and a person representative of relief organizations and shall be appointed in such method as the Council of the League of Nations shall from time to time determine. The member appointed by the Council and the Chairman of the Commission shall enjoy diplomatic privileges and immunities in Greece.

V. The members of the Refugees Settlement Commission appointed by the Hellenic Government may at any time be replaced by that Government with the consent of the Council of the League of Nations; the other two members may only be replaced by the Council of the League of Nations.

VI. The salaries of the two members of the Refugees Settlement Commission appointed by the Hellenic Government shall be fixed by that Government; the salaries of the other two members shall be fixed by the Council of the League of Nations. The salaries of all members shall be payable out of the funds of the Commission, but the Hellenic Government shall refund to the Commission the amount of the two salaries fixed by it.

VII. The first appointments of members of the Refugees Settlement Commission shall be made not later than September 30th, 1923. Thereafter, if any vacancy on the Commission is not filled by the competent authorities, the Council of the League of Nations shall be competent forthwith to appoint a person to act and to exercise the full powers of the member whom he succeeds until such time as the competent appointing authority shall itself make an appointment. The Commission shall enter upon its functions as soon as all four members have been appointed. In the event of temporary absence, the absent member shall designate a substitute who shall have the right to vote; failing which the Chairman or the member acting as Chairman shall designate such a substitute. In the event of the absence of the chairman, the chair shall be taken by the member appointed by the Council of the League of Nations, who shall have the same voting rights as the Chairman. The presence of three members or their substitutes including always the two members not appointed by the Hellenic Government or their duly appointed substitutes, shall be necessary to form a quorum and validate decisions of the Settlement Commission.

VIII. The Commission shall take all its decisions by a majority vote of the members present at the meeting. In the event of the votes being equally divided, the Chairman shall have a second vote. Subject to any provisions in these statutes, the Settlement Commission shall establish its own rules of Procedure.

IX. The Chairman, or in his absence his substitute, will convene all meetings of the Settlement Commission, sign all documents and correspondence and be responsible for the execution of the decisions of the Settlement Commission.

X. The Refugees Settlement Commission shall have power to appoint and dismiss such personnel, either Greek or (when necessary for special reasons) of foreign nationality as it may require for the discharge of its functions. The work of the Commission will be carried on as far as possible with the assistance of Greek central and local administrative authorities and of private organizations.

XI. The expenses of the Commission shall be payable out of the funds at its disposal or out of its income.

XII. The functions of the Refugees Settlement Commission shall be, by means of the lands assigned to it, the funds placed at its disposal and its own income, to promote the establishment of refugees in productive work either upon the land or otherwise in Greece.

XIII. The Refugees Settlement Commission shall receive and hold in full ownership the lands which the Hellenic Government undertakes to transfer to it under the Protocol signed on behalf of Greece at Geneva on September 29th, 1923, and shall apply such lands for the purpose specified in Article XII above. The lands shall primarily be applied to the settlement of refugees thereon either as tenants or as owners, on the terms fixed by the Commission, but the Commission may, in its discretion sell land by it to persons not refugees, provided that any sums raised by the Commission from the sale of such land shall be paid into a special account and applied, by way of a sinking fund, to the redemption of the loan or loans referred to in Article XVI of these Statutes. The Commission shall sell land if such sale becomes necessary under the provisions of Article XVI.
Sales of land to persons not possessing Greek nationality shall require the consent of the Hellenic Government except in the case contemplated by the last sentence of the preceding paragraph.

XIV. The Refugees Settlement Commission shall receive and apply for the purpose specified in Article XII above, any advances obtained by the National Bank of Greece for the purposes of establishment of refugees in productive work in Greece, and the proceeds of the loans which the Hellenic Government undertakes to raise and pay over to the Commission under Protocol signed on behalf of Greece at Geneva on September 29th, 1923.

XV. The income and funds of the Refugees Settlement Commission may not be expended on the relief of distress or other charitable purposes as distinct from the settlement in productive work of the persons assisted. All assistance given shall be given on terms involving ultimate repayment.

XVI. In event of the revenues assigned by the Hellenic Government to the services of the loan in accordance with the protocol signed at Geneva on September 29th, 1923 being insufficient, the International Commission shall call upon the [Refugees] Settlement Commission to pay of its income or other funds, or if necessary from the realisation of its property, such as may be necessary to meet any deficit on the services of the loan. Further, it shall at all times be the duty of the Settlement Commission to pay to the International Financial Commission for application to the services of the loan any sums which the Settlement Commission may find possible to contribute for this purpose out of its current income without prejudicing the effective performance of its functions. In the event of the International Financial Commission having in its possession sums exceeding the amount necessary for the service of the loan, the Financial Commission will refund these sums to the Hellenic Government.

XVII. The Refugees Settlement Commission shall communicate every three months a report upon its operations to the Hellenic Government and the Council of the League of Nations and shall simultaneously publish such report. The Council of the League of Nations, acting, if need be, by a majority vote, shall have the right to consider the reports of the Commission and to make such measures thereon as it may consider proper.

The Commission shall annually publish and forward to the Council of the League of Nations and to the Hellenic Government, audited accounts of its income and expenditure.

XVIII. The Council of the League of Nations, acting, if need be, by a majority vote, may at any time enquire by such method as it determines into the manner in which the Refugees Settlement Commission is discharging its functions, and the necessary cost of such enquiries shall be payable to the Secretary-General of the League by the Commission out of funds at the disposal of the Commission or out of its current income.

XIX. The Refugees Settlement Commission may be dissolved when in the opinion of the Council of the League of Nations, acting if need be, by a majority vote, its services are no longer required, subject to the establishment of arrangements approved by the representatives of the lenders to secure that the assets and income of control are at the disposal of the International Financial Commission for the purpose of enabling the latter to meet the service of the loans (or to accelerate as far as possible the amortization of the loans) raised by the Hellenic Government in accordance with the Protocol signed on its behalf at Geneva on September 29th, 1923 until such loans have been repaid in full.

XX. After the dissolution of the Refugees Settlement Commission and the repayment in full of the loans mentioned in Article XIX above, the balance still remaining of all assets which have belonged to the Commission shall become the absolute property of the Hellenic State.

XXI. In the event of any difference as to the interpretation of these Statutes, the opinion of the League of Nations will be accepted.

XXII. In the event of any difference between the French and English texts on these Statutes, the English shall be considered to be authentic text.

XXIII. This Annex shall be ratified and the ratification shall be deposited at the Secretariat of the League of Nations at the same time as the ratification of the Protocol to which this Annex is attached.

In faith whereof, the undersigned, duly authorized for this purpose, has signed the present Annex.

Done at Geneva on the twenty-ninth day of September 1923, in a single copy which shall be deposited with the Secretariat of the League of Nations, and shall be registered by it without delay.

(signed) A. Michalakopoulos.

Declaration signed on behalf of Great Britain, France and Italy

The undersigned, representatives, of the Governments of Great Britain, France and Italy, duly authorised by their respective Government, hereby agree that the International Financial Commission referred to in the Protocol relating to the Settlement of refugees in Greece and the creation for this purpose of a Refugee Settlement Commission, which has been approved by the Council of the League of Nations and executed on behalf of the Hellenic Government, shall discharge the duties which the said Protocol contemplates shall be performed by it; and they undertake on behalf of their respective Governments that the necessary instructions will be given by these Governments to their representatives upon the said International Financial Commission.

In witness whereof, the undersigned, duly authorized for this purpose, have signed the present declaration.

Done at Geneva on the twenty-ninth day of September 1923, in a single copy of which shall be deposited with the Secretariat of the League of Nations and shall be registered by it without delay.

RENNELL RODD (Great Britain).
DUPUY (France).
GARBASSO (Italy).

Appendix D
Members of the Refugee Settlement Commission

Chairmen

HENRY MORGENTHAU, from November 1923 to April 1924 and from August 19, 1924, to August 25, 1924.[1]

CHARLES P. HOWLAND, from January 1925 to May 1926; also during September 1926.

CHARLES B. EDDY, from October 1926 to December 1930.

Vice-Chairmen

JOHN CAMPBELL, from January 1924 to January 1927.

JOHN HOPE SIMPSON, from January 1927 to December 1930.

Substitutes

ALFRED BONSON, from July 1924 to April 1925, and from July to October 1925.

B. H. HILL, from June 1927 to December 1928 (at various times).

ROBERT GRAVES, from May to October 1926; from November 1929 to January 1930, and from May to October 1930.

ROYALL TYLER, from August 1923 to September 1927.

FRANCIS CUNLIFFE-OWEN, from July to September 1924.

Appendix D

Members appointed by the Greek Government

ETIENNE DELTA, from October 1923 to September 1925.
PERICLES ARGYROPOULOS, from October 1923 to August 1924.
THEODORE EUSTATHOPOULOS, from August 1924 to September 1925.
ACHILLES LAMBROS, from September 1925 to December 1930.
A. A. PALLIS, from September 1925 to December 1930.

Substitutes

DEMETRIUS TANTALIDES, during October 1925.
JACQUES DAMALAS, from December 1924 to March 1925.
ALEXANDER PASTATIS, October 1926.
MILTIADIS NEGROPONTE, from January to July 1924.

Appendix E
Balkan Peace: The Influence of American Economic Participation via Greece

It may be assumed that not only Mr. Venizelos, but all of the best minds of Greece consider Balkan peace as one of their principal foreign policies.[1] By force of arms they can have but little hope of forwarding this policy. Nor can it be secured simply by agreements, for these recorded understandings are but stage setting. The drama itself can only be consummated by the actors themselves. Any peace, especially Balkan peace, can only be obtained and maintained by work. Like all other problems the essential of the solution is work—work on the spot.

The Greeks are beginning to understand this, though perhaps they are, as yet, only groping. It is not too much to say that their inspiration comes in general from American example and in particular from the continuous every-day effect of the American economic participation in the upbuilding of Greece.

They are beginning to be curious as to the Pan-American conferences and the fact that these conferences produce certain mutual understandings and powerful personal friendships which, even though differences exist, are far better than the general attitude of glaring inarticulately at each other from a distance—the old Balkan method. They are talking about the probable benefits of Pan Balkan Athletic games. It will be observed that these conferences and games involve the idea of work and personal cooperation—team work—not the mere signing of agreements.

Appendix E

This Greek interest in American ideals springs not merely from long distance observation and historical study, but from our influence on the spot—contact with resident Americans, daily experience with our methods enmeshed with the daily life of Greeks in many parts of their Republic. On the streets of Athens and Saloniki, in their principal hotels, public offices, banks and business houses, resident Americans are now seen in considerable numbers. They are the local representatives and employees of tobacco, oil, engineering and banking firms. (These are all private enterprises, as this report is not concerned with educational, welfare and refugees institutions, all quasi-public bodies and all influential.) The tobacco men now extend their personal activities to the countryside and small towns of Thrace and Macedonia. The engineers are personally known throughout the Valleys of the Vardar and of the Struma, and in all the region beyond Kiphissia, toward Marathon, where the great dam for the new water supply of Athens is being built.

Without claiming any unusual qualities for these men it is safe to say that their usual American methods and American outlook have made an impression. The Greek has noticed that when these Americans start out to do a thing, results actually arrive. He has found their methods successful and their propositions and contracts fair. He knows that they are grinding no axe of territorial gain or of balance of power. The effect is a psychological one, noticeable only in processes of evolution—hence slow.

This process has begun in Greece where economic interests are now very large. It is affecting the Greeks and through them, the Balkan situation. If and when our people acquire large economic influence in other Balkan countries, the peace of this part of Europe, and of all Europe, will receive a greater insurance than is now in sight from any other source. This is not a thing that can be planned and directed, as it is but a probable evolution growing out of private activity in the due course of business. But it is a process to be borne in mind, observed and, so far as practicable, encouraged. Our attention may very well be devoted, in part, to observing whether the achievement of Balkan peace in the future may not be in the ratio of American economic penetration.

EDWARD DAVIS,
Colonel, Cavalry,
Military Attaché.

228

Appendix F
Letter from Morgenthau to Hull

NEW YORK, N.Y., MARCH 29, 1928[1]

HON. CORDELL HULL,
    Washington, D.C.

DEAR SIR:

Having given some study for the past five years to the matter of the obligation of the United States to Greece under the war-credits agreement of February 10, 1918 and with the cooperation of some others who have been in close touch with the situation, I beg to submit a few brief observations on the report of the minority members of the Ways and Means Committee on H. R. 10760, which is a bill to compromise the questions arising out of the war-time agreement and to fund the indebtedness of Greece to the United States.

I cite the principal objection made by the minority. Those objections are as follows:

1. That the representatives of the United States have taken the position in the negotiations running over eight years that the United States has been absolved from the obligations of the 1918 agreement.
   It will appear that, until politics came into the case, the opposite was true.

The brief written in controversy with Greece has no more merit than the further points I am about to mention.

2. That the advances called for by Greece under the agreement were not for war purposes; that this will be a peace-time loan, and not within the welfare clause of the Constitution. This is not a new loan, but the settlement of a war-time obligation. Greece's part of the contract was performed during the war when she mobilized her entire resources of men and material and broke the Macedonian front. In order to do this she issued bank notes of the National Bank of Greece in the amount of 250,000,000 drachmas against the promised United States credit of $48,236,629 which was intended to be the "cover" for the bank note issue. Receiving $15,000,000 from the United States she retired 77,337,500 drachmas, but there remained outstanding 172,262,500 drachmas corresponding to the balance of the credit of $33,236,629 granted by the United States. The failure of the United States to make good this credit was a main cause of the collapse of the drachma. The Greek expenditures were all for war-time purposes and precisely within the four corners of the 1918 agreement:

a. The American financial representative at Athens, Mr. [Alexander] Weddell, so certified after examination of the vouchers.

b. The Treasury representative, Mr. [Albert] Rathobone, directed the opening of the credit on Mr. Weddell's certification.

c. Mr. Norman Davis, in the Department of State, expressed himself in writing to the effect that the Treasury can not "legally or morally cancel its obligation to complete the loan to Greece under the terms stipulated."

d. The Department of State and the President on December 31, 1920, formally expressed the opinion "that the credit obligation negotiated with the Venizelos Government should be considered as still binding on this Government," and on January 19, 1921, The Secretary of the Treasury confirmed this opinion by letter to Senator John Sharp Williams.

3. That the loan was a joint one on the part of Great Britain, France, and the United States; that France advanced nothing; and that this had the legal effect of releasing the United States "from further obligation under the tripartite agreement."

The answer is that the loan was not joint. There was not to be a series of combined advances by the three governments but separate advances were to be "in equal shares" in the language of the agreement. The advances were made separately. No one of the three great powers in making its advances paid any attention to what the others were doing, the United States no more than the others. Each of the three opened a credit on its treasury books for its equal share. The United States advanced $15,000,000 over a period of a year, taking no account of the fact that

France had advanced nothing. Great Britain more than doubled the advances of the United States without waiting to see what France was doing or the United States. Greece similarly subdivided the loan on her books and made a separate account for each country.

If the thing had not been this way, if the agreement were for a joint loan and had been so handled by the three great powers, then Greece had the legal right—the author of the minority report [Congressman Charles Robert Crisp] is too good a lawyer not to know this—to demand the full 750,000,000 francs of the entire loan from any one of the three lenders, could now demand it from the United States, leaving the one which bore the whole burden to collect from the other two their respective thirds by what the law calls "the right of contribution." The objection is tantamount to offering Greece a check of the United States for the whole unpaid balance of 750,000,000 francs, leaving us to collect from France and Great Britain.

Neither the language of the agreement or the acts of the parties under it afford the slightest ground for any such interpretation. Each of the three great powers had a separate policy in regard to its own advances. Great Britain and France made heavy advances in material in which the United States did not share. The United States on its part negotiated some new terms in 1919, as to a part of its own advances, which it would have had no right to do if it had been jointly bound with the other two lenders. (This is referred to on page 27 of the print of the minority report.)

4. That the loan being joint, a release by Greece of Great Britain from her obligation to continue her advances released the United States as a matter of law.

Answer:

a. I have shown that the obligation was not joint, but several; the rule of law cited does not apply.

b. There was no release by Greece of Great Britain. Great Britain gave Greece permission to negotiate a $15,000,000 loan on the London market [December 1921], in return for which Greece was to release the British Government from its separate obligation under the 1918 agreement, but the $15,000,000 loan was never made.

c. This agreement required the assent of the Greek Parliament, or Boule, the equivalent of an act of Congress, and that was never given. There was never in law anything more than a negotiation between Greece and Great Britain.

5. That Greece obtained a loan of $8,000,000 in Canada in December 1923, "contrary to her expressed covenant that she would not make another

exterior loan without the assent of the United States, France, and Great Britain.''

When Greece borrowed in Canada she gave no new security at all; the "security" or the "exterior loans" of Greece is all in the hands of an International Financial Commission sitting in Athens. Whenever Greece gives "security" for an "exterior loan" she and the lender agree that the International Financial Commission shall hold certain Greek revenues, which are under their direct control, as security for the loan and that the International Financial Commission shall "serve" the loan by paying interest and amortization direct to the lenders out of the revenues. Greece is the pledger, the International Financial Commission a pledge-trustee for the lender who is the beneficiary of the pledge.

The word "security" in the agreement of 1918 was used in its exact legal sense. In the French text the phrase was "aucun gage nouveau ne pourra être affecté à un umprunt extérieur." "Un gage affecté" is the precise equivalent of the English "pledged security." In the Canadian loan agreement Greece gave no "security," "pledge," or "lien." She agreed that out of the surplus revenues coming to her own treasury from the International Financial Commission she would guarantee the payment of the Canadian loan. This is no more than an agreement by a debtor to pay his debt out of his own revenues; it is neither "security" nor a "lien" nor a "gage affecté."

6. That Greece broke the agreement by failing to pay interest on the $15,000,000 already advanced.

Greece paid interest until the spring of 1922, two and a half years after the last of the United States advances, and would have gone on paying interest had not the representative of the Greek Government, sent to Washington expressly to obtain the continuance of the advances, found that neither the Secretary of the Treasury nor any other American official was prepared to go on with the agreement by continuing the advances. On this basis it is unfair to charge Greece with a breach of the agreement. Per contra, it would appear that if Greece had paid interest, notwithstanding the refusal of the United States to go on with the advances, Greece would have recognized that the obligation of the United States had come to an end.

7. That Greece did not come forward to fund her war debt of $15,000,000. This is a political not a legal objection, for there is no provision on this subject in the agreement. The objection becomes absurd when it is known that Greece was the first to send a commission to the United States to settle a war debt. The Greek commission arrived in Washington in the winter of 1921 and remained until the midsummer of 1922; it left because the United States was at that time not ready to discuss the Greek debt, and the commission was never officially received.

8. That the drachma is now worth 1.33 cents, and the to-day $15,000,000 "would purchase and retire all the drachmas issued by the Bank of Greece on this credit."

   As the fall of the drachma is largely due to the failure of the United States to continue the advances which were to be "cover," for Greece's increased note issue, this objection of the minority amounts to saying that the United States may take advantage of its own wrong: that having arranged for the note issue and having failed to protect buying in the notes at the market price to which they have fallen, owing to the unsecured inflation for which it is responsible.

9. That the agreement was made when Greece was friendly to the Allies and that the "consideration of the agreement was negatived when the Greek Government became unfriendly upon the return of King Constantine."

   There is nothing in the agreement about the kind of government Greece is to have for the indefinite future. Greece loyally complied with the terms of the agreement by putting all her resources into the war. Her effort was largely responsible for the success of a major operation and the collapse of Bulgaria in September 1918. King Constantine returned to Greece in December 1920, two years after the war was over. Since then several Greek elections have been held, going one way or the other, and Greece has become a republic. None of these internal affairs of Greece has the slightest bearing on her war-time effort. It is extraordinary that the minority report should quote Mr. [Herbert Adams] Gibbons on this subject, for as he says, "the United States used the change of government as an excellent pretext for not allowing Greece to draw further upon the credit granted her as a war measure."[2] The position of the United States on this point is exactly what Mr. Gibbons calls it—pretext is another word for subterfuge, an effort to find a way out of the situation where no clear ground of escape exists.

Very sincerely yours,

H. MORGENTHAU.

Notes

In citing works in the notes, short titles have generally been used. Works frequently cited have been identified by the following abbreviations:

AYE	Archeion tou Ypourgeiou Exoterikon (Archives of the Foreign Ministry)
BFDC	Bureau of Foreign and Domestic Commerce
DBFP	Documents on British Foreign Policy
FL	Forced Loan
FO	Foreign Office
GPO	Government Printing Office
MID	Military Intelligence Division
NA	National Archives
PW	Public Works
RL	Refugee Loan
RSC	Refugee Settlement Commission
SV	Struma Valley
WC	War Credits

Preface

1. Brainerd P. Salmon, ed., "American Interests in Greece," *Glimpses of Greece* (Washington, D.C.: Hellenic Information Bureau, 1928), 37.

Introduction

1. Stephen A. Larrabee, *Hellas Observed: The American Experience of Greece, 1775–1865* (New York: New York Univ. Press, 1957), 3. Many books, pamphlets, and articles in Greek and English deal with the attitude of the United States government towards the Greek War of Independence and with the role that prominent Americans played in that conflict. The Center for Neo-Hellenic Studies in Austin, Texas, under the direction of the late Professor George G. Arnakis, has made valuable contributions to the historiography of American philhellenism during the Greek Revolution and the Cretan revolt against the Turks. Two useful studies are by Myrtle A. Cline, *American Attitude toward the Greek War of Independence* (Atlanta: Higgins-McArthur Co., 1930), and H. J. Booras, *Hellenic Independence and America's Contribution to the Cause* (Rutland, Vt.: Tuttle Company, 1934).

2. Trade with the Greek islands and the mainland was secondary to the trade with Asia Minor. American shippers generally bypassed the area of the Aegean and went directly to the international port of Smyrna. See Samuel E. Morison, *Maritime History of Massachusetts, 1783–1860* (Boston: Houghton Mifflin Company, 1921), chap. 18.

3. *Foreign Relations of the United States* (1866), 2:253. It is with Tuckerman's appointment (June 1868) that formal Greek-American relations can be said to have begun. The United States recognized the Greek government in 1833. It is not clear why thirty-five years passed before the State Department formalized that recognition.

4. In contrast to the American effort of the 1820s the American response to the Cretan uprising was limited. The area of activity centered in New York and New England. Arthur J. May, "Crete and the United States, 1866–1869," *Journal of Modern History* 16 (December 1944):286–93. For an account of American influence in Greece during the 1860s see E. Marcoglou, *The American Interest in the Cretan Revolution, 1866–1869* (Athens: National Centre of Social Research, 1971), chaps. 5–6, 59–60, 125–31.

5. The American School of Classical Studies in Athens, for example, dates from this period. See Louis E. Lord, *A History of the American School of Classical Studies at Athens, 1882–1942* (Cambridge, Mass.: Harvard Univ. Press, 1947).

6. Quoted in Larrabee, *Hellas Observed*, 294.

7. For a critical analysis of missionary activity in Greece see Charles K. Tuckerman, *The Greeks of To-Day* (New York: G. P. Putnam and Sons, 1872), 211–30. For an analysis of the problem from the missionary point of view see Julius Richter, *A History of Protestant Missions in the Near East* (New York: Revell, 1910).

8. The appeal was in the form of a small book. See C. N. Maniakes, *America and Greece* (Athens: Anestis Constantinides, 1899). This book is essentially an appeal for additional philanthropic and financial assistance from the Western Powers, but particularly from the United States.

9. Arnold J. Toynbee et al., *The Balkans: A History of Bulgaria, Serbia, Greece, Rumania, Turkey* (Oxford: Claredon Press, 1915), 248-49. See also Theodore Saloutos, *They*

Notes to Chapter 1

Remember America: The Story of the Repatriated Greek-Americans (Berkeley and Los Angeles: Univ. of California Press, 1956). Many books and articles treat Greek immigration and its impact on American life. For a comprehensive account see Theodore Saloutos, *The Greeks in the United States* (Cambridge, Mass.: Harvard Univ. Press, 1964).

10. For a first-hand account of the circumstances that led to the purchase of the ships, see Henry Morgenthau, *Ambassador Morgenthau's Story* (Garden City: Doubleday, Page & Co., 1918), 48–56.

Chapter 1

1. The legal justification for the Protecting Powers' intervention in Greek affairs rested on the Treaties of London of 7 May 1832 and of 14 November 1863, and for the Ionian Islands, of 29 March 1864. Article 4 of the Treaty of 7 May 1832, states in part: "Greece, under the sovereignty of Prince Otto of Bavaria and under the guarantee of the three Courts, shall form a monarchial and independent state." Precisely what "guarantee" meant never was defined explicitly. This ambiguity left much room for interpretation; hence, the pervasive influence of France, Great Britain, and Russia in Greek politics. This onerous provision was renounced by France and Great Britain in the Treaty of Lausanne. For a survey of this and related problems, see Theodore A. Couloumbis; John A. Petropulos; and Harry J. Psomiades, *Foreign Interference in Greek Politics: An Historical Perspective* (New York: Pella Publishing Company, 1976).

2. Bentinck to MacDonald, Athens, 30 August 1924, FO 371/9896, no. 555. For an historical summary of this problem and an analysis of British motives see "Memorandum on the History of Guarantee to Greece by [the] Three Protecting Powers" by Headlam Morley, London, 20 June 1922, FO 371/7584, Registry No. C 8953/13/19.

3. See chap. 3, note 2.

4. Near East Relief, *Report to Congress for 1924* in Microcopy No. 443, file no. 868.48/918.

5. Marjorie Housepian Dobkin, *Smyrna 1922: The Destruction of a City* (1966; reprint, Kent, Ohio: Kent State Univ. Press, 1988), 72.

6. For an illuminating discussion of the role of the United States Navy in protecting American Commerce, see Office of Naval Intelligence, *The United States Navy As An Industrial Asset: What the United States Navy Has Done for Industry and Commerce*, revised to July 1, 1924 (Washington: GPO, 1924). For Greece and the Eastern Mediterranean, see pp. 1–12. A useful article on the same subject is by Allan Wescott, "The Struggle for the Mediterranean," *Our World* (February 1923): 11–17.

7. Unpublished manuscript of Jefferson Caffery, *Adventures in Diplomacy*, 2:9. Jefferson Caffery Papers, Southwestern Archives, University of Louisiana, Lafayette, La.

8. Bentinck to MacDonald, Athens, 30 August 1924, FO 371/9896, no. 555.

9. Edward Mead Earle, *Turkey, the Great Powers and the Bagdad Railway: A Study in Imperialism* (New York: Macmillan Company, 1923), 338; George S. Gibb and Evelyn Knowlton, *History of the Standard Oil Company (New Jersey): The Resurgent Years, 1911–1927*, vol. 2 (New York: Harper and Brothers, 1956) 272; Bentinck to Curzon, Athens, Spring/Summer 1923, FO 371/8832, no. unavailable.

10. Earle, *Turkey, the Great Powers and the Bagdad Railway*, 339. To promote American business in the Near East, numerous Chambers of Commerce were established in Greece

and elsewhere. Although the American Chamber for the Levant was headquartered in Constantinople, its agents played an active role in Greece. They worked closely with American commercial attachés, trade commissioners, and officials in the American consulates.

11. James A. Field, *America and the Mediterranean World, 1776–1882* (Princeton, N.J.: Princeton Univ. Press, 1969), 338. The phrases "negligible factor" and "rare sight indeed" are exaggerations. A fundamental reason for the tendency to underestimate the importance of American commerce with Greece before 1919 is the unreliability of Greek statistics and the methods employed in recording and valuing imports and exports. Shipments of manufactured articles from the United States reached Greece, but they often lost their nationality when they were credited to intermediate ports rather than to the original country. Thus, in the process of transhipment a port such as London, Hamburg, Trieste, or Marseilles was recorded in Greek statistics as the port of origin.

Chapter 2

1. This rejection wounded the pride of the Greeks and added one more factor to the subsequent breach between Constantine and Venizelos. Memorandum from Greenway to Chamberlain, Athens, 27 March 1926, FO 371/11334, Registry No. C 3257/67/19.

2. See Robert Rhodes James, ed., *Winston S. Churchill: His Complete Speeches, 1897–1963*, vol. 3 (New York: Chelsea House Publishers, 1973), 2611.

3. Not all the members of the Franco-British coalition were equally active in the coercion of Greece. Tsarist Russia, the third member of the guarantor powers, was a reluctant participant in this affair because of the dynastic ties between King Constantine and Tsar Nicholas II and because of fear that Greece's participation in the war would be rewarded at the expense of Russian claims. Italy, the fourth member of the Entente, had no legal grounds for intervention. Nevertheless, she proclaimed her moral solidarity with the Allies, participated actively in the Allied blockade of Greece, and gave her full support to the coercive measures imposed by the General Staffs of the Allies.

4. Douglas Dakin, *The Unification of Greece, 1770–1923* (New York: St. Martin's Press, 1972), 203; Bernadotte Schmitt, *The Coming of the War,* 2 vols. (New York: Howard Fertig, 1966), 2:448–49.

5. Schmitt, *The Coming of the War,* 2:453.

6. Memorandum from Greenway to Chamberlain, Athens, 27 March 1926, FO371/1134.

7. Dakin, *The Unification of Greece,* 208; John Campbell and Philip Sherrard, *Modern Greece* (New York and Washington, D.C.: Frederick A. Praeger, Publishers, 1968), 120. For an analysis of the constitutional issues involved in the controversy, see Nicholas Kaltchas, *Introduction to the Constitutional History of Modern Greece* (New York: Columbia Univ. Press, 1940; reprint ed., New York: AMS Press, 1970), 137–47.

8. See Saloutos, *The Greeks in the United States,* chaps. 6, 7, 10 and 246–57.

9. Two good studies of the role of the Great Powers in Greece during the early years of the war are by George B. Leon, *Greece and the Great Powers, 1914–1917* (Thessaloniki: Institute for Balkan Studies, 1975) and Christos Theodoulou, *Greece and the Entente: August 1, 1914–September 25, 1916* (Thessaloniki: Institute for Balkan Studies, 1971). For

the details of the Allied landings see John E. Kehl, American Consul at Salonika, to Lansing, 1 November 1915, NA 763.72/2288.

10. Gerald to Lansing, 5 January 1916, NA 763.72/2235; Kehl to Lansing, 5 June 1916, NA 763.72/2782.

11. The exact date appears uncertain. The Greek Foreign Minister, Stephen Skouloudis, puts it on the 6th. Skouloudis to Droppers, 15 June 1916, NA 763.72/2757; Leon puts it on the 7th. Leon, *Greece and the Great Powers*, 367; and the American minister gives no date in his dispatches.

12. See Droppers to Lansing, 8 June 1916, NA 763.72112/2616 and Leon, *Greece and the Great Powers*, 367.

13. Ibid.; Skouloudis to Diplomatic Officers in neutral countries, 15 June 1916, NA 763.72/2757. The Greek chargé in Washington left a copy of the protest at the State Department on 19 June.

14. When this practice continued unabated in the ensuing months, the American Minister, Garrett Droppers, joined the neutral ministers of Spain and Holland in delivering a written protest to the Foreign Ministry against the reckless and lawless methods countenanced by the Greek government in suppressing the Venizelists. Droppers to Lansing, 4 December 1916, NA 868.00/83.

15. This concern did not prove unfounded. When Constantine regained his throne in 1920 and the United States refused to recognize his regime and to release all or part of the remaining credits established under the 1918 Tripartite Loan, the Greek government adopted retaliatory measures in the form of high tariffs on certain American goods sold in Greece. The tariff on oleomargarine, for example, was increased 300 percent. U.S. Congress, Senate, *Loans to Foreign Governments: Greece* (Section 99), 67th Cong., 2nd sess., S. Doc. 86, 1921, 180. See also the letter from the American legation to the State Department on p. 203 of the same document.

16. Droppers to Lansing, 17 April 1917, NA 868.00/102. In fairness to Droppers it must be noted that similar sentiments were expressed within the Division of Near Eastern Affairs. One memorandum reads: "Consul Kehl has throughout manifested a spirit of hostility towards the Venizelist Government. His attitude would seem to be a reason as to why it might be advisable for the United States to have a diplomatic representative at Saloniki." A. P. (identity uncertain) to Phillips and Adee, 18 April 1917, NA 868.00/102.

17. Memorandum from A. P. to Phillips and Adee, 18 August 1917, NA 868.00/102; Kehl to Lansing, 11 May 1917, NA 868.00/114; and unnumbered memorandum from A. P. to Carr, 22 June 1917.

18. Letter from Politis to Kehl, Salonika, 17/30 December 1916, Foreign Ministry #589 enclosed in Kehl to Lansing, 8 January 1917, NA 868.00/95.

19. Ibid; Polk, the acting secretary of state, to Kehl, 21 October 1916, unnumbered; Kehl to Lansing, 23 October 1916, NA 763.72/2981.

20. See Saloutos, *The Greeks in the United States*, chaps. 7 and 10; see also personal note from William Phillips, assistant secretary of state, to Lansing, 4 April 1917, unnumbered; Lansing to Droppers, 8 December 1916, NA 868.00/83; Lansing to Droppers, 14 April 1917, unnumbered; Lansing to Droppers, 4 April 1917, NA 868.00/100; and Droppers to Lansing, 1 May 1917, NA 868.00/105.

21. The British, in order to combat Royalist propaganda, established an intelligence

service with Compton Makenzie as its first director. For the story of the Allied Secret Service in Greece during the First World War and after see Sir Basil Thomson, *The Allied Secret Service in Greece* (London: Hutchinson & Co., 1931); quoted material, pp. 169–70.

22. Droppers to Lansing, 23 October 1916, NA 868.00/84. The reference to Mexico is not clear. Someone in the department penciled a question mark beside "Mexico." Droppers was probably expressing the opinion that in comparison to Greek politics the traditional chaotic political conditions in Mexico were less pernicious.

23. Droppers to Lansing, 19 June 1917, NA 868.00/32.

24. Droppers to Lansing, 24 December 1917, NA 868.00/157. It has been alleged that Hibben's Royalist sentiments were nurtured by a decoration from King Constantine and by a monthly stipend from the public treasury. These were the conclusions of the Parliamentary Commission of Investigation, which was created by the Venizelists after the king's departure in 1917 to look into alleged corruption inside Constantine's government. Droppers to Lansing, 29 October 1917, NA 868.00/146.

25. Paxton Hibben was more than a journalist and a passing figure in the course of Greek-American diplomacy. He was also a lawyer, an American diplomat (having served as secretary and chargé d'affaires in Petrograd, Mexico City, and several capitals in South America), and he was an officer in the United States Army during the War. From 1920 to 1922 he served with the Near East Relief. Subsequently, he served with the Military Mission to Armenia and as secretary of the American Committee for the Relief of Russian Children. He was, above all, a radical; but a benign radical as the sources seem to suggest. From 1917 to 1924 he was a veritable gadfly on the side of government officials in the Foreign Ministry and the Department of State. He was persistent in his efforts to promote and defend the rights of those whom he perceived to be the "underdog." For a biographical sketch of this interesting and controversial figure, see the *New York Times*, 6 December 1928, 9 December 1928, and 13 December 1928.

26. Droppers to Lansing, 24 December 1917, NA 868.00/157.

27. Paxton Hibben, *King Constantine and the Greek People*, (New York: Century, 1920), ix, 492, 496. It is probable that this allegation is not entirely the result of a vivid imagination. In November 1917 Hibben was commissioned a First Lieutenant in the United States Army and advanced to Captain in May 1919. During the war and after his discharge from the army, he was an outspoken advocate of the recognition of the Soviet Union by the United States. Because of the frequent public expression of his views, he was stripped of his commission and a court of inquiry was convened in 1924 to look into his activities. A few months later, however, his commission was renewed, The *New York Times*, 6 December 1928. Another case in point is George Horton's *The Blight of Asia*. Horton's outspoken indictment of American and British policy before and during the Smyrna crisis was a source of embarrassment to the State Department. It allegedly attempted to buy up the entire edition in order to contain any possible damage to the American "image." See Marjorie Housepian, "George Horton and Mark L. Bristol: Opposing Forces in U.S. Foreign Policy, 1919–1923," *The Bulletin of the Centre of Asia Minor Studies* 4 (1983):147.

28. Droppers to Lansing, 24 December 1917, NA 868.00/157.

29. Ibid. A sense of the urgency that surrounded these activities and the intensity of the efforts to sway American public opinion can be obtained from Mrs. Kenneth (Dēmētra) Brown, *Constantine: King and Traitor* (New York: John Lane Company, 1918) and *In*

the Heart of German Intrigue (Boston and New York: Houghton Mifflin Company, 1918).

30. Droppers to Lansing, 23 October 1916, NA 868.00/84.

31. Ibid; Droppers to Lansing, ca. 23 November 1916, NA 868.00/89.

32. Droppers to Lansing, 19 June 1917, NA 868.00/123; Droppers to Lansing, 28 May 1917, NA 868.00/123; Droppers to Lansing, ca. 23 November 1916, NA 868.00/89.

33. For a detailed discussion of the effect of the propaganda in the U.S. see Saloutos, *The Greeks in the United States*, chap. 7; Timagenis to Lansing, 2 May 1917, NA 868.00/106; A. P. to Carr, 11 May 1917, NA 868.00/106.

34. Lansing to Vouros, 18 June 1917, NA 868.00/130; Greek chargé to Lansing, 29 July 1917, NA 868.00/130.

35. There is an excellent book which contains a wealth of anecdotal information relative to America's role in the establishment of educational and philanthropic institutions, health facilities, social centers, and many other social services in the period between 1909 and 1960. The author had a first-hand knowledge of many of the events described in this book and was on intimate terms with most of the American officials who served in Greece during the 1920s and 1930s. See Stavros S. Papadakēs, *Synchronoe amerikanoe philellēnes: anamnēseis misou aeona* [Contemporary American philhellenes: memoirs of a half century] (Athens: M. Pechlibades, 1967).

36. For the full text of the conversation, see Droppers to Lansing, 11 February 1917, NA 711.68/1.

37. Droppers reported that numerous British and French troops were killed in the confrontation, and the situation, therefore, became very critical. The American minister requested that an American cruiser be stationed near Athens to be ready for any contingency. Droppers to Lansing, 2 December 1916, NA 868.00/82. The State Department's answer to this request is significant because it illustrates the lengths to which the American government would go to avoid political involvement. At a time when other legations were making plans for the evacuation of their nationals and members of their staffs, Lansing answered: "Navy Department and Department agree inadvisable to send [a cruiser] to Athens." Then, almost as an afterthought, he added: "Are you in imminent danger?" Telegram from Lansing to Droppers, 4 December 1916, unnumbered. The American minister's version of the disturbances of 1 December 1916 can be found in Droppers to Lansing, 13 January 1917, NA 868.00/94.

38. In February 1897 an insurrection erupted in Crete, which was designed to liberate the island from Turkish domination and to annex it to Greece. The government in Athens sent ships and troops in order to placate public opinion at home. Great Britain, France, and Italy, fearing that this revolt would destroy the balance of power in the Balkans by inducing an uprising in Macedonia, established a blockade on 21 March to check the Cretan movement. The American embassy in London was immediately informed of this action. Carter to Sherman, 21(?) March 1897, unnumbered. The blockade was applied to all ships under the Greek flag. All other ships were permitted to enter ports occupied by the Great Powers and land their merchandise, but only if it was not intended for Greek troops or for the interior of the island. Secretary of State John Sherman protested to the British ambassador in Washington. He stated that since the United States was not a signatory of the Treaty of Berlin (1878), it would not concede "the right [to the Great Powers] to make such a blockade . . . [and reserved for itself] the consideration of all

international rights and of any question which may in any way affect the commerce or interests of the United States." Sherman to Sir Julian Pauncefote, 26 March 1897, unnumbered.

39. Lansing to Jusserand, 21 December 1916, NA 763.72112/3203.

40. See chap. 2, note 3 for Tsar Nicholas' role in the matter of Constantine's abdication. George Bentērēs, *Ē Ellas tou 1910–1920* [Greece, 1919–1920], 2 vols., 2nd ed. (Athens: Ikaros, 1970), 2:308; Leon, *Greece and the Great Powers,* 469, 472.

41. Droppers to Lansing, 18 June 1917, NA 868.00/131.

42. Ibid; Jonnart represented the Allied Powers in the discussions between the Royalist government in Athens and the Allied Command in Salonika—he was also given the task of delivering the ultimatum to the Foreign Ministry; Droppers to Lansing, 15 June 1917, NA 868.00/131.

43. For a detailed discussion on the legal issues raised by Constantine's failure to sign formal articles of abdication, see a dispatch from Capps to the acting secretary of state, 16 January 1921, NA 868.00/251.

44. Quoted in Dakin, *The Unification of Greece,* pp. 215–16.

45. The letter, dated 6 July 1917, was delivered by the Greek minister in Washington to the Department of State on 8 September 1917; NA 868.0076/10. The sources give no indication why two months passed before the letter was delivered.

46. The letter, dated 1 October 1917, was sent to the American minister in Athens to be delivered to the minister of foreign affairs; 6 October 1917, NA 868.001A12/18.

Chapter 3

1. Droppers to Lansing, 16 July 1917, NA 868.51WC/2.

2. Greece emerged from the Greco-Turkish War of 1897 with her foreign and domestic finances in total disarray. After the conclusion of that conflict, the Great Powers established an International Financial Commission (1898) whose responsibility was to oversee the conduct of Greece's foreign finances. To this commission were assigned the revenues from monopolies, taxes on tobacco, stamp duties, and import duties levied at the port of Piraeus. Import duties were expected to raise 39,600,000 drachmas per year. If the yield fell below this sum, then the import duties from other Greek ports could be tapped to make up the difference. The internal debt was to remain under the control of the Greek government, and the cost of the service of internal loans was to be covered by any surpluses not required by the IFC. If, however, surplus revenues exceeded the sum of 28,900,000 drachmas, the difference between the two figures could be legally spent by the IFC according to a specified formula. Thirty percent was to be used to pay off the interest on foreign loans at a higher rate than had originally been agreed; 30 percent was to be used for amortization purposes; and the remaining 40 percent was to be turned over to the Greek treasury. For the administration of these revenues, a regulatory agency was created under the control of the commission.

The interests of the IFC were to take precedence over the requirements of the Greek treasury until the public debt had been stabilized and the claims of foreign creditors had been satisfied. The commission had enormous power which left a legacy of bitterness in Greece. It was believed generally that this power was often used not to regulate, but to punish and coerce. The existence of the IFC had a profound influence on Greek-

American affairs after 1922, since much of what transpired between Greece and the United States involved financial and economic matters. After the First World War only France, Great Britain, and Italy retained their membership in the IFC. For the history of this and related problems, see John A. Levandis, *The Greek Foreign Debt and the Great Powers, 1821–1898* (New York: Columbia Univ. Press, 1944).

3. Droppers to Lansing, 11 July 1917, NA 868.51WC/1.

4. Droppers to Lansing, 16 July 1917, NA 868.51WC/2.

5. Ibid.

6. Ibid.

7. Charles Seymour, ed., *The Intimate Papers of Colonel House*, 2 vols. (Boston and New York: Houghton Mifflin Company, 1926), 1:372.

8. Memorandum by Droppers enclosed in Droppers to Lansing, 16 July 1817, NA 868.51WC/2; Droppers to Lansing, 17 September 1917, NA 868.51WC/9. General Ludendorff has testified to the effectiveness of the Greek army on the Macedonian front against the Bulgarian forces. See Erich von Ludendorff, *Ludendorff's Own Story*, 2 vols. (New York and London: Harper & Brothers Publishers, 1919), 1:340, 346–47; 2:162, 165; and William Miller, *Greece* (New York: Charles Scribner's Sons, 1928), 59–60.

9. Droppers to Lansing, 17 September 1917, NA 868.51WC/9.

10. AYE, 1917/A/7, note verbale from Droppers to Politis, Athens, 24 July/6 August 1917; AYE, 1917/A/7, memorandum from Droppers to Politis, Athens, 30 July/12 August 1917.

11. AYE, 1917/A/7, Droppers to Politis, Athens, 24 July/6 August 1917; Droppers to Lansing, 19 August 1917, NA 868.51WC/5.

12. AYE, 1917/A/7, Negropontis to Venizelos, Athens, 3/16 November 1917.

13. For a summary of Greek efforts in the negotiations, see memorandum by the Greek minister, 18 September 1917, NA 868.51WC/10; AYE. 1917/A/7, Roussos to the foreign minister, Washington, D.C., 23 September 1917; AYE., 1917/A/7, foreign minister to Major General Broque, Athens, 10/23 November 1917; and AYE. 1917/A/7, Negropontis to Venizelos, Athens, 3/16 November 1917.

14. Two commissions were established in Athens to oversee the disposition of the proceeds from the loan. The Inter-Allied Financial Commission was to determine what credits were to be put at the disposal of the Greek government, while the actual spending of the credits was to be controlled by an Inter-Allied Military Commission. Both were composed of French, British, American, and Italian representatives.

15. The loan was granted in several installments whose total reached the sum of 600,000,000 francs, approximately $116,000,000.

16. Lansing to Droppers, 8 September 1917, NA 868.51WC/7.

17. U.S. Congress, Senate, *Loans to Foreign Governments: Greece*, 67th Cong., 2nd sess., S. Doc. 86, 1921, 185, and Kellogg to Skinner, 2 February 1928, NA 868.51WC/492b.

18. The British and French financial representatives signed on 10 February with no reservations, while Oscar T. Crosby, the American representative, signed it ad referendum. The reason for this technical procedure was the need to give American officials time to include an addendum which placed a limit on the amount of time that the United States government would be obligated to honor the terms of the loan. On 13 February, Crosby signed the agreement on the basis of the reservations contained in the addendum.

19. The credits were issued in the following installments: 20 June 1918, $15,790,000;

3 December 1918, $23,764,036; 25 March 1919, $3,858,930; and 31 July 1919, $4,823,663.05. The negotiations relative to the opening of these credits were extremely complex and technical. A good and succinct summary of the correspondence regarding these credits is in U.S. Congress, Senate, *Loans to Foreign Governments: Greece* (Section 99) 67th Cong., 2nd sess., S. Doc. 86, 186–97.

20. Charles P. Howland, *Survey of American Foreign Relations, 1928–1931*, 4 vols. (New Haven: Yale Univ. Press, 1928–31), 3:428.

21. Letter from Tsamados to Lansing, 3 September 1917, U.S. Congress, Senate, *Loans to Foreign Governments: Greece*, 198.

22. For a summary of the correspondence relating to these points see U.S. Congress, Senate, *Loans to Foreign Governments: Greece*, 198–203.

23. It should be noted that of the $48,236,629 provided for by the Tripartite Loan as the share of the United States, only $43,900,000 were finally approved allowable expenditures by the Inter-Allied Financial Commission at Athens.

Chapter 4

1. The *Balkan Post*, 5 June 1920, cited in Granville to Curzon, Athens, 21 July 1921, FO 371/6096, no. 319.

2. Hamilton Fish Armstrong, *Peace and Counterpeace, from Wilson to Hitler: Memoirs of Hamilton Fish Armstrong* (Harper & Row Publishers, 1971), 147; Miller, *Greece*, 61. Venizelos sent several telegrams from Paris (both public and secret) expressing his disgust at the excesses committed in his name. But on his return to Athens on 30 August considerations of practical politics prevailed, and he publicly embraced the architect of this policy of repression, M. Repoulés, to show his confidence in him. Granville to Curzon, Athens, 21 July 1921, FO 371/6096, no. 319.

3. *New York Times*, 14 November 1920.

4. The sources do not contain any specific promise by Dēmētrios Gounaris, leader of the Royalist opposition, or by any of his chief associates relative to demobilization and peace; but it was universally believed at the time that a Royalist victory at the polls and the return of Constantine would lead to that result. Granville to Curzon, Athens, 21 July 1921, FO 371/6096, no. 319.

5. *New York Times*, 10 November 1920, 21 October 1920.

6. Even the British minister shared in this optimism, a fact which led him to send inaccurate and misleading political analyses to the Foreign Office. Only R. S. Hudson, second secretary of the British legation, offered a dissenting opinion which was brushed aside. DBFP, First Series, 12:508. The attitude of the British Minister is puzzling, since the British legation seems to have been aware, as early as May, of the growing opposition to Venizelos. See Annual Report for 1920 from Granville to Curzon, Athens, 21 July 1921, FO 371/6096, no. 319.

7. In December 1915 Venizelos made a statement whose publication was withheld at his request. Subsequently, however, he gave an almost identical statement to *Le Temps* based on the notes from his first interview. He said, "Greece is not ready for a republic and may not be ready for centuries. I have never believed a republic suitable as a government for Greece at this epoch of her history." He went on to add that if a republic were established, he would be chosen president, thereby bringing an end to his Liberal Party,

for there would be no one to succeed him as its leader. "Greece would [then] be in the same position of Mexico under Porfirio Diaz. That was bad for Mexico and it would be even worse for Greece." Hibben, *Constantine I and the Greek People*, 579. See also J. Gennadius, "The Truth about Constantine and Venizelos," *Current History* 16 (August 1922):810.

8. *New York Times*, 16 November 1920; Dakin, *The Unification of Greece*, 228.

9. Capps to Bainbridge Colby, Secretary of State, 15 November 1920, NA 868.00/222; 18 November 1920, NA 868.00/226; Miller, *Greece*, p. 62.

10. For summaries relative to this problem see Charles Cheney Hyde, *International Law: Chiefly As Interpreted by the United States*, 3 vols., 2nd ed. (Boston: Little, Brown, and Company, 1947), I:161–69; Logan, "The Recognition of Mexico," *American Society of International Law: Proceedings* 17 (1924):109–15; Henry L. Stimson, "The United States and the Other American Republics," *Foreign Affairs* 9 (April 1931):v–viii; and Lawrence Dennis, "Revolution, Recognition and Intervention," *Foreign Affairs* 9 (January 1931):204–21.

11. Paul Leicester Ford, ed., *The Writings of Thomas Jefferson*, 10 vols. (New York and London: G. P. Putnam's Sons, 1892), 6:199; Dennis, "Revolution, Recognition and Intervention," 204.

12. Memorandum from Adee to the Secretary of State, *Foreign Relations of the United States* (1913), 100.

13. Dennis, "Revolution, Recognition and Intervention," p. 205.

14. For an incisive analysis of the pitfalls and contradictions inherent in Britain's Greek policy from 1920 to 1922 see a memorandum by Harold Nicolson entitled: "Future Policy towards King Constantine," DBFP, First Series, 12:550–53.

15. Granville to Curzon, Athens, 21 July 1921, FO 371/6096. no. 319.

16. AYE., 1922/A/7, French Legation to Greek Foreign Ministry, Athens, 3 December 1920; Miller, *Greece*, 64. A somewhat liberal translation of the full text of the note can be found in *Current History* 13 (January 1929):64. The correct date of the document is 3 December 1920, not 2 December as indicated in the *Current History* article.

17. Miller, *Greece*, 63. Capps reported that the percentages in favor of Constantine were 75 percent in Old Greece and approximately 55 percent in New Greece. Capps to the Acting Secretary of State, 6 December 1920, 868.00/232. The latter figure is more surprising, since New Greece was a Venizelist stronghold.

It has been charged that the plebiscite was conducted dishonestly because in many districts the number of votes ranged from 110 to 130 percent of the registered voters. "In other words," wrote one American journalist, "every Royalist voted as often as he pleased, and he pleased quite frequently." Kenneth L. Roberts, "They Sometimes Come Back," *The Saturday Evening Post*, September 10, 1921, 53. The British minister in Athens reported that "the plebiscite was little more than a farce." Granville to Curzon, Athens, 21 July 1921, FO 371/6096, no. 319.

18. A major source of this uncertainty was King Alexander, who made it known that he regarded himself as a temporary substitute for his father who had never ceased to be king. Granville to Curzon, Athens, 21 July 1921, FO 371/6096, no. 319.

19. Capps to Colby, 18 November 1920, NA 868.00/226.

20. Granville to Curzon, Athens, 21 July 1921, FO 371/6096, no. 319; *Times* (London), Special Supplement, 1 January 1921, 2:b. Immediately after the return of Constantine the ministers of Great Britain and France were ordered to leave Athens, but the

orders of recall were subsequently revoked; probably because the Italian minister informed the British legation of his government's intention to keep a diplomatic representative in Greece while at the same time withholding recognition from Constantine's government. Capps to Colby, 21 December 1920, NA 868.001C76/19. The French, British, and American legations continued to conduct business unofficially with Rallis' ministry, but refused to have anything to do with Constantine and his court.

21. *Current History* 13 (January 1921): 62–63.

22. Letter from Davis to Wilson, 28 December 1920, NA 868.001C76/49.

23. AYE, 1922/A/7, Dracopoulos to Rallis, Washington, 18/31 December 1920.

24. Capps to Colby, 30 December 1920, NA 868.00/248; Robbins to Davis, 13 January 1921, unnumbered; Davis to Capps, 30 December 1920, NA 868.001C76/19; Davis to Capps, 7 January 1921, NA 868.001C76/20.

25. AYE, 1922/A/7, Dracopoulos to the Foreign Ministry, Washington, 8 January 1921.

26. Capps to Colby, 16 January 1921, NA 868.00/251. In November 1921 Harold Nicolson wrote: "M. Jonnart . . . appears to have given some verbal assurances that the King would doubtless be allowed to return to Greece after the war if the Greek people so desired, [while His Majesty's] . . . Government for their part have not actually pledged themselves to forbid the return of King Constantine." DBFP, First Series, 12:514.

27. Capps to Colby, 18 January 1921, NA 868.001C76/22.

28. This decision is corroborated by British archival material. See Annual Report from British Legation to the Foreign Office, Athens, ca. Spring 1923, FO 371/8832, no. unavailable.

29. Davis to Capps, 15 January 1921, NA 868.001C76/21; AYE, 1922/A/7, Dracopoulos to the Foreign Ministry, Washington, 15 January 1921; AYE, 1922/A/7, Dracopoulos to the Foreign Ministry, Washington, 14 January 1921; Davis to Capps, 15 January 1921, NA 868.001C76/21.

30. *New York Times*, 15 January 1921, 31 January 1921.

31. Harrison to Warren D. Robbins, 14 May 1921, NA 868.001C76/55.

32. While the Government of the United States had formally recognized Alexander, it did not go on record as having withdrawn its recognition from Constantine. The only American response to the December plebiscite was the interruption of normal relations on 6 December 1920.

33. The negotiations on this technical point are long and tedious. For a succinct summary of this issue see Robbins to Davis, 19 January 1921, NA 868.001C76/50; Davis to Robbins, 26 January 1921, NA 868.01/232; Capps to Colby, 25 February 1921, NA 868.001C76/29; and Hall to Colby, 16 March 1921, NA 868.001C76/71.

34. The letter is dated 10/23 December 1920, but it was not delivered to the State Department by Dracopoulos until 2 March 1921. Apparently, the letter was held in reserve to be used only as a last resort. Division of Near Eastern Affairs to Fletcher, 7 March 1921, NA 868.001C76/48. For the full text of the letter see Dracopoulos to the Secretary of State, 2 March 1921, NA 868.001C76/30.

35. Letter from Bliss to Senator Henry Cabot Lodge, 15 March 1921, NA 868.001C76/39A; *New York Times*, 15 March 1921.

36. Harrison to Robbins, 14 May 1921, NA 868.001C76/55.

37. Memorandum from Robbins to Davis, 8 January 1921, NA 868.00/248; AYE, 1922/A/7, Dracopoulos to the Foreign Ministry, Washington, 6 January 1921.

38. Allan Westcott, "The Struggle for the Mediterranean," *Our World*, February 1921, 14.

39. In the decade following the fall of Porfirio Diaz, diplomatic relations between the United States and Mexico deteriorated. The countries of Europe sought to take advantage of the situation and make greater commercial inroads in Mexico and elsewhere in Central America. See George D. Beelen, "The Harding Administration and Mexico: Diplomacy by Economic Persuasion," *The Americas* 41 (October 1984): 177–89 and the sources therein cited.

40. Smaller shares were held by German, Dutch, Belgian, Swiss, and Spanish nationals. The Belgians were often instrumental in prodding the French to press the Mexican issue.

41. Memorandum by Fletcher of a conversation with the French Ambassador, 6 March 1922, NA 868.01/231; Dulles(?) to Hughes, 10 July 1922, NA 868.01/83.

42. For the British position see memorandum by Undersecretary of State Fletcher of a conversation with Sir Henry Getty Chilton, counselor to the British embassy in Washington, 21 October 1921, NA 868.01/228; British Ambassador to Fletcher, 16 February 1922, NA 868.01/82; memorandum by Fletcher of a conversation with the British Ambassador, 17 February 1922, NA 868.01/81; and British Ambassador to Fletcher, Acting Secretary of State, 25 February 1922, NA 868.01/83.

43. See Annual Report from Granville to Curzon, Athens, 21 July 1921, FO 371/6096, no. 319; memorandum from Davis to the Secretary of State, 21 January 1921, NA 868.001C76/41.

44. Memorandum from Robbins to Fletcher, 2 November 1921, NA 868.01/78. In October 1921 Vouros submitted to the State Department a lengthy memorandum in which he argued that the United States had been misinformed regarding the events which transpired from the electoral defeat of Venizelos to the restoration of Constantine. The document is undated.

45. Dulles, "Recognition of New States and Governments: Greece," *American Society of International Law: Proceedings* 18 (1924):107.

46. Caffery to Hughes, 23 March 1922, NA 868.001C76/42.

47. AYE, 1920–1922/A/7, Vouros to the Foreign Ministry, Washington, 7/20 April 1921; AYE, 1921/A/VIII, Vouros to the Foreign Ministry, Washington, 4/17 May 1921; AYE, 1922/A/7, Vouros to the Foreign Ministry, Washington, 7/20 April 1921; AYE, 1922/A/7, Gennadius, Dracopoulos, and Vouros to the Foreign Ministry, Washington, 9 June 1922; and AYE, 1922/A/7, Baltatzēs to Vouros, Athens, 19 April 1921.

48. Interview with an American correspondent of the *Chicago Tribune* (Paris edition) and published in the *Eleutheron Vēma*, 18 September 1922; memorandum by Dulles of a conversation with Gennadius, 25 April 1922, NA 868.01/143.

49. AYE, 1920/A/7, S. G. Pezas to the Foreign Ministry, Rio de Janeiro, 20 August 1921; AYE, 30 November 1921.

50. Illustrative of this shift in emphasis is the fact that in three weeks (18 January to 11 February 1922), the State Department received 416 telegrams (711.68P81/1 to 711.68P81/416) bearing the names of many thousands of Greeks and Americans. This phase of Greek-American diplomacy will be treated in relation to the Forced Loan of 1922.

51. [Charles Evans Hughes], "Recent Questions and Negotiations: Greece," *Foreign Affairs* 2 (no. 2, 1923): xx.

52. *Eleutheron Vēma*, 18 September 1922.

Chapter 5

1. Bentinck to Curzon, Athens, ca. Spring/Summer 1923, FO 371/8832, no. unavailable.

2. Ibid.

3. Evidence has been uncovered which seems to indicate that certain British officials hinted to Gounaris that a campaign against Kemal would have their approval, though they could not guarantee outright material support. Kousoulas, *Modern Greece*, 123.

4. Konstantinou Th. Rentē, *Ē exoterikē politikē tēs ellados meta tēn 1ēn noembriou* [The foreign policy of greece after november 1st (1921)] (Athens: Ioannou Batsou, 1922): 102; *New York Times*, 1 January 1922.

5. Wheeler, chargé d'affaires *ad interim* in London, to Hughes, 13 January 1922, NA 868.51WC/247.

6. Memorandum from Young to Robbins, Harrison, and Dearing, 3 March 1923, NA 868.51WC/262; Rentē, *Ē Exoterikē politikē tēs Ellados*, 99, 103.

7. E. I. Malainou, *Istoria ton xenikon epembaseon* [History of foreign interventions], vol. 7 (Athens: n.p., 1963), 7:207.

8. In the absence of an accredited minister, Hall was in charge of the American legation. His tenure in Greece had been marred by controversies that went back to the days when he served under Garrett Droppers. Illustrative of his attitude toward the Royalists is a dispatch to the secretary of state in which he wrote: "A more stubborn and worthless good for nothing set of people would be hard to imagine." Hall to Hughes, 12 April 1921, NA 868.00/unnumbered; see also chap. 2, note 25.

9. Memorandum by Robbins, 27 October 1921, NA 868.01/58.

10. Allen W. Dulles, head of the Division of Near Eastern Affairs, admitted in May 1922 that American recognition should have been granted immediately upon the return of the king. The problem had then become intertwined with other political, economic, and territorial considerations which could not help but influence American policy. Memorandum by Dulles to the Undersecretary of State, 3 May 1922, NA 868.00176/79.

11. Ibid. Hibben's recommendations included Papafrangos, Philip Dragounis, and Alexander Mercati, a confidant of the Royal family. Hibben was an interesting figure who appears frequently in the documents in various contexts, often playing the role of the gadfly, to the consternation of American officials.

12. Memorandum of a conversation between L. R. Robinson and Young, 3 March 1922, NA 868.51/422; memorandum of a conversation between Salmon and officials of the Office of the Foreign Trade Adviser, Department of State, 12 December 1921, NA 868.51/380.

13. The plan called for the creation of a syndicate which would loan the Greek government ten to thirty-five million dollars in twenty-year bonds. Letter from Eastman, Dillon & Co. (investment bankers) to Hughes, 3 January 1922, NA 868.51/383; letter from Hoover to Eastman, Dillon & Co., 3 January 1922, NA 868.51/389; and memorandum from Hughes to Hoover, 4 January 1922, NA 868.51/389.

14. Memorandum of a conversation between Salmon and officials of the Foreign Trade Adviser, Department of State, 12 December 1921, NA 868.51/380.

15. Venizelos was married in London on 9 September. He traveled throughout the United States, Panama, South America, and Cuba. He spent the winter in Santa Barbara, California and took particular pleasure in the comforts of the famous health spa in Hot Springs, Arkansas.

16. Hughes wrote: " 'It is believed that this visit would be unfortunate, not because of any lack of esteem, but because of speculations and misunderstandings to which it might give rise. [I] Suggest that you advise informally against visit at this time, if you have the opportunity to do so without giving offense.' " Telegram from Hughes to American Embassy, 23 September 1921, quoted in Saloutos, *The Greeks in the United States*, 197.

17. Hughes to Caffery, 15 April 1922, NA 868.01/1.

18. Memorandum from Robbins to Young, 18 January 1922, NA 868.51WC/249; Caffery to Hughes, 3 March 1922, NA 868.51WC/263.

19. The Forced Loan of 1922 as it was carried out in Greece had no precedent in modern history. Other kinds of forced loans, however, were not new to Americans living abroad. For an historical summary of this problem see a memorandum from the Solicitor of the State Department to Nielsen, 21 April 1922, NA 868.51FL, 1922/12 1/2. For the funding operation carried out in Czechoslovakia under the Law of February 1919 there is a brief discussion of the differences between that law and its Greek counterpart in BFDC, *Operations and Consequences of the Greek Forced Loan Law*, prepared by P. L. Edwards, Trade Information Bulletin No. 68 (Washington: GPO, 1922), 9–10. It was primarily for this stroke of inventive genius that Protopapadakēs later found himself facing a firing squad. See Laughlin to Kellogg, 29 January 1926, NA 868.51FL, 1926/3.

20. An English translation of the Forced Loan Law is attached to a dispatch from Caffery to Hughes, 10 May 1922, NA 868.51FL, 1922/19.

21. A detailed analysis of all the technical aspects of the Forced Loan is available in BFDC, *Operation and Consequences of the Greek Forced Loan*, 1–10, and ii.

22. Memorandum from the Solicitor of the State Department to Hill, NA 868.51FL, 1922/34; Bentinck to Curzon, Athens, ca. Spring/Summer 1923, FO 371/8832, no. unavailable; Horton to Hughes, 21 August 1922, NA 868.51FL, 1922/42.

23. This was a legitimate complaint, and Caffery readily agreed with Gounaris. The American chargé reported that claims for exemptions were "enormous," while illicit efforts were made by many naturalized Greek-Americans to disguise the permanent nature of their residence in Greece. Caffery to Hughes, 24 April 1922, NA 868.51FL, 1922/13.

24. Atherton to Hughes, 16 November 1923, NA 868.51FL, 1922/65, enclosure 1. From September 1922 to November 1923 the file on the Forced Loan is extensive, but it adds little to the understanding of the overall problem. The documents are basically recitations of specific measures taken to ensure satisfaction for individual claims.

25. The Department of Commerce considered the matter serious enough to publish the booklet cited in note 21 and to provide an English translation of the Forced Loan Law for the benefit of American importers and exporters. The influence of this law is also analyzed in BFDC, *Business Practices in Greece*, prepared by E. A. Plitt, Trade Information Bulletin No. 472 (Washington: GPO, 1927).

26. Memorandum by Edwards attached to Caffery to Hughes, 12 July 1922, NA 868.51FL, 1922/35.

27. The following documents give a summary of the issues surrounding the Forced Loan of 1926: Laughlin to Kellogg, 24 January, NA 868.51FL, 1926/1; and H. S. Gould to Kellogg, 5 October 1928, NA 868.51FL, 1926/13.

Chapter 6

1. The problem was far more complex, involving conflicting territorial and commercial aspirations of the Allies. See Michael Llewllyn Smith, *Ionian Vision: Greece in Asia Minor, 1919-1922* (London: Allen Lane, Division of Penguin Books, Ltd., 1973).

2. The effectiveness of the army was greatly compromised by the expulsion of competent Venizelist officers from the General Staff. This purge was based partly on traditional political hostility and partly on the well-founded suspicion that unscrupulous Venizelists would attempt to undermine the discipline and loyalty of the army. Bentinck to Curzon, Athens, ca. Spring/Summer 1923, FO 371/8832, no. unavailable.

3. Of the three, Plastiras and Gonatas wielded the most power; hence, the customary omission of Fokas' name when referring to the Revolutionary Committee. Eventually, several other officers were added. The Committee was dissolved the day before the execution of the "Six," though Plastiras remained in charge of the government, exercising dictatorial powers.

4. Bentinck to Curzon, Athens, ca. Spring/Summer 1923, FO 371/8832, no. unavailable.

5. Throughout this chapter the terms "revolution" and "revolutionary" will be treated as proper nouns. Plastiras and Gonatas conceived their movement as an entity possessing all the attributes of a formal and established institution.

6. S. S. Papadakis, "The Greek Treason Trials," *Current History* 17 (January 1923):673; Caffery to Hughes, 4 October 1922, NA 868.00/311; Bentinck to MacDonald, Athens, 30 August 1924, FO 371/9896, no. 555; Caffery to Hughes, 17 October 1922, NA 868.00/317.

7. Caffery to Hughes, 17 October 1922; NA 868.00/317; Bentinck to Curzon, Athens, ca. Spring/Summer 1923, FO 371/8832, no. unavailable.

8. Caffery to Hughes, 23 October 1922, NA 868.00/328; Caffery to Hughes, 17 October 1922, NA 868.00/317; Caffery to Hughes, 4 October 1922, NA 868.00/311; memorandum from Dulles to the Undersecretary of State, 13 October 1922, NA 868.00176/79.

9. The Committee arrived on the evening of 14 September. The intention of the authorities was to take the ex-ministers the next day aboard the battleship *Lemnos*. They were to be given a speedy "trial" and then shot on the spot. A general amnesty would immediately follow the executions. When Plastiras informed the British and French Ministers of the plan, he was warned that such an illegal and criminal act would have serious consequences for the national interests of Greece. Gregorios Daphnēs, *Ē Ellas metaxy dyo polemon* [Greece between two wars], 2 vols. (Athens: Ikaros, 1955), 1:12-13; Bentinck to Curzon, Athens, ca. Spring/Summer 1923, FO 371/8832, no. unavailable. Apparently, the decision to deal harshly with Constantine's ministers was reached early in the revolutionary movement. Plastiras, while still in Chios, gave a dramatic speech in which he concluded by shouting: " 'Death to the traitors!' " Papadakis, "The Greek Treason Trials," 673.

10. *New York Times*, 30 November 1922.

11. Daphnēs, *Ē Ellas*, 1:12–13.

12. On 27 November several hundred Venizelist officers presented to the Revolutionary Committee a demand for the immediate execution of the chief political prisoners. In the event that their demand was denied, they threatened to retaliate by taking the lives of the committee's members. Caffery to Hughes, 28 November 1922, NA 868.00/322; Dakin, *The Unification of Greece*, 230; and Miller, *Greece*, 72; Bentinck to Curzon, Athens, ca. Spring/Summer 1923, FO 371/8832, no. unavailable.

13. A statement to this effect was made by the Prime Minister, Alexander Zaïmis, in *Proïa*, 16 May 1927.

14. Bristol to Hughes, 17 November 1922, NA 868.00/319. In an apparent effort to add weight to their protests, the British and French ministers attempted not merely to persuade, but to pressure Caffery to lodge an informal and personal protest with the Foreign Ministry. Caffery to Hughes, 26 October 1922, NA 868.00/301.

15. This interpretation of French policy is based on British sources. Bentinck to Curzon, Athens, ca. Spring/Summer 1923, FO 371/8832, no. unavailable. The French minister's initial response to the arrests was an expression of compassion for the arrested ministers and their families. He cooperated with his British colleague in extracting a promise from the Revolutionary leaders that the ministers would be properly tried. He was genuinely anxious to get the Royal family away without bloodshed. This attitude, however, was not approved in Paris.

16. Daphnēs, *Ē Ellas*, 1:17.

17. Caffery to Hughes, 4 November 1922, NA 868.00/338; Caffery to Hughes, 22 November 1922, NA 868.00/358; Caffery to Hughes, 2 November 1922, NA 868.00/308; *New York Times*, 5 November 1922; and Bristol to Hughes, 17 November 1922, NA 868.00/319.

18. Hughes to Caffery, 1 November 1922, NA 868.00/301; Caffery to Hughes, 2 November 1922, NA 868.00/308; Bentinck to Curzon, Athens, ca. Spring/Summer 1923, FO 371/8832, no. unavailable. Reflecting upon the crisis many years later Caffery wrote: "It was none of my business, but in answer to a round-about inquiry of mine, I received a note . . . from an important revolutionary, saying that they would be legally tried." Caffery, *Adventure in Diplomacy*, 1:7–8. It is unfortunate that Caffery has so little to say about this and other important matters in which he took an active interest. His unpublished memoirs for this period are little more than an informal travelogue.

19. A variety of restrictions were imposed on the defense, some of which were absurd. The president of the court, for example, could forbid questions and statements by the accused and their attorneys solely for the purpose of saving time. Caffery commented that the trial was hardly an example of objective jurisprudence. "The proceedings," he wrote, "were a poor showing against the accused." Caffery to Hughes, 6 December 1922, NA 868.00/361. For a dissenting opinion see Daphnēs, *Ē Ellas*, 1:12.

20. Caffery to Hughes, 14 December 1922, NA 868.00/347; Caffery to Hughes, 15 December 1922, NA 868.00/378. The contents of these documents were published in the Parisian newspaper, *Matins*. They created a furor, to the embarrassment of the British who had opposed their publication.

21. Bristol to Hughes, 15 November 1922, NA 868.00/320.

22. Daphnēs, *Ē Ellas*, 1:10, 14–15.

23. *New York Times*, 30 November 1922.

24. Hughes to Caffery, 1 December 1922, NA 868.00/324.

25. Letter from Harding to Hughes, 5 December 1922, NA 868.00/325. Harding's assertion is not entirely correct. It is true that the issue did not become the subject of sensational journalism, but it was duly mentioned in many leading American newspapers on numerous occasions. There is no doubt, however, that in sensitive matters affecting the Near East, the Harding administration frequently indulged in news manipulation and suppression. See Dobkin, *Smyrna 1922.*

26. Caffery to Hughes, 11 December 1922, NA 868.00/340.

27. *New York Times*, 30 November 1922.

28. Reference to Hibben's telegram (dated 29 November 1922) is made in a letter from Harding to Hughes, 1 December 1922, NA 868.00/324; Paxton Hibben, "Betrayal of Greece by Lloyd George," *Current History* 17 (January 1923):347.

29. *New York Times*, 20 December 1922; Thomson, *The Allied Secret Service in Greece*, 270–71.

30. Letter from Hughes to Harding, 2 December 1922, NA 868.00/324; [Charles Evans Hughes], "Recent Questions and Negotiations: Greece," xx; Hughes to Bristol, 23 January 1924, NA 711.67/46a.

31. Daphnes, *Ē Ellas*, 1:20, 11.

32. This statement reflects official policy, not personal sentiment. Caffery was greatly saddened by the tragic fate of the six men. He felt especially sorry for Baltatzes, who had been most cooperative with him under trying circumstances. Caffery, *Adventure in Diplomacy*, 2:8.

33. Bentinck to Curzon, Athens, ca. Spring/Summer 1923, FO 371/8832, no. unavailable. The phrase, "exceptional position" is probably an allusion to Caffery's role as the representative of a nation which was not a party to the Treaty of Sèvres—a fact which contributed to the popular perception that American influence was totally benign. "To sum up," the chargé concluded, "I should say the Greeks regard the United States as a thoroughly benevolent Power from whom much is to be hoped and nothing feared."

34. [Hughes], "Recent Questions and Negotiations: Greece," xix; Hughes to Bristol, 23 January 1924, NA 711.67/46a.

35. Caffery, *Adventure in Diplomacy*, 2:8–9 ("black claims" is probably a reference to the Forced Loan of 1922).

36. [Hughes], "Recent Questions and Negotiations," xxi.

37. Memorandum from Dulles to Phillips and Bliss, 14 November 1922, NA 868.01/137.

38. Vice-Consul in Salonika to the State Department, 12 May 1923, NA 868.00/403.

39. The following anecdote is revealing. A Russian woman relief worker, decidedly British or American in appearance, had her path blocked by a small boy whom she pushed aside. "I say, madam," the boy snapped, "do you think you can push me aside just because you're an American?" The boy then turned to several bystanders who complemented his indignation with some unpleasant remarks. "A month ago," the Vice-Consul wrote, "such an episode would not have occurred." Ibid.

40. Atherton to Hughes, 27 August 1923, NA 868.01/166; Bentinck to MacDonald, Athens, 30 August 1924, FO 371/9896, no. 555.; see a report from the American military attaché in Athens to the State Department, 4 September 1923, MID, Factor no. 3850.

41. An analysis of the ramifications of French influence in the months preceding the establishment of the republic can be found in a report from the American military attaché, 4 September 1923, MID, Factor no. 3850; Bentinck to MacDonald, Athens, 30 August 1924, FO 371/9896, no. 555; and in W. J. Rapp, "The New Greek Republic," *Current History* 20 (May 1924):254–62. Rapp spent considerable time in Greece with Near East Relief.

42. Atherton to Hughes, 27 August 1923, NA 868.01/166.

43. American Vice-Consul in Salonika to the State Department, 8 December 1923, NA 868.00/59. For an incisive and scholarly analysis of refugee influence in Greek politics during the interwar period see George Th. Mavrogordatos, *Stillborn Republic: Social Conditions and Party Strategies in Greece, 1922–1936* (Berkeley: Univ. of California Press, 1983), 182–225.

44. Memorandum from Dulles to Phillips, 17 September 1923, NA 868.51C/341.

45. Dr. Arthur N. Young, an eminent economist and a leading authority on international finance and economics, had a long and distinguished career in government service. From 1922 to 1929 he was economic adviser to the Department of State and was thus familiar with the questions of reparations, commercial negotiations, foreign loans, and intergovernment debts. He was an expert assistant to the World War Foreign Debt Commission during the negotiations for the settlement of war debts (1925–26) between the United States and several debtor nations. He was, therefore, an influential figure in the shaping of America's Greek policy throughout the 1920s.

46. Memorandum from Dulles and Young to Hughes, 27 June 1922, NA 868.01/144; memorandum from Young to White and Phillips, 25 October 1923, NA 868.01/181.

47. Memorandum from Young and Phillips to the Division of Near Eastern Affairs, 26 October 1923, NA 868.01/181.

48. For a detailed analysis see S. Victor Papacosma, *The Military in Greek Politics: The 1909 Coup d'état* (Kent, Ohio: Kent State Univ. Press, 1977).

49. Many years later Count Sforza confessed that the murders had been ordered by Mussolini. D. George Kousoulas, *Modern Greece: Profile of A Nation* (Charles Scribner's Sons, 1974), 131.

50. Papacosma, *The Military in Greek Politics*, 30–31, 85, and 151–52.

51. In September 1922, while still in Chios, Plastiras delivered a fiery oration in which he concluded by shouting: "Hurrah for the Republic!" Papadakis, "The Greek Treason Trials," 673. This was probably the first meaningful statement after 1920 which gave a hint that the subject of the republic was no longer academic.

52. *Eleutheron Vēma*, 1 November 1922. A copy of the same article can also be found in Atherton to Hughes, 8 November 1923, NA 868.00/441, enclosure 5; Bentinck to MacDonald, Athens, 30 August 1924, FO 371/9896, no. 555.

53. *Eleutheros Logos*, 17 November 1923; *Eleutheron Vēma*, 17 November 1923. On 29 November Henry Morgenthau, president of the Refugee Settlement Commission, informed Atherton that the Bank of England agreed to advance £1,000,000 (which composed part of the refugee loan being negotiated) to his commission only on condition that Morgenthau give his "personal conviction" that no republic would be established through unconstitutional means. Atherton to Hughes, 30 November 1923, NA 868.00/445.

54. *Enosis tou Ellēnismou*, 7 November 1923; Atherton to Hughes, 8 November 1923, NA 868.00/441; Atherton to Hughes, 30 November 1923, NA 868.00/445. Plastiras

told Atherton that the British chargé informed the Foreign Ministry of his government's opposition to the establishment of a republic by means of a coup d'état. He assured the American chargé that this would not happen.

55. Bentinck to MacDonald, Athens, 30 August 1924, FO 371/9896, no. 555; personal letter (dated 13 November 1923) from Atherton to Dulles attached to a memorandum from Young to Phillips, 30 November 1923, NA 868.01/185. When the French minister became "mixed up" in the affair by expressing pro-Royalist sentiments, he "received a sharp rap on the knuckles from Paris."

56. Personal letter (dated 13 November 1923) from Atherton to Dulles. When the Corfu incident and the counterrevolution erupted, Plastiras went to the American legation and "explained the whole situation fully and stated that any personal opinion that I [Atherton] cared to express . . . would be gratefully received."

57. Bentinck to MacDonald, Athens, 30 August 1924, FO 371/9896, no. 555.

58. Ibid. The Duke of York, Prince Arthur, and the Duke of Connaught were mentioned most frequently. The American chargé also reported that "frequent statements were made . . . that if the monarchy must be retained, then the King ought to be replaced by an English Prince." Atherton to Hughes, 7 November 1923, NA 868.00/443.

59. Dēmokratia, 18 December 1923; 19 December 1923; the Chicago Tribune article is quoted in the Eleutheron Vēma, 22 December 1923.

60. O'Donohue to the State Department, 5 December 1923, NA 868.00/458; Myron T. Herrick to Hughes, 27 December 1923, NA 868.01/187.

61. There is some confusion regarding the exact date of British recognition. American sources and Morgenthau put it on the eleventh of January, while British sources put it on the fifteenth.

62. This account is based on Morgenthau's own story. While Morgenthau had the tendency to exaggerate his interpretations to enhance his own role, his account of his activities can be accepted as reliable. Those portions of his story that can be checked against American and British documents, as well as against the personal accounts of contemporaries, emerge essentially accurate.

63. On 10 January the New York Times published an article headlined: "Morgenthau Insists on Greek Plebiscite." Morgenthau justified his intervention in Greek politics "only because of the urgency of the refugee situation." He warned that no American bank would float a large refugee loan "until a plebiscite has been held and Greece gets a stable Government."

64. Quoted in Morgenthau, I Was Sent to Athens, 140. See also an article entitled "Morgenthau Sounds Britain for Greeks," New York Times, 6 February 1924.

65. Morgenthau, I Was Sent to Athens, 141–42. Morgenthau's role in Greek political intrigue is an interesting story; see especially 118–66.

66. Cheetham to Chamberlain, 15 May 1925, Athens, FO 371/10771, no. 153.

67. Memorandum by Dulles of a conversation with Morgenthau, 17 May 1924, NA 868.51SC/192; see Morgenthau, I Was Sent to Athens, 154–56; Papadakēs, Synchronoe amerikanoe philellēnes, 3, 115.

68. Morgenthau, I Was Sent to Athens, 164–66.

69. Bentinck to MacDonald, Athens, 30 August 1924, FO 371/10771, no. 153.

70. Memorandum from Dulles to Hughes, 16 January 1924, NA 868.01/192; New York Times, 17 January 1924.

71. Letter from Hughes to Coolidge, 25 January 1924, NA 868.01/196a. Hughes

suggested that "Mr. Atherton . . . could be instructed to take up formal relations with the Minister of Foreign Affairs pending the appointment of a Minister. This action would be similar to that recently taken in the case of Mexico." Ibid. Obregón's government was recognized on 31 August 1923.

72. Ibid.

73. Daphnēs, Ē Ellas, 1:245. The results of the plebiscite showed 758,472 (70 percent) votes for the republic and 325,322 (30 percent) for the monarchy.

Chapter 7

1. Letter from Horton to Bristol (20 May 1920) attached to a dispatch from Bristol to Hughes, 25 September 1920, NA 868.01/23. George Horton, the American consul general in Smyrna, was unceasing in his efforts to promote an American mandate for "the whole of [the] Turkish Empire . . . giving security and justice to all concerned. . . ." He intimated prophetically that American aloofness would have disastrous consequences. For the full story see James B. Gidney, A Mandate for Armenia (Kent, Ohio: Kent State Univ. Press, 1967). For a documented summary of the positions of President Wilson and the American delegation relative to Greek territorial claims see Paul C. Helmreich, From Paris to Sèvres (Columbus: Ohio State Univ. Press, 1974), 41–42, 86, 92–105, 125, 154–55, and 158 and the references therein cited.

2. The American Vice-Consul and Delegate of the United States High Commissioner to Turkey to Hughes, 12 October 1922, NA 868.48/232.

3. Letter from Harding to Hughes, 20 May 1922, NA 867.4016/498; George Horton, The Blight of Asia (New York: Bobbs-Merrill Company, 1926), 123.

4. Letter from Hughes to Senator Lodge, Foreign Relations of the United States (1922), 2:452n. Landing parties of American bluejackets were stationed at various points throughout the city for this purpose, but no marines were sent ashore. The entire American force numbered 93 men, including officers.

5. Phillips to Bristol, 5 September 1922, NA 767.68/276.

6. Phillips to Hughes, 5 September 1922, NA 767.68/275. Phillips recommended to Hughes that all orders sent to Smyrna be vague. If it became necessary for American forces to land, the commanding officer responsible for the landing could then be made the scapegoat in the event of undesirable consequences.

7. Esther Pohl Lovejoy, Certain Samaritans (New York: Macmillan Company, 1933), 137–38, 146. American organizations included in the committee were the American Red Cross, American Women's Hospitals, Y.M.C.A., Y.W.C.A., Near East Relief, and the American Foreign Missions Board.

8. Bristol to Hughes, 6 September 1922, NA 868.48/83. Bristol has not always been treated kindly by historians. Evidence suggests that the admiral was inclined to be anti-Greek and pro-Turkish, though it can also be argued that Horton tended to be anti-Turkish, anti-American Indian, and anti-Negro. For two illuminating letters regarding the philosophical differences between the two men relative to Near Eastern affairs see two enclosures in Bristol to the Secretary of State, 26 September 1920, NA 868.01/23. Bristol made sincere efforts to intercede on behalf of the Christians in Anatolia, to prevent massacres, and to report the facts objectively. See Bristol to Hussein Raouf, president of the Turkish Council of Ministers, 8 September 1922, NA 867.4016/664, enclosure no. 2; Bristol to the Acting Secretary of State, 14 September 1922, NA 867.4016/664. For a

critical interpretation of Admiral Bristol's activities and his attitude toward the matter of evacuation see Dobkin, *Smyrna 1922*, and "George Horton and Mark L. Bristol: Opposing Forces in U.S. Foreign Policy, 1919–1923," *Bulletin of the Centre for Asia Minor Studies*, 4 (1983): 131–58; John Thomas Malakasses, "American Diplomatic Relations with Greece during the Last Part of Wilson's Administration and the Beginning of Harding's: The First Active American Invervention in the Internal Affairs of Greece," *Dodone* 5 (1976):47–74.

9. Bristol to Hughes, 6 September 1922, NA 868.48/83.

10. James L. Barton, *Story of Near East Relief, 1915–1930* (New York: Macmillan Company, 1930), 152–53. The group included several volunteers and two nurses. It was under the direction of Dr. Wilfred Post, the Near East Relief's managing director, and C. Caflin Davis, an official of the American Red Cross.

11. Testimony of Mrs. Elenē Pilafa, who witnessed the episode. "In my opinion," she told the author, "the Americans were our salvation." Athens, Greece, 3 July 1974.

12. Papadakēs, *Synchronoe amerikanoe philellēnes*, 85. These extralegal activities became the subject of exaggerated news reporting in the American press, to the irritation of the State Department. The acting secretary of state wrote Bristol: "Press reports indicate that the only relief work being done in Smyrna is by Near East Relief, the Red Cross, and your destroyers, and that the only foreign forces ashore are American sailors." Phillips to Bristol, 19 September 1922, NA 868.48/118. The quote from Caffery's memoirs may be found in *Adventure in Diplomacy*, 2:4.

13. Bentinck to Curzon, Athens, ca. Spring/Summer 1923, FO 371/8832, no. unavailable. Much praise also was given to the British and Japanese who took refugees aboard, while considerable bitterness was expressed at the indifference of the French and Italian navies.

14. See articles in *Nea Alētheia* (Salonika), 18/31 October 1922; *Makedonia* (Salonika), 14/27 October 1922; and *Estia* (Athens), 14/27 October 1922 enclosed in Leland B. Morris, American Consul in Salonika, to Hughes, 3 November 1922, NA 868.48/368. As commentary on the attitude of the Greek press Morris wrote: "There is no question . . . the real appreciation by all classes . . . of the American help received and contemplated."

15. On 14 September American destroyers took charge of the evacuation and within six weeks succeeded in evacuating approximately 300,000 people from various points along the western coast of Asia Minor. Bristol Papers, Manuscript Div., Library of Congress. Bristol to Hughes, 2 November 1922, NA 868.48/220. When ships of Greece and other nations finally were permitted to enter the harbor of Smyrna for evacuation purposes, it was American convoys that provided the direction and protection. For a statistical analysis, see a report by the American senior naval officer at Smyrna to Bristol, which was attached to a dispatch from Frederic R. Dolbeare, the Acting High Commissioner at Constantinople, to Hughes, 25 November 1922, NA 868.48/291. A descriptive analysis of the evacuation procedures is included in Bristol to Hughes, 25 September 1922, NA 868.48/14.

16. Other countries eventually did make some contributions to the relief effort, but they were in no hurry to do so. As of 9 February 1923, for example, little work for the refugees was being done by other nations. The British were just beginning "to show some activity through the establishment of the 'Save the Children Fund.' " Caffery to Hughes, 9 February 1923, NA 868.48/367.

Notes to Chapter 7

17. Bentinck to Curzon, Athens, ca. Spring/Summer 1923, FO 371/8832, no. un-available; letter from Nansen to Bristol attached to a dispatch from Bristol to Hughes, 11 October 1922, NA 868.48/221, enclosure no. 1.

18. Quoted in a letter from Lane Ross Hill, official of the American Red Cross in Greece, to the State Department, 11 November 1922, NA 868.48/297.

19. Quoted in Dimitri Pentzopoulos, *The Balkan Exchange of Minorities and Its Impact upon Greece* (Paris: Mouton & Co., 1962), 77.

20. Bristol to Hughes, 18 September 1922, NA 868.48/113.

21. Bristol to Hughes, 22 September 1922, NA 868.48/129.

22. The American Red Cross, Near East Relief, Y.M.C.A., Y.W.C.A., Federal Council of Churches, Knights of Columbus, American Relief Administration, Jewish Distribution Committee, and numerous other organizations comprised the President's committee.

23. The text of the president's statement is in Hughes to Bristol, 9 October 1922, NA 868.48/180a. For a summary of the negotiations leading to the White House agreement of 7 October see a letter and four enclosures from John Barton Payne, chairman of the American Red Cross, to the members of the Central Committee of the Red Cross, 18 July 1924, NA 868.48/860.

24. Maynard Barnes, Vice-Consul of Smyrna, to Hughes, 4 November 1922, NA 868.48/273. President Harding appointed his private secretary, Will H. Hays, to promote the drive. Hays was president of a syndicate made up of the largest movie studios in the United States. One of the most interesting "side stories" of Greek-American commercial relations in the 1920s was the lively competition between American and European filmmakers for the attention of Greek audiences.

25. ARC, *Annual Report for the Year Ended June 30, 1920* (Washington: The American Red Cross, 1920), 115.

26. A good summary of the work of the Red Cross in Greece from January 1918 to June 1922 can be found in ARC, *Annual Report(s) for the Year(s) Ended June 30, 1918,* 156; *1920,* 115–16; and *1922,* 72–73. Valuable and illuminating information is available in the pamphlets of the Red Cross cited in the bibliography.

27. Much friction often developed between the two sides; while the refugees, no doubt as a result of the despair and shock that attended their uprooting, often seemed defensive, resentful, and oblivious to the efforts being made on their behalf. There was also the problem of corruption, which reached the highest levels of the government. Caffery seriously considered the use of his influence to remove from office Dr. Apostolos Doxiades, the minister of public assistance, whose incorruptibility is open to question; but ultimately he decided against it. Caffery to Hughes, 25 January 1923, NA 868.48/342. The British minister referred to the Greek minister as "A Thracian who did well in office." Bentinck to Curzon, Athens, ca. Spring/Summer 1923, FO 371/8832, no. unavailable.

28. Robert L. Daniel, *American Philanthropy and the Near East, 1820–1960* (Athens, Ohio: Ohio Univ. Press, 1970), 59, 167.

29. Assimilation was a serious problem. It entailed the meshing of two cultures, despite the existence of many similarities between the two peoples. Horton's assertion that "there is about as much difference between an Anatolian Greek and a Hellenic Greek as there is between an Athens fly and a Smyrna fly" is not true. Horton's quote is in a letter from Horton to Bristol (29 May 1920) attached to a dispatch from Bristol to the Secre-

tary of State, 25 September 1920, NA 868.01/23. For an analysis of the fundamental differences between the two Greek peoples see Dimitri Pentzopoulos, "The Social and Cultural Impact," *The Balkan Exchange of Minorities and Its Impact on Greece*, 199–219. It is significant that the author chose "The Refugees Accept Greece" as the title of part 2 of his book.

30. Atherton to Hughes, 8 October 1923, NA 868.47/632.

31. Report from R. Knapp, Managing Director of the NER in Greece, to Atherton, 23 May 1923, NA 868.48/504.

32. Computed from data in U.S. Congress, Senate, *Report of the Near East Relief for the Year Ended December 31, 1923*, 68th Cong., 1st sess., S. Doc. 111 1924, 11.

33. The fame of the Perkins Institute was long established, partly as a result of the work of Dr. Samuel Gridley Howe and Michael Anagnos. The former was a philhellene who served as surgeon general of the Greek forces in the War of Independence. During the Cretan Revolution of 1866, he sailed again for Greece. There he met Anagnos whom he induced to come to the United States to become a teacher of the deaf and blind; eventually Anagnos also became his son-in-law. On the death of Dr. Howe, Anagnos became director of the institute. The institute's most famous pupil was Helen Keller.

34. Thurber became one of the most famous and beloved American relief workers in Greece. When he died in Athens (31 May 1930), his funeral was a veritable spectacle as thousands attended the services and took part in the procession. The dignitaries present included Venizelos and the American minister, Robert P. Skinner. See Barton, "Tribute to America," *Story of Near East Relief*, 476–79.

35. Daniel, *American Philanthropy in the Near East*, 167; Payne to Phillips, 1 March 1923, NA 868.48/387.

36. U.S. Congress, Senate, *Report of the Near East Relief for the Year Ended December 31, 1923*, 68th Cong., 1st sess., S. Doc. 111, 1924, 5.

37. See Near East Relief, *Report to Congress for 1924* in Microcopy no. 443, file no. 868.48/918.

38. Letter from Charles V. Vickrey to Phillips, 8 March 1923, NA 868.48/392. Vickrey's figures are taken from a report by NER to Congress. For the full text see U.S. Congress, senate, *Report of the Near East Relief for the Year Ended December 31, 1922*, 67th Cong., 4th sess., S. Doc. 343, 1923. A copy of the same report is attached to a letter from Phillips to Vickrey, 12 March 1923, NA 868.48/392.

39. This figure has been computed by comparing the data referenced in note 38 with the *Report of the Near East Relief for the Year Ended December 31, 1923*, 7.

40. *Report of the Near East Relief for the Year Ended December 31, 1923*, 3–4, 15.

41. Barton, *Story of Near East Relief*, x. The introduction to this book was written by President Coolidge.

42. Lovejoy, *Certain Samaritans*, 7.

43. Ibid., 145.

44. Ibid., 205.

45. Kenneth Scott Latourette, *World Service: A History of the Foreign Work of the Young Men's Christian Associations of the United States and Canada* (New York: Association Press, 1957), 384. For a brief account of the Y.M.C.A.'s work in Greece from 1892 to 1955 see 384–87.

46. Papadakēs, *Synchronoe amerikanoe philellēnes*, 32–34.

47. Report by D. O. Hibbard, Director of the Y.M.C.A. in Athens, to Caffery enclosed in Caffery to Hughes, 5 February 1923, NA 868.48/368. There is an intimate historical sketch (replete with interesting anecdotal material) of the Y.M.C.A.'s work in Greece in Papadakēs, *Synchronoe amerikanoe philellēnes*, 35–53.

48. A detailed summary of the committee's work is enclosed in a consular report from Leland B. Morris, American Consul in Salonika, to Hughes, 11 June 1923, NA 868.48/571.

49. See the *Second Annual Report of the Athens American Relief Committee on Conditions in Greece and the Greek Islands* (dated 13 November 1923) attached to a letter from the ARC to Phillips, 27 December 1923, NA 868.48/656.

50. Atherton to Hughes, 8 October 1923, NA 868.48/632, enclosure no. 1; Atherton to Hughes, 8 October 1923, NA 868.48/632.

51. A summary of the work of private Greek agencies is found in Morgenthau, *I Was Sent to Athens*, 71–78. The Refugee Settlement Fund was supplanted on 31 October 1923 by the Refugee Settlement Commission.

52. Atherton to Hughes, 8 October 1923, NA 868.48/632, enclosure no. 1. The dollar equivalents are based on 58.34 drachmas to the dollar, the average for 1923.

53. ARC, *Annual Report for the Year Ended December 31, 1922*, 56; report by Hays to Harding enclosed in Hays to Phillips, 28 November 1922, NA 868.48/300.

54. Tsamados to Dulles, 28 January 1923, NA 868.48/337.

55. Payne to Phillips, 19 February 1923, NA 868.48/351, enclosure. The ARC, NER, and several other American agencies continued to offer aid in certain cases involving new and unforseen emergencies. In the winter of 1923–24, for example, a malaria epidemic broke out among the refugees, primarily among those settled in Macedonia. The ARC made a gift of ten tons of quinine. In addition, 1,000,000 five-grain tablets were given to the AWH, which continued to maintain a number of small hospitals. Three thousand cases of condensed milk also were given to the Greek government and to the AWH for hospital use. In all, the expenditures for Greek refugees from July 1923 to June 1924 amounted to $200,000. Beyond these gifts, 160 bails of clothing (approximately 50,000 garments) were distributed. ARC, *Annual Report for the Year Ended June 30, 1924*, 65–66.

56. Atherton to Hughes, 11 July 1923, NA 868.48/576 and one enclosure.

Chapter 8

1. For a detailed analysis of the role of other governments, as well as the commission's work and accomplishments, see the RSC's quarterly reports in League of Nations, *Official Journal*, 5th–11th Years, 1924–1930; League of Nations, *Greek Refugee Settlement* (English translation); Morgenthau, *I Was Sent to Athens*; Charles B. Eddy, *Greece and the Greek Refugees* (London: George Allen & Unwin, Ltd., 1930); C. P. Howland, "Greece and Her Refugees," *Foreign Affairs* 4 (July 1926): 613–23; Stephen P. Ladas, *The Exchange of Minorities: Bulgaria, Greece and Turkey* (New York: Macmillan Company, 1932); and Dimitri Pentzopoulos, *The Balkan Exchange of Minorities and Its Impact upon Greece* (Paris: Mouton & Co., 1962).

2. For the full text of the convention see Fred L. Israel, ed., *Major Treaties of Modern History, 1648–1967*, 4 vols. (New York: Chelsea House Publishers in association with

McGraw-Hill Book Co., 1967), 4:2301–68. There remains considerable doubt as to how the idea of an exchange of populations, and in particular its compulsory character, originated. Although there is evidence that Venizelos talked about the possibility of a forced exchange as early as 1914, Dr. Fridtjof Nansen, the renowned explorer and the chief representative of the League in matters affecting refugees, is often given the credit. The editor of *Forum* has written: "This plan was not, as some have said, suggested by Dr. Nansen. It's in fact a Greek and Turkish proposition . . . which was discussed years ago, both in Turkey and in Greece." Quoted from an editorial addendum in Fridtjof Nansen, "Re-Making Greece," *Forum* 71 (January 1924), 23. One must assume that the publication of this assertion had the approval of Dr. Nansen.

3. Exact figures are not available. The League of Nations estimated the number of Greek refugees at 1,400,000. League of Nations, *Greek Refugee Settlement*, 12. The neutral members of the mixed commission for the Exchange of Greek and Turkish Populations set the number of Turkish refugees at 354,647. Eddy, *Greece and Her Refugees*, 202.

4. NER was also anxious to reexamine its commitment. It was prepared to continue its child welfare work and its support of 65,000 dependent orphans in Greece and elsewhere in the Near East, as well as its supplementary child welfare work for a larger number. However, NER officials wanted to terminate the emergency relief to adult refugees of whom approximately 100,000 had received aid throughout the winter of 1922–23. Hughes to the British Ambassador, Sir Auckland Geddes, 31 March 1923, NA 868.51RSC/13.

5. Memorandum by H. D. Dwight, Chief of the Division of Near Eastern Affairs, to Phillips, 28 August 1923, NA 868.51RSC/130; Dolbeare to Hughes, 29 June 1923, NA 868.51RSC/130; Atherton to Hughes, 17 May 1923, NA 868.51RSC/42.

6. Hughes to Geddes, 31 March 1923, NA 868.51RSC/13.

7. The reader familiar with the issues surrounding the settlement of the refugees might find this assertion provocative. No attempt is being made to minimize the role of European Governments; for, after all, the RSC was the offspring of the League of Nations. The point to note is that the unofficial and active participation of the United States Government was a significant factor in the creation of the RSC.

8. Geddes to Hughes, 9 April 1923, NA 868.51RSC/28; the American Ambassador to France, Herrick, to Hughes, 6 April 1923, NA 868.51RSC/22; the French Ambassador, Jusserand, to Hughes, 5 May 1923, NA 868.51RSC/38; AYE, 1923/A5/VI, Romanos to the Foreign Ministry, Paris, 6 April 1923. The French government was willing to help to the extent of utilizing "a certain number of Armenian and particularly Greek refugees," if the United States would pay for their transportation; and then only after a few shipments of from 100 to 200 persons had proven the refugees' usefulness as farm workers.

9. The Italian Ambassador to Hughes, 26 April, 1923, NA 868.51RSC/37.

10. The British Ambassador, H. G. Chilton, to Dulles 25 May 1923, NA 868.51RSC/51; memorandum from Dwight to Phillips, 28 August 1923, NA 868.51RSC/130.

11. Memorandum from Dulles to Phillips, 23 May 1923, NA 868.51RSC/45. Dulles' suggestions were significant because, in essence, they embodied the general guidelines relative to the establishment of the RSC and the granting of the Refugee Loan of 1924. These suggestions were not novel because they were based partly on the recommenda-

tions of William N. Haskell, Commissioner of the ARC in Greece. Nevertheless, they do demonstrate the role of the State Department in the inception of the idea of the Refugee Settlement Commission.

12. Memorandum from Dulles to Phillips, 23 May 1923, NA 868.51RSC/45. Dulles' concern was not without foundation. Continuous efforts were made by the Foreign Ministry in Athens, the Greek legation in Washington, and Venizelos at Lausanne to combine the issue of the remaining 1918 credits with the concurrent refugee loan negotiations. Toward this end, a definite plan of attack was devised which was directed at influential Americans and at the traditional philhellenism of American religious groups.

13. Bentinck to Curzon, Athens, ca. Spring/Summer 1923, FO 371/9896, no. 555; Atherton to Hughes, 24 May 1923, NA 868.51RSC/50.

14. Letter from Hughes to Harding, 28 May 1923, NA 868.51RSC/55; letter from Harding to Hughes, 6 June 1923, NA 868.51RSC/57. President Harding was eager to send an American diplomat to act in behalf of the ARC, "If the Red Cross does not have a suitable man. . . . There is an American interest in the solution of the refugee problem in the Near East."

15. For an intimate, first-hand account of the American role at Lausanne and the separate peace negotiations between the United States and Turkey see Joseph C. Grew, *Turbulent Years: A Diplomatic Record of Forty Years, 1904-1945*, 2 vols., Walter Johnson, ed. (Boston: Houghton Mifflin, 1952), 1:chaps. 18-21, and Richard Washburn Child, *A Diplomat Looks at Europe* (New York: Duffield and Company, 1925). Child, the American ambassador to Italy, was put in charge of the American delegation during the first phase of the Lausanne conference (20 November 1922 to 4 February 1923).

16. Dolbeare to Hughes, 29 June 1923, NA 868.51RSC/82.

17. Ibid.

18. Memorandum from Dwight to Phillips, 28 August 1923, NA 868.51RSC/130.

19. Atherton to Hughes, 17 May 1923, NA 868.51RSC/42; Grew to Hughes, 26 June 1923, NA 868.51RSC/72. Space does not permit even a cursory account of this interesting aspect of American influence in Greece at this crucial point, but it must be noted that many Americans went to Greece, each hoping to be of some assistance. Most of these people viewed the refugee question as a crusade in which the crescent and the cross were once again the main protagonists. An "American Committee for Aid to Greece and to the Refugees of the Near East" was established under the auspices of the American Friends of Greece with Dr. Edward Capps as its president. The committee sought to unify the philhellenic elements in Greece and the United States into concerted action for the purpose of inducing the State Department into a more direct, aggressive role in the matter of refugee settlement. The group published a manifesto entitled, *Preliminary Plan for the Organization of An American Committee to Aid Greece and the Refugees*. See letters from R. Fulton Cutting to Phillips, 20 August 1923, NA 868.51RSC/124, enclosure; Milton W. Ailes (secretary of Capps' American Committee and president of Riggs National Bank in Washington, D.C.) to Phillips, NA 868.48/620, two enclosures. Cutting and Ailes were important financiers from New York and Washington, D.C., respectively. See also Atherton to Hughes, 6 September 1923, NA 868.48/625 to which are attached six enclosures giving detailed information of the role of private American citizens.

20. Colonel Logan's appointment to the American delegation at Geneva was important for two reasons. Logan was a banker with considerable experience in international finance and in matters affecting refugees. From June 1921 to June 1923 he was adviser to

the American Relief Administration in connection with Russian relief. He was principal assistant to Herbert Hoover in relief operations in Europe after the Armistice, while at the same time he was in charge of coordinating the operations of technical advisers to the various new states of central and eastern Europe. It is important to remember that a refugee loan under the auspices of the League of Nations was being negotiated as a necessary corollary to a successful settlement plan. Since the likelihood of American participation in such a loan was becoming increasingly probable, competent American representation was indispensable.

21. Memorandum from Dwight for Phillips, 28 October 1923, NA 868.51RSC/130.

22. Ibid.; Herrick to Hughes, 17 July 1923, NA 868.51RSC/101.

23. Memorandum from Dwight for Phillips, 28 August 1923, NA 868.51RSC/130.

24. Nansen, "Re-Making Greece," 19. The last part of Nansen's statement refers to the disparity between the $48,236,629 in credits that were opened on the books and the $15,000,000 that had actually been advanced. By 1924 it was privately conceded in financial circles that any future refugee or stabilization loan agreement would release the United States government from that obligation.

25. Aide-Memoire from the State Department to the British Embassy, 10 September 1923, NA 868.51RSC/134; Hughes to the American Ambassador in France, Herrick, for Logan, 17 July 1923, NA 868.51RSC/100; memorandum from Dwight for Phillips, 28 August 1923, NA 868.51RSC/130. NER was also asked to appoint a representative, but it, too, refused. Memorandum from Dwight for Phillips, 5 September 1923, NA 868.51RSC/132.

26. While the State Department maintained an official aloofness, the American legation in Athens and Admiral Bristol in Constantinople applied strong pressure on the Greek government to seek solutions to its own problems. See Atherton to Hughes, 7 August 1923, NA 868.48/582; Atherton to Hughes, 6 August 1923, NA 868.51RSC/118; and Bristol to Hughes, 6 August 1923, NA 868.48/578.

27. Letter (dated 14 May 1923) from Haskell to Herbert Hoover, Secretary of Commerce, attached to a letter from Christian A. Herter, Assistant to Hoover, to Dulles, 22 June 1923, NA 868.46/546.

28. Under pressure from American public opinion (especially from church organizations) and on the promise that a refugee loan would soon be granted, the ARC finally compromised its initial intransigence by making smaller contributions "for a strictly limited period only." The NER continued its work for the orphans, but refused to assume any additional obligation for adult relief work. Aide-Memoire from the State Department to the British Embassy, 10 September 1923, NA 868.51RSC/134.

29. Memorandum from Dulles to Tsamados, 12 September 1923, NA 868.51RSC/140; memorandum from Dwight for Phillips, 28 August 1923, NA 868.51RSC/130. Tsamados cannot be blamed entirely for assuming the existence of some collusion between the State Department and American relief agencies. Atherton frequently and "unofficially" (to use his word) exerted a heavy hand in the entire matter of refugee settlement, while Bristol persistently pressed for the speedy transfer to Greece of all refugees who still remained outside the country. There is circumstantial evidence which suggests that Colonel Haskell had considerable influence on Atherton's thinking.

30. Hughes to Bristol, 7 August 1923, NA 868.48/578.

31. Atherton to Hughes, 17 May 1923, NA 868.51RSC/42.

32. The file on this problem is extensive. It is also revealing, because it reflects the deep

interest of the United States government in Greek internal affairs, despite its public statements to the contrary. Most of the pertinent documents are found in Rolls 21, 22, and 34 of Microcopy no. 443. See also "Smyrna Refugee Situation Solved by Assimilation," 5 January 1924, 1–2; "Evidence Shows Greek Refugee Views Conflict," 12 January 1924, 1–2; and "Full Report of Athens American Committee's Greek Refugee Survey," 19 January 1924, 1, 8–9 in *The Red Cross Courier*; and AYE, 1924/A.A.K., Brainerd P. Salmon to D. Kalopothakēs, Chief, Section of the Press, Ministry of Foreign Affairs, Athens, 14 January 1924.

33. League of Nations, Council, *Official Journal* 4th Year, no. 11 (November 1923), 1356.

34. Morgenthau, *I Was Sent to Athens*, 238.

35. Letter from Acheson to Dulles, 14 September 1923, NA 868.51RSC/141.

36. Memorandum from Dwight to Phillips, 28 August 1923, NA 868.51RSC/130.

37. Sidney O'Donohue, American Vice-Consul in Salonika, to the State Department, 20 November 1923, NA 868.00/456.

Chapter 9

1. This chapter is confined to the American participation in the Refugee Loan of 1924. For a detailed, authoritative account surrounding the negotiations in their international setting see Morgenthau, *I Was Sent to Athens*, 175–235 and League of Nations, Council, *The Settlement of the Refugees: Scheme for an International Loan*, C. 524. M. 1924. II [A], Geneva, October 30, 1924.

2. The Bank of England advanced an additional sum of £1,000,000 in May 1924. A similar amount was advanced by the Greek government through the National Bank of Greece in July, as well as an additional £700,000 in later installments. In this way, a total of £3,700,000 was put at the disposal of the RSC. This sum was to be repaid from the impending Refugee Loan. Since almost the entire amount was spent by December 1924, the Refugee Loan, in effect, provided only an additional £6,300,000 for refugee settlement. This detail was a significant factor in the negotiations for the Refugee and Stabilization Loan of 1928.

3. Memorandum from Dulles to Phillips, Harrison and Young, 8 November 1922, NA 868.48/287.

4. Grew and Child to Hughes, 25 November 1922, NA 767.68119/203.

5. Atherton to Hughes, 26 June 1923, NA 868.51RSC/73. See also Pentzopoulos, "The Social and Cultural Impact," *The Balkan Exchange of Minorities and Its Impact upon Greece*, 199–219.

6. Morgenthau, *I Was Sent to Athens*, 175; Atherton to Hughes, 24 May 1923, NA 868.51RL, 1924/8.

7. Memorandum by "K.C.", 16 May 1923, NA 868.51RL, 1924/5.

8. A summary of the Allied-American confrontation at Lausanne is appropriate at this point insofar as it helps to place the Refugee Loan of 1924 in its international setting. See J. C. Grew, *Turbulent Era*, 1:475–85. For the official correspondence see *Foreign Relations of the United States* (1923), 2:879–1040.

9. When the revision of the Treaty of Sèvres became inevitable, the British high commissioner at Constantinople was troubled by the realization that the "United States Government [could] reap . . . all the benefits of being an associated Government of

victorious powers and of . . . [its] independent position in not being a party to the treaty of Sèvres." DBFP, First Series, 17:308.

10. Memorandum from the State Department to the British Embassy, 31 March 1923, NA 767.68119/500a.

11. For the British rationale see DBFP, First Series, 18:680.

12. Hughes to the Special Mission in Lausanne, 30 June 1923, NA 868.51RSC/85. Colonel Logan replaced Frederic R. Dolbeare who had been attending the meetings since 15 June in a consultive capacity.

13. At the center of Greek-American commercial relations was the renewal of certain treaties dating back to 1837 and the granting of most favored-nation treatment to the United States. Although Greek-American commercial relations in the interwar period were not divorced from the events described in this book, they were extremely technical and sufficiently apart from the main course of events to justify independent treatment.

14. Hughes to Special Mission at Lausanne, 30 June 1923, NA 868.51RSC/85; Grew to Hughes, 3 July 1923, NA 868.51RSC/88. In the early stages of the negotiations American officials were inclined to use the term *relief* loosely, when it was obvious that relief was precisely what the refugee loan was designed to avert.

15. DBFP, First Series, 17:13. British-American commercial relations were not amicable where the Near East was involved. This was particularly true in matters dealing with the production of petroleum. Curzon telegraphed to the British High Commissioner in Constantinople: " 'It has been represented to the United States Government [by the American High Commissioner in Constantinople] that great friction exists between the Allied and American authorities at Constantinople and that the former use their paramount position wholly in their own interests.' " DBFP, First Series, 17:308n. The British High Commissioner labeled this assertion as "sheer libel." DBFP, First Series, 17:308.

16. Hughes to Special Mission at Lausanne, 30 June 1923, NA 868.51RSC/85.

17. On 30 August Nicholas Politis, former minister of foreign affairs, delivered a lengthy lecture at the University of Geneva which was a model of fanciful optimism. A copy of the lecture is attached to a dispatch from Atherton to Hughes, 23 November 1923, NA 868.51/769.

18. Tsamados to Dulles, 24 July 1923, NA 868.51RL, 1924/12; Dulles to Tsamados, 7 August 1923, NA 868.51RL, 1924/12 1/2; and Tsamados to Dwight, 18 August 1923, NA 868.51RSC/123. The first formal request by the Greek government was made to the League of Nations on 2 February 1923. Eddy, *Greece and the Greek Refugees*, 55–56. The first request to the United States government was in the form of an informal appeal by the Greek chargé on 24 July 1923, NA 868.51RL, 1924/12.

19. See Article IV of the Agreement enclosed in Artherton to Hughes, 20 September 1923, NA 868.51/755.

20. Hughes to Harvey, 10 October 1923, NA 868.51/755.

21. Bemis, A *Diplomatic History of the United States*, p. 707.

22. DBFP, First Series, 17:26; Young to Hughes, 1(?) December 1923, NA 868.51RL, 1924/26.

23. Letter from Calvert to Dwight, 19 November 1923, NA 868.51/767.

24. Letter from Dulles to Hughes, 28 November 1923, NA 868.51/767.

25. Ladas estimates that as of November 1923 the Greek government had spent about 550,000,000 drachmas. Ladas, *The Exchange of Minorities*, 633.

26. Morgenthau, *I Was Sent to Athens*, 112.

27. League of Nations, Council, *Official Journal*, 5th Year, No. 10 (October 1924), 1300.

28. For a comparison of the amended text with the original see League of Nations, Council, "Amendments to the Protocol of September 29th, 1923 Concerning the Settlement of the Greek Refugees," 5th Year, no. 10 (October 1924), Appendix 677. C. 490. 1924; II.C C. S. 9, 1558–63; or League of Nations, Council, "Memorandum Addressed to the Financial Committee on September 18th, 1924 by Emmanuel Tsouderos, Greek Minister of Finance," *The Settlement of the Greek Refugees: Scheme for An International Loan*, C. 525, M. 187, 1924, II [A] (October 30, 1924), 29–33, 5.

29. Tsouderos, memorandum of September 18, 1924, in *The Settlement of the Greek Refugees*, October 30, 1924, 35. The exact figures are as follows:

I.	Public Revenues free of all charges (i.e., controlled by the IFC):	
	A. Monopolies in the new provinces (salt, matches, playing cards, cigarette paper)	55,000,000
	B. New customs duties (Canea, Samos, Chios, Mitylene, and Syra)	55,727,000
	C. Tobacco monopolies in the new provinces	210,930,000
	D. Stamp duties in the new provinces	50,600,000
	E. Alcohol in the whole of Greece	170,000,000
	Total	542,257,000
II.	Excess revenue after deducting the sums pledged for the servicing of prior liens	671,717,963
	Total of I and II	1,213,974,963

30. Pentzopoulos, *The Balkan Exchange of Minorities and Its Impact on Greece*, 88. From the point of view of the National Bank of Greece this estimate was conservative. The Bank appraised the value of the land to be at least £6,000,000 higher.

31. Xanthopoulos to Hughes, 9 October 1924, NA 868.48/879; letter from Xanthopoulos to Hughes, 9 October 1924, NA 868.51RL, 1924/40; memorandum by Dulles of a conversation with Xanthopoulos (10 November), 11 November 1924, NA 868.51RL, 1924/40.

32. Laughlin to Hughes, 30 September 1924, NA 868.51/839; Hughes to Xanthopoulos, 14 November 1924, NA 868.48/879. See also Appendix F for discussion in the House of Representatives, 1928, concerning Greece's indebtedness to the U.S.

33. Note from Xanthopoulos to Hughes, 9 October 1924, NA 868.48/879; note from Hughes to Xanthopoulos, 14 November 1924, NA 868.48/879.

34. Memorandum by Dulles of a conversation with Rife, 25 November 1924, NA 868.51RL, 1924/46. The offer by Hambros Bank was the result of the close business connections with the New York firm. Hambros also played a significant role in the negotiations that led to the second £1,000,000 advance by the Bank of England in May 1924. See memorandum by Dulles of a conversation with Rife, 25 November 1924, NA 868.51RL, 1924/47.

35. Letter from Speyer & Company to Hughes, 12 December 1924, NA 868.51RL, 1924/54.

36. Hughes to Laughlin, 6 December 1924, NA 868.51RL, 1924/48.

37. Equivalent to $11,000,000; computed at the rate of $4.7826 per pound sterling.

38. Ladas, *The Exchange of Minorities*, 635.

39. Ibid.

40. André Andreades, *Les effects économiques et sociaux de la guerre en Gréce* [The economic and social effects of the war on Greece] (Paris: Les Presses Universitaires de France, 1928), 101; Atherton to Hughes, 31 January 1924, NA 868.51/785.

41. Adamantios Th. Polyzoides, "Greece in the Agonies of Revolutionary Conflict," *Current History* 21 (December 1924): 401; Stylianos Ep. Gonatas, *Apomnēmoneumata Stylianou Ep. Gonata ek tou stratiotikou kae politikou dēmosiou biou apo tou 1897 mechri tou 1957* [Memoirs of Stylianos Ep. Gonatas from his military and political public life from 1897 to 1957] (Athens: n.p., 1958), 321.

42. Under the circumstances the Department of Commerce considered the public debt of Greece important enough to publish a detailed analysis of this problem. See U.S., Department of Commerce, Bureau of Foreign and Domestic Commerce, *Public Debt of Greece*, Bulletin no. 321, (Washington, D.C.: GPO, 1925). The figure assumes a population of 6,000,000, including the refugees.

43. Report by R. O. Hall attached to a dispatch from Laughlin to Hughes, 27 January 1925, NA 868.51RL, 1924/61(?).

Chapter 10

1. The annual reports from the British legation in Athens from 1920 to 1928 contain numerous references to the expanding role of American commercial influence in the Eastern Mediterranean and the concerns to which it gave rise in the Foreign Office. See especially the annual reports for 1927 and 1928.

2. Harrison to Warren D. Robbins, 14 May 1921, NA 868.001C76/55.

3. W. L. Lowrie, American Consul General, to Hughes, 28 September 1922, NA 868.5034/7. The exact figures are as follows: United States, 243; Great Britain, 206; France, 84; Switzerland, 21; Belgium, 14; Sweden, 13; Italy, 13; and Denmark, 5. Lowrie's source was the Ministry of Finance. These figures can be misleading. They give no indication of amounts of capital involved, but in terms of foreign branches established in Greece, Great Britain probably had the greatest number. There is also the conspicuous absence of a listing of German firms. Nevertheless, the figures as they stand are significant. The American commercial attaché, R. O. Hall, gave some credibility to these figures when he wrote: "Largely because of our good will in Greece, we have sold more goods to Greece—*for years at a time*—than any other nation has" [document's emphasis]. Memorandum by Hall enclosed in a letter to Dulles, 9 January 1926, NA 868.51WC/405. The consul general's figures are supported in a general way by the British chargé in Athens who expressed the hope that given some internal stability "British firms will again begin to take an interest in putting contracts in Greece . . . and that the field will no longer be left open to French and American competitors." Bentinck to MacDonald, Athens, 30 August 1923, FO 371/9896, no. 555.

4. Had British intervention through the IFC not prevented a $54,000,000 public works loan between the Greek government and Seligman & Company of New York in 1929, the total would have reached the sum of $149,000,000. Skinner to Kellogg, 28 January 1929, NA 868.51PW/2.

5. Elliot Grinell Mears, *Greece Today: The Aftermath of the Refugee Impact* (Stanford, Calif.: Stanford Univ. Press, 1929), vi, 268; Leften S. Stavrianos, "The United States and Greece," *Essays in History and International Relations in Honor of George Hubbard Blakeslee.* Dwight E. Lee and George E. McReynolds, eds. (Worcester, Mass.: Clark Univ. Publications, 1949), 42.

6. Walter E. Spear, "The Public Works of Modern Greece," *Boston Society of Civil Engineers Journal* 8 (June 1921): 223.

7. Loraine to Chamberlain, Athens, 1 March 1929, FO 371/13659, no. 87.

8. Ibid.

9. Robert P. Skinner, "America Faces East," *Queen's Quarterly* 54 (Summer 1947): 159.

10. Political analysis by Colonel Edward Davis for the War Department, 17 May 1929, MID, G-2 Report no. 3850. Skinner was extremely aggressive in this respect. He implored officials in the State Department to enunciate a definite, forceful policy regarding "the relations of foreign loans to industrial prosperity in the United States." He suggested legislation that would require American financial houses to withhold their support from governments which refused to "patronize the American market." Skinner to Kellogg, 15 March 1928, NA 868.51/1090.

11. Political analysis regarding the Balkan situation by Davis for the War Department, 27 May 1929, MID, G-2 Report no. 3820.

12. Skinner to Kellogg, 8 February 1928, NA 868.002/129. The British minister appears to suggest that political maneuvering by Skinner was a contributory factor in the fall of Zaïmis' ministry. Loraine to Austen Chamberlain, Athens, 1 March 1929, FO 371/13659, no. 87.

13. R. W. Gausmann, general manager of the Athens Waterworks Company, "Operation of the Athens Water Supply," *American Waterworks Association Journal* 27 (November 1935): 1459.

14. The 1922 per capita daily consumption (before the arrival of the refugees) was a meager 2 1/2 gallons according to Gausmann. A representative of Ulen & Company gives a figure of 1 1/2 gallons. Compare Ibid. Gausmann's account with W. P. Christie, "Athens to Relieve Its Thirst," *American City* 44 (January 1931): 95.

15. Walter E. Spear, "The Public Works of Modern Greece," *Boston Society of Civil Engineers Journal* 8 (June 1921): 206.

16. Dēmētrios G. Skouzēs and Dēmētrios Al. Gerontas, *To chroniko tēs ydreuseos ton athēnon* [Annals of the waterworks of Athens] (Athens: n.p., 1963), 112–13. This is an excellent social and, often, amusing history of Athens' water supply system from antiquity to our own time.

17. Armstrong, *Peace and Counterpeace*, 155; Daphnēs, *Ē Ellas*, 1:269; Skinner, "America Faces East," *Queen's Quarterly*, 165; Mears, *Greece Today*, 98.

18. Agamemnon Schlieman, Greek Minister, to the Secretary of State, 26 October ("November?" has been handwritten above the month) 1914, NA 868.15/unnumbered. The minister was the son of Heinrich Schlieman, the archaelogist who discovered Troy. See also George H. Moses to the Secretary of State, 15 March 1912, NA 868.151 Greek Series/unnumbered; and George H. Davis to the Acting Secretary of State, Norman H. Davis, 12 January 1921, NA 868.51/1. Eight hundred men were used and more than 2,000,000 drachmas spent.

19. See letters from Ford, Bacon, and Davis to Capps, 12 January 1921, NA

868.151/1 and the Bank of Piraeus to Ford, Bacon and Davis, 10 December 1920, NA 868.151/1.

20. Letter from Henry C. Ulen to Severo Mallet-Prevost, Counsel for Ulen & Company, attached to a memorandum from the Division of Near Eastern Affairs regarding a conversation between State Department officials and Mallet-Prevost, 2 June 1925, NA 868.151/58. Ulen & Company was established in 1897. By 1929 the firm had completed public works projects totaling a contract value of $900,000,000. Ulen & Company, *The New Water Supply for Athens, Piraeus and Environs* (Athens: A Pallis) 10. For a summary of the Company's record see a letter from Julius Klein, Director of Ulen & Company, to Dulles, 5 March 1924, NA 868.151/4.

21. Memorandum from the Division of Near Eastern Affairs, 6 November 1924, NA 868.151/6; Daphnēs, *Ē Ellas*, 1:269.

22. Memorandum from the Division of Near Eastern Affairs, 6 November 1923, NA 868.151/6.

23. In 1919 McArthur was a member of McArthur, Perks & Company of New York, which went into bankruptcy as a result of certain speculative enterprises in Cuba. McArthur's business practices did not inspire confidence. His association with the Chester Concession and the Ottoman-American Development Company raised many questions. See memorandum from the Division of Near Eastern Affairs, 23 January 1925, NA 868.151/24 and a letter from N. C. Ulen to the Department of State, 25 February 1925, NA 868.151/14. Somewhat curious is the fact that the letterheads of both Ulen & Company and McArthur show the same address in New York City—120 Broadway.

24. Letter from Case to Ulen & Company, 19 January 1925, NA 868.151/23.

25. Letter from Henry C. Ulen to Mallet-Prevost, 2 June 1925, NA 868.151/58. Ernest L. Connant, an agent of McArthur, assured Dulles "that Speyer & Co. would take the bonds necessary to carry through the enterprise." Memorandum by Dulles, 30 January 1925, NA 868.151/25.

26. Loraine to Chamberlain, Athens, 17 January 1928, FO 371/12924, no. 18; 1 March 1929, FO 371/13659, no. 87.

27. Kellogg to Simopoulos, 5 May 1925, NA 868.151/21. On 9 May a provisional contract for $1,000,000 was signed between Ulen & Company and the Greek government. Its purpose was the financing of provisional works to insure a supply of water until the completion of the permanent water supply facilities. American consent was granted with the same reservations relative to the 1918 Loan. Kellogg to Simopoulos, 23 May 1925, NA 868.151/35. Copies of both contracts can be found in Microcopy 443, Roll 14.

28. Letter from Curtis, Mallet-Prevost, Colt and Mosley to Kellogg, 27 July 1925, NA 868.151/62.

29. Christie, "Athens to Relieve Its Thirst," 97. The American minister estimated the total cost at about $11,300,000. Skinner to Stimson, 5 June 1931, NA 868.151/90.

30. Skinner, "America Faces East," 165; Skinner to Stimson, 5 June 1931, NA 868.151/90. Attached to this dispatch is an attractive, multicolored commemorative certificate (in English and Greek) in which "The Hellenic Government . . . expresses to Ulen and Company its complete gratification. . . . " In the 1930s relations between Ulen & Company and the Greek government were frequently marred by bickering over water rates and by many other technical issues. These problems, however, have little historical significance.

31. For technical and detailed summaries regarding the aspects of financing and construction see Ulen & Company, *The New Water Supply for Athens, Piraeus and Environs* (1929 and 1931 editions); Christie, "Athens to Relieve Its Thirst;" R. W. Gausmann, "Pos elythē to zētēma tēs ydreuseos ton athēnon kai tou piraios" [How the water supply problem of Athens and Piraeus was solved], *Ergasia*, 2 (November 20, 1932): 1458–59; Andreas Michalakopoulos, (identical title to the above), *Ergasia* 2 (November 27, 1932): 1490–91; and A. K. Georgalas, (identical title to the above), *Ergasia* 2 (December 4, 1932): 1525–26.

32. League of Nations, Council, *Official Journal*, 6th Year, no. 4 (April 1925), Annex 734, "Fifth Quarterly Report of the Commission," C. 112, M. 53, II:509.

33. An authoritative and detailed article on the subject is by A. Domesticos, director-general of agriculture and land settlement in Macedonia, "Productive Works in Greece," *International Labour Review* 30 (November 1934):601–21. The words *plain* and *valley* are used interchangeably when discussing topographical features of the Balkan Penninsula.

34. Skinner to Kellogg, 17 June 1928, NA 868.51SV/4; Ward P. Christie, "Reclaiming Macedonia's Plains," *Constructor* 13 (October 1931): 24; Percy Loraine to Chamberlain, Athens, FO 371/13659, no. 87.

35. Domesticos, "Productive Works in Greece," 604. There are some discrepancies in the figures, though they do not affect the total picture. I have relied on those authorities who can be expected to possess the most accurate data. For detailed, descriptive accounts of the work itself, see Ralph H. Chambers, vice-president, The Foundation Company of New York, "Greece Engaged on Huge Reclamation Project," *Civil Engineering* 3 (April 1933): 217–21; report no. 63 by the American consul in Salonika, Robert F. Fernald, 28 October 1925, NA 868.6113/unnumbered; a summary by The Foundation Company enclosed in a report from Charles J. Pisar, American consul in Salonika, 29 September 1930, NA 868.6113/39; "Saloniki Plain Reclamation Project," report by the American consul, 28 April 1932, NA 868.6113/41; and "Vardar River Drainage Project," memorandum by the chief of the Division of Near Eastern Affairs, 15 December 1932, NA 868.6113/45.

36. On the basis of British archival material it is virtually certain that the same political pressure was applied by the American legation in the negotiations surrounding these projects as was applied in the reclamation of the Struma Valley. See annual reports of 1927 and 1928 from Loraine to Chamberlain, Athens, 17 January 1928, FO 371/12924, no. 18 and 1 March 1929, FO 371/13659, no. 87.

37. Memorandum by Dulles of a conversation with Remington, 5 November 1925, NA 868.6113/11. When one of the members of the Greek cabinet went to Macedonia to mollify public opinion, "he found the people and the local press in a state of frenzy that not even the dictatorial powers of General Pangalos could suppress."

38. Memorandum by Dulles, 30 June 1925, NA 868.151/25; memorandum by Dulles 5 March 1925, NA 868.6113/39.

39. Memorandum by Dulles of a conversation with Remington, 5 November 1925, NA 868.6113/11; consular report by Pisar, 28 April 1932, NA 868.6113/4. The rate of 33 percent assumes that one-third of the expenditures in item III were made in the United States. The high rate in item V reflects a clause in the contract which stipulated that as much of the money as possible would be spent in Greece. If one uses the sum of items I through IV as the base for computing the percentages, America's share in the purchase jumps to 62 percent. The exact figures are as follows:

I. Purchases in the United States (chiefly excavating and earthmoving machinery)	$2,055,011.11 (19.00%)
II. Purchases in other foreign countries	1,971,795.50 (18.23%)
III. New York and London expenses	264,490.00 (2.44%)
IV. Contractor's fees	1,393,561.72 (12.88%)
V. Balance (salaries, labor, local purchases, etc.)	5,133,186.38 (47.45%)
Total	$10,818,044.71 (100.00%)

40. As of 29 September 1930 the countries which had gained the largest orders were: the United States ($1,400,000), Italy ($180,000), Germany ($170,000), Great Britain ($150,000), and Greece ($150,000). Cunsular report by Pisar, 29 September 1930, NA 868.6113/39.

41. Note from Grew to Howard, 1 September 1926, NA 868.51WC/437; aide-memoire from the State Department to the British Embassy, 27 December 1926, NA 868.51WC/443.

42. MacVeagh to Hull, 23 July 1938, NA 868.6113/50.

43. Domesticos, "Productive Works in Greece," *International Labour Review*, 604–5. For a comprehensive, technical account of the engineering problems, see Christie, "Reclaiming Macedonia's Plains," *Constructor*, 24–26.

44. Skinner to Kellogg, 6 May 1928, NA 868.51SV/12.

45. Loraine to Chamberlain, Athens, 1 March 1929, FO 371/13659, no. 87.

46. Letter from Hoover to Kellogg, 14 October 1927, NA 868.51SV/unnumbered; letter from Capps to Undersecretary of State, Olds, 9 November 1928, NA 868.51SV/3; Skinner to Kellogg, 6 May 1928, NA 868.51SV/12; Kellogg to Skinner, 7 May 1928, NA 868.51/12; Loraine to Austen Chamberlain, Athens, 1 March 1929, FO 371/13659, no. 87.

47. Skinner to Kellogg, 2 July 1928, NA 868.51/1106. According to the British minister in Athens, Skinner's activities involved the use of unethical business practices and political blackmail. Loraine to Chamberlain, Athens, 1 March 1929, FO 371/13659, no. 87.

48. Skinner to Kellogg, 10 December 1928, NA 868.51SV/28.

49. Ibid.

50. A list of the major pieces of equipment used shows that all were American or German. Christie, "Reclaiming Macedonia's Plains," 26; MacVeagh to Hull, 20 March 1939, NA 868.51SV/97; MacVeagh to Hull, 20 March 1939, NA 868.51SV/97, enclosure.

Chapter 11

1. A comprehensive discussion of all the legal, political, and financial considerations inherent in this problem is not possible within the limits of this chapter; in any case, such a treatment would serve to distract from a clear understanding of Greek-American relations in the 1920s. There is extensive documentary material on this topic. For an exhaustive account see the publications of the United States Congress and the Treasury Department cited in the bibliography. For a succinct and lucid analysis for the period to January 1926 see a copy of a report by R. O. Hall, American commercial attaché in Athens, to the

Secretary of Commerce, Herbert Hoover, enclosed in a letter to Dulles, 9 January 1926, NA 868.51WC/405.

2. Charles P. Howland, "War Credits and War Debts of Greece," *American Foreign Relations*, 4 vols. (New Haven: Yale Univ. Press, 1928–31), 3:479.

3. This point became a controversial issue during hearings by the Ways and Means Committee on Greece's indebtedness to the United States. Edward Capps wrote to the committee's chairman, Representative William R. Green: "I never at any time received instructions from the [State] department to make any representations to the Greek Foreign Office on the subject of the proposed recall of Constantine, nor did I ever make any such representations. The attitude of the Department of State was consistently that the succession to the throne after the death of King Alexander was no affair of the United States." *Greek Debt Settlement*, 72–73.

4. Hughes to Laughlin, 6 December 1924, NA 868.51RL/48. The Greeks later insisted that they were never told of any change in American policy. The sources, however, give strong indication that the Foreign Ministry was informed. The problem, no doubt, was the result of the department's failure to put the warning in writing. See "Additional Memorandum by the Greek Delegation on the Reply of the World Foreign Debt Commission in Respect of the Greek Indebtedness to the United States," *Greek Debt Settlement*, 71.

5. *Congressional Record*, 70th Cong., 2nd session, 1928, 352; Van S. Merle-Smith, Third Assistant Secretary of State, to Kelly, 31 December 1920, NA 868.51WC/449.

6. Letter from Hall to Dulles, 9 January 1926, NA 868.51WC/405, enclosure; memorandum by an unidentified official in the Division of Near Eastern Affairs (pencilled initials illegible), 31 December 1920, NA 868.51WC/449, enclosure.

7. Copy of a report from Hall to Hoover enclosed in a letter from Hall to Dulles, 9 January 1926, NA 868.51WC/405.

8. For the text of the commission's position see "Memorandum of the World War Foreign Debt Commission in Reply to the representations made by the Greek Delegation," *Greek Debt Settlement*, 51–59. A copy is also found in Microcopy 443, Roll 36, dated 6 January 1926, and bearing the file number 868.51WC/408.

9. For a brief résumé of both sides of the issue see Appendix F.

10. Relations with France became embittered as the French government attempted to coerce the Greeks, through its membership in the IFC, to relinquish all claims to the French credits, and thus to escape entirely the terms of the Tripartite Loan. Loraine to Chamberlain, Athens, 17 January 1928, FO 371/12924, no. 18.

11. This release proved abortive because the British loan ultimately failed to materialize. See chapter 5.

12. *Greek Debt Settlement*, 55; copy of a report from Hall to Hoover enclosed in a letter from Hall to Dulles, 9 January 1926, NA 868.51WC/405. Congressman Burton was responsible for the introduction of the bill to settle the differences arising out of the Tripartite Loan. He was also a member of the World War Foreign Debt Commission.

13. *Greek Debt Settlement*, 62. The Greek delegation, in effect, raised a well-known technical point in international law.

14. Testimony by Mills, *Greek Debt Settlement*, 23; letter from Hall to Dulles, 9 January 1926, NA 868.51WC/425, enclosure; *Congressional Record*, 70th Cong., 2nd session, 1928, 361.

15. The problem centered on the last sentence of Article 4. The French text reads: "Jusqu'au remboursement des dites obligations aucun gage nouveau ne pourra être affecté à un enprunt extérieur sans l'assentiment des Gouvernement des États-Unis, de France et de Grande Bretagne." See point 5, Appendix F.

16. Letter from Hall to Dulles, 9 January 1926, NA 868.51WC/405, enclosure.

17. *Greek Debt Settlement*, pp. 6–7. The sole exception was Congressman Charles Robert Crisp, leader of the opposition on the Ways and Means Committee and author of the minority report for the House of Representatives.

18. Ibid., 19.

19. Of this number 550,635 were settled on farms and 72,230 found homes and jobs in cities and towns. League of Nations, *Official Journal*, 7th Year, no. 7 (July 1926), Annex 874, "Tenth Quarterly Report," C. 308, M. 1926, 2:925.

20. The full text is in "Agreement for the Settlement of the War Debt of Greece to Great Britain" enclosed in a dispatch from F. A. Sterling, Counselor to the American Embassy in London, to Kellogg, 20 April 1927, NA 868.51WC/1005; Loraine to Austen Chamberlain, Athens, 17 January 1928, FO 371/12924, no. 18.

21. Skinner to Kellogg, 25 May 1927, NA 868.51WC/474.

22. Skinner to Kellogg, 9 June 1927, NA 868.51WC/476; memorandum by Shaw, 8 June 1927, NA 868.51WC/475 1/2; memorandum by Shaw of a conversation with Undersecretary Mills, 7 July 1927, NA 868.51WC/476 1/2.

23. Simopoulos represents a pleasant aberration. He was the first Greek career diplomat to view Washington, not as a "provincial" post to be endured temporarily, but as the capital of a great country which merited close attention from the Foreign Ministry. With his appearance the contacts between the Greek legation and the State Department achieved a higher level of professionalism and mutual respect. During the turbulent debt negotiations, he earned the confidence of the chief of the Division of Near Eastern Affairs, who wrote: "Mr. Simopoulos gave me to understand that attempts were still being made to take the financial negotiations out of his hands. He said that some day if the question was finally settled he would tell me of the terrible experience that he had undergone and was still undergoing in this connection [because of his efforts to be objective]. I listened with sympathy . . . as I have many reasons for believing that he spoke with complete truth." Memorandum by Shaw of a conversation with Simopoulos, 30 August 1927, NA 868.51WC/478 3/4.

24. "Resolution adopted at the Sixth Meeting of the Forty-sixth Session of the Council, September 15th, 1927," League of Nations, *Official Journal*, 8th Year, no. 10 (October 1927), 1134.

25. For a comprehensive account of the negotiations and the pertinent documents, see League of Nations, *Greek Stabilization and Refugee Loan-Protocol and Annexes* (Geneva, November 14th, 1927), 1–43.

26. *Greek Debt Settlement*, 1. The exact figures are as follows:

Principal amount	$15,000,000.00
Interest accrued and unpaid on the principal to December 15, 1922 at a rate of 4 1/4%	744,333.79
Total	$15,744,333.79

Accumulated interest at 3% annually from December 15, 1922 to January 1, 1928	<u>2,383,588.88</u>
Total	$18,127,922.67

To be paid in cash by the Greek government upon execution of the agreement	<u>2,922.67</u>
Total indebtedness to be funded	$18,125,000.00

27. *Greek Debt Settlement*, 7. In the process of the negotiations the final figure was rounded off to $12,167,000. The face value of the loan was computed as follows:

Advances by Great Britain		$31,826,910
Advances by the United States	$15,000,000	
Interest owed by Greece at 5% annual interest rate to January 1, 1928	4,659,836	
Total owed by Greece		<u>19,659,836</u>
Face value of the loan		$12,167,074

28. Ladas, *The Exchange of Minorities*, 638.

29. *Congressional Record*, 70th Cong., 2nd sess., 1928, 349–81.

30. For the full text see *Agreement between the Governments of the Hellenic Republic and the United States of America, May 10, 1929*, Microcopy 443, Roll 37, NA 868.51WC/527. For the president's statement see reference cited in note 1.

31. In the absence of a monograph on Greek-American Relations from 1930 to 1940, the reader is referred to John O. Iatrides, ed. *Ambassador MacVeagh Reports, 1933–1947* (Princeton, N. J.: Princeton Univ. Press, 1980). This volume is a compilation of diplomatic dispatches, entries from the diaries of Ambassador MacVeagh, and personal letters from MacVeagh to President Roosevelt.

32. The Refugee Settlement Commission was dissolved on 31 December 1930.

33. It is probable that there is more diplomatic material available for the 1930s than for the 1920s.

34. Daphnēs, *Ē Ellas*, 2:103.

35. This figure was the subject of considerable discussion between the Treasury and State Departments. Shortly before Greece abandoned the gold standard, Venizelos declared in Parliament that the Greek reserve had shrunk from $30,000,000 in September 1931 to approximately $13,000,000. The figure was probably scaled down for effect. Furthermore, "The official figures of the Bank of Greece indicate a larger sum of money on hand." Chargé d'affaires, Morris, to Kellogg, 24 May 1932, NA 868.51RL, 1924/94.

36. Aide-memoire (dated 7 May 1932) from the American legation to the Greek ministry of Foreign Affairs, attached to a dispatch from Morris to Kellogg, NA 868.51/1246, enclosure no. 3. The same document is listed as "enclosure 2" in NA 868.51RL, 1924/94.

37. Ibid., enclosure 1.

38. "Greek External Debt Service," *The Near East and India* 41 (September 15, 1932):754.

39. Secretary of State, Stimson, to Morris, 28 September 1932, NA 868.51WC/551a. The date, 10 May 1929, refers to the day the 1928 Agreement was signed by the president.

40. "Support of American Holders of Greek Bonds," a memorandum by the Economic Adviser of the Department of State, 1 May 1935, NA 868.51/1437; for the text of the agreement see U.S. Department of State, *United States Treaties and Other International Agreements* (Washington, D.C.: GPO, 1968), 17:2331–37.

Epilogue

1. For a list of all American organizations functioning in Greece in the immediate post-World War II period, see a letter from George E. Edman, First Secretary of the American Embassy in Athens to the *New York Times*, June 7, 1948.

2. For extensive, incisive analyses and differing viewpoints on Britain's policy in Greece see John O. Iatrides, *Revolt in Athens: The Greek Communist "Second Round",* *1944–1945* (Princeton, N.J.: Princeton Univ. Press, 1972); Phyllis Auty and Richard Clogg, eds., *British Policy towards Wartime Resistance in Yugoslavia and Greece* (New York: Harper & Row, 1975); G. M. Alexander, *The Prelude to the Truman Doctrine: British Policy in Greece, 1944–1947* (Oxford: Clarendon Press, 1982); and John O. Iatrides, ed., *Greece in the 1940's: A Nation in Crisis* (Hanover and London: Univ. Press of New England, 1981).

3. Cordell Hull, *The Memoirs of Cordell Hull,* 2 vols. (New York: Macmillan Co., 1948), 2:1451–59; *Foreign Relations of the United States* (1944), 5:117–18 and 125–27.

4. *Foreign Relations of the United States* (1943), 4:126–52 passim; Auty and Clogg, eds., *British Policy towards Wartime Resistance in Yugoslavia and Greece,* 147–66 passim.

5. John O. Iatrides, *Revolt in Athens,* 81–83.

6. *Foreign Relations of the United States* (1943), 4:126–27.

7. *Foreign Relations of the United States* (1943), 4: 2–3. Another revealing example is the attitude of the American minister, Lincoln MacVeagh. During the turbulent events of December 1944, "he was so neutral that he would not allow British troops to draw water from his well [in his garden]." Elisabeth Barker, *Churchill and Eden at War* (New York: St. Martin's Press, 1978), 196–97.

8. Iatrides, ed., *Greece in the 1940's,* 133. See also pp. 109 and 230 and the sources cited therein.

9. For an analysis of American policy in the deliberations of the Security Council see John C. Campbell, *The United States in World Affairs, 1945–1947* (New York: Published for the Council of Foreign Relations by Harper, 1947).

10. The final report of the Allied Mission concluded that the election results reflected accurately the views of the Greek people. It was defended strongly in the United States. See U.S. Department of State, *Report of the Allied Mission to Observe the Greek Elections,* Pub. no. 2522 (Washington, D.C.: Department of State, 1946).

11. *Foreign Relations of the United States* (1946), 7:137–207 passim (allegations by the opposition that the balloting was rigged were confirmed in confidential reports by British and American observers, 204–7); Richard Clogg, *A Short History of Modern Greece* (Cambridge and New York: Cambridge Univ. Press, 1979), 158.

Notes to Appendixes

12. Quoted in Lawrence S. Wittner, "American Policy toward Greece" in *Greece in the 1940's*, ed., John O. Iatrides, p. 232.

13. Ibid., 232–33; *New York Times*, October 12, 1946. Caffery was then Ambassador to France. He promised that the "United States would lend its support in accordance with its solemn undertakings under the United Nations."

14. Great Britain, Parliament, *Report of the British Parliamentary Delegation to Greece, August 1946* (London: His Majesty's Stationery Office, 1946), 15.

15. For a summary of the economic mission's report see James Byrnes, *Speaking Frankly*, (New York: Harper, 1947), 898–909; for a summary of the negotiations, see Byrnes, *Speaking Frankly* 302–3; for a detailed account, see United Nations, Security Council, *Official Records*, 1st year, 2nd series, no. 24–28, 529–701.

16. Theodore A. Couloumbis, *Greek Political Reaction to American and NATO Influences* (New Haven and London: Yale Univ. Press, 1966), 39.

17. For a succinct summary see S. Victor Papacosma, "Greece and NATO," in *NATO and the Mediterranean*, ed. Lawrence S. Kaplan, Robert W. Clawson, and Raimondo Luraghi (Wilmington, Del.: Scholarly Resources, Inc., 1985), 189–213. For an extensive treatment see Theodore A. Couloumbis and John O. Iatrides, eds., *Greek-American Relations: A Critical Review* (New York: Pella Publishing Company, 1980).

18. Couloumbis, *Greek Political Reaction to American and NATO Influences*, 78.

19. For a candid discussion of this sensitive issue see an interview with Robert V. Keeley by Maria Garoufalē, "Den mporoume na gyrisoume piso [We cannot turn back]," *Eleutherotypia*, July 14, 1986, 18–19, 44.

Appendix A

1. U.S. Congress, Senate, *Loans to Foreign Governments: Greece* (Section 99), 67th Cong., 2nd sess., S. Doc. 86, 1921, 180–82.

Appendix B

1. League of Nations, Council, "Minutes of the Twenty-Sixth Session of the Council," *Official Journal* (4th Year, No. 7), Annex 580, November 1923, 1506–8.

Appendix C

1. League of Nations, Council, "Minutes of the Twenty-Sixth Session of the Council," *Official Journal* (4th Year, No. 7), Annex 580, November 1923, 1508–10.

Appendix D

1. This members' list is taken from Charles B. Eddy, *Greece and the Greek Refugees* (London: George Allen & Unwin, Ltd., 1931), Appendix F.

Appendix E

1. Colonel Edward Davis, American Military Attaché, U.S. War Department, 17 May 1929, MID, G-2, Report No. 3820.

Appendix F

1. *Congressional Record*, 70th Cong., 2nd sess., vol. 70, December 10, 1928, 370-71.
2. Herbert Adams Gibbons, *Venizelos*, 2nd ed. (Boston and New York: Houghton Mifflin, 1923), 290–91.

Selected Bibliography

UNPUBLISHED DOCUMENTS

United States

Department of Commerce. Bureau of Foreign and Domestic Commerce. *Records of the Bureau of Foreign and Domestic Commerce, 1921–1948*. Record Group 151. Central File, No. 443.1. Washington, D.C.: The National Archives.

_____. *Records of Commercial Attachés, 1934–1938*. Record Group 151. Washington, D.C.: The National Archives.

Department of State. *Records of the Department of State Relating to Internal Affairs of Greece, 1910–1929*. Microcopy No. 443. Forty-five rolls. Washington, D.C.: The National Archives.

_____. *Records of the Department of State Relating to Internal Affairs of Greece, 1930–1940*. Group 59. Washington, D.C.: The National Archives.

_____. *Records of the Department of State Relating to Political Relations between Greece and Other States 1910–1929*. Group 59. Microcopy No. 476. Six rolls. Washington, D.C.: The National Archives.

_____. *Records of the Department of State Relating to Political Relations between the United States and Greece, 1910–1929*. Group 59. Microcopy No. 475. Three rolls. Washington, D.C.: The National Archives.

Military Intelligence Division. *Correspondence, 1917–1940: Records of the War Department, General and Special Staffs.* Record Group 165. Washington, D.C.: The National Archives.

Great Britain

Historical Section of the Foreign Office. *Annual Reports for 1920 to 1928.* The annual reports of the British legation in Athens for the 1920s contain lengthy, detailed analyses of virtually every aspect of Greek life. They filled many gaps left open by American sources.

Greece

Ministry of Foreign Affairs. Records Relating to the Relations between Greece and the United States, 1917–1925. Envelopes Nos. A/4/XII, A/7, A/5/ii, A/5/VII, B/35, B/59, A/5/VIII, Θ/230, A/5/VI, A/9, A/2, A/19, A/5/XII, A/5/11, and A.A.K. Athens: AYE [Archives of the Ministry of Foreign Affairs].

Manuscript Collections

Lafayette, Louisiana. The University of Southwestern Louisiana. Southwestern Archives. The Unpublished Memoirs of Jefferson Caffery.
Washington, D.C. Library of Congress. Manuscript Division.
  Calvin Coolidge Papers.
  Cordell Hull Papers.
  Charles Evans Hughes Papers.
  Henry Morgenthau, Sr. Papers.
  Woodrow Wilson Papers.
  Mark L. Bristol Papers.
  Arthur Nichols Young Papers.

Interviews

Pilafa, Elenē. Refugee. Interview, 3 July 1974.

PUBLISHED SOURCES

United States

U.S. House of Representatives. *Greek Debt Settlement: Hearings before the Committee on Ways and Means of the House of Representatives on H.R. 10760.* 70th Cong., 1st sess., 1928.
_____. *Report to Accompany H.R. 10760.* Report No. 953, 70th Cong., 1st sess., 1928.
_____. Resolution 254, 70th Cong., 2nd sess., December 10, 1928. *Congressional Record,* vol. 70.

_____. Committee on Finance. *Settlement of the Indebtedness of the Hellenic Republic: Report.* Washington, D.C.: Government Printing Office, 1929.

U.S. Senate. *Funding of Greek War Debt to the United States.* 70th Cong., 1st sess., S. Doc. 51, 1928.

_____. *Loans to Foreign Governments: Greece* (Section 99). 67th Cong., 2nd sess., S. Doc. 86, 1921.

_____. *Report of the Near East Relief for the Year Ending December 31, 1922.* 67th Cong., 4th sess., S. Doc. 343, 1923.

_____. *Report of the Near East Relief for the Year Ending December 31, 1923.* 68th Cong., 1st sess., S. Doc. 111, 1924.

Department of Commerce. Bureau of Foreign and Domestic Commerce. *Business Practices in Greece.* Trade Information Bulletin No. 472. Washington D.C.: Government Printing Office, 1927.

_____. *Commerce Yearbook,* 1922–1932. Washington, D.C.: Government Printing Office. 1923–33.

_____. *Foreign Commerce and Navigation of the United States,* 1920–1940. 22 vols. Washington, D.C.: Government Printing Office, 1921–42.

_____. *Foreign Commerce Yearbook,* 1933–1939. 6 vols. Washington, D.C.: Government Printing Office, 1934–42.

_____. *Operation and Consequences of the Greek Forced Loan Law.* Trade Information Bulletin No. 68. Washington, D.C.: Government Printing Office, 1922.

_____. *Public Debt of Greece.* Trade Information Bulletin No. 321. Washington, D.C.: Government Printing Office, 1925.

_____. *Statistical Abstract of the United States.* Nos. 40–63. Washington, D.C.: Government Printing Office, 1918–41.

_____. *Trade Financing in Egypt, Greece and Turkey.* Trade Information Bulletin No. 506. Washington D.C.: Government Printing Office, 1927.

Department of State. *Diplomatic List.* [Volumes for January 1917 to December 1940.] Washington, D.C.: Government Printing Office, 1917–40.

_____. *Foreign Relations of the United States* (1897–1947). Washington, D.C.: Government Printing Office, 1898–1971.

_____. Historical Office. *Chiefs of Missions, 1778–1973.* Compiled by Richardson Dougal and Mary Patricia Chapman. Washington, D.C.: Government Printing Office, 1973.

_____. *Papers Relating to the Foreign Relations of the United States: The Lansing Papers,* 1914–1920. 2 vols. Washington, D.C.: Government Printing Office, 1939–40.

_____. *Report of the Allied Mission to Observe the Greek Elections.* Washington, D.C.: Department of State, 1946.

_____. *Treaties and Other International Agreements of the United States of Amer-

ica, 1776–1949. Vol. 8. Compiled by Charles I. Bevans. Washington, D.C.: Government Printing Office, 1971.

———. *United States Treaties and Other International Agreements*. Vol. 17, Part 2. Washington, D.C.: Government Printing Office, 1968.

———. Office of Press Relations. *Press Conferences of the Secretaries of State, 1922–1973*. Microfilm Rolls 1–9 [1922–40]. Wilmington, Del.: S R Scholarly Resources, Inc., n.d.

Department of the Treasury. *Annual Report of the Secretary of the Treasury on the State of Finances for Fiscal Year Ended June 30, 1928*. Exhibits Nos. 36–38. Washington, D.C.: Government Printing Office, 1928.

———. *Annual Report of the Secretary of the Treasury on the State of Finances for Fiscal Year Ended June 30, 1929*. Exhibits Nos. 22–26. Washington, D.C.: Government Printing Office, 1929.

———. *Annual Report of the Secretary of the Treasury on the State of Finances for Fiscal Year Ended June 30, 1932*. Exhibit No. 35. Washington, D.C.: Government Printing Office, 1932.

Greece

Library of Parliament. *Ai Ellenikai kybernēnseis kai ta proedreia boulēs kai gerousias, 1926–1959*. [The Greek Governments and the Presidencies of the Chamber of Deputies and the Senate, 1926–1959]. Athens: Greek Government Printing Office, 1959.

Ministère des Affaires Étrangeres. *La Grèce et la crise mondiale* [Greece and the World Crisis]. Athens: The Ministry for Foreign Affairs, 1933.

———. *La Grèce actualle* [Present-day Greece]. Athens: Constantinople Press, 1933.

Ministry of Social Welfare. *Stegasis aston prosfygon, 1922* [Sheltering of Urban Refugees, 1922]. Athens: M. Paxlibanidēs & Co., n.d.

———. *The Refugee Problem in Greece*. Athens: n.p., 1949. Royaume de Grèce. *Loi et cahier des charges pour l'alimentation d'eau et constrution d'egouts dans les villes d'Athénes et du Pirée* [Law and Official Report Regarding the Water Supply and the Construction of Sewers in the Cities of Athens and Piraeus]. Athènes: Imprimerie P. D. Sakelarios, 1914.

Great Britain

Department of Overseas Trade. *Report on Economic and Commercial Conditions in Greece* [Title varies slightly for some years]. London: His Majesty's Stationery Office, 1919–39. It is not clear whether volumes were published for 1925–26, 1929–31, and 1934–36.

Foreign Office. *Documents on British Foreign Policy, 1919–1939*. First Series.

Vols. 8, 12, 17 and 18. London: Her Majesty's Stationery Office, 1958, 1962, 1970, and 1972.

Naval Intelligence Division. *A Handbook of Greece*. 3 vols. At the Chapel River Press, Andover, Hants: His Majesty's Stationery Office, 1945.

Parliament. *Report of the British Delegation to Greece, August, 1946*. London: His Majesty's Stationery Office, 1946.

Canada

Department of Trade and Commerce. Commercial Intelligence Service. *Greece As A Market*. Compiled by Henri Turcot. Ottawa, Canada: F. A. Acland, Printer to the King, 1931.

League of Nations

Assembly. Second Committee. *Greek Loan*. A. 91, 1927, II. Geneva: Imp. Jent s.a. September 21, 1927.

_____. *Greek Refugee Settlement and Greek Stabilization Loan*. A. 58, II. Geneva: Imp. Jent, s.a., September 15, 1928.

Council. *Greek Refugee Settlement* (Trans.). II, 32. Economic and Financial, 1926. Geneva, 1926.

_____. *Greek Stabilization and Refugee Loan: Protocol and Annexes Approved by the Council of the League of Nations and signed by the Hellenic Government on September 15, 1927*. C. 556, M. 198, 1927, II. Geneva: League of Nations, 1927.

_____. *Official Journal*. 3rd–11th Year. Geneva: League of Nations, 1922–30.

_____. *Report on the Work of the High Commission for Refugees Presented by Dr. F. Nansen to the Fourth Assembly*. A. 30, 1923, XII. Geneva: League of Nations, 1923.

_____. *The Settlement of Greek Refugees: Scheme for An International Loan*. C. 524, M. 187, II. Geneva: League of Nations, October 30, 1924.

Financial Committee. *Report to the Council of the Twenty-Eighth Session of the Committee*. A. 53, 1927, II. Geneva: League of Nations, 1927.

Greek Refugee Settlement Commission. *Greece: Report on the Liquidation of the Refugee Settlement Commission*. C. 67, M. 28, II. Geneva: League of Nations, 1931.

United Nations

Security Council. *Official Records*. 1st year, 2nd series. Nos. 24–28.

Memoirs, Biographies, and Published Private Papers

Andrew, Prince of Greece. *Towards Disaster: The Greek Army in Asia Minor in 1921*. London: Murray, 1930.

Armstrong, Hamilton Fish. *Peace and Counterpeace, from Wilson to Hitler: Memoirs of Hamilton Fish Armstrong.* New York: Harper & Row, Publishers, 1971.

Barton, James L. *Story of Near East Relief, 1915–1930: An Interpretation.* New York: The Macmillan Company, 1930.

Bicknell, Ernest P. *Pioneering with the Red Cross.* New York: The Macmillan Company, 1935.

———. *With the Red Cross in Europe, 1917–1922.* Washington, D.C.: The National Red Cross, 1938.

Byrnes, James. *Speaking Frankly.* New York: Harper, 1947.

Child, Richard Washburn. *A Diplomat Looks at Europe.* New York: Duffield and Company, 1925.

Elliot, M. D., Mabel, Evelyn. *Beginning Again at Ararat.* New York: Flemming H. Revell, 1924.

Ford, Paul Leicester, ed. *The Writings of Thomas Jefferson,* 10 vols. New York and London: G. P. Putnam's Sons, 1892.

Gibbons, Herbert Adams. *Venizelos.* 2nd ed. Boston and New York: Houghton Mifflin Company, 1923.

Gonatas, Stylianos, Ep. *Apomnēmoneumata stylianou ep. gonata ek tou stratiotikou kai politikou dēmosiou biou apo tou 1897 mechri tou 1957* [Memoirs of Stylianos Ep. Gonatas from His Military and Political Public Life from 1897 to 1957]. Athens: n.p., 1958.

Grew, Joseph C. *Turbulent Years: A Diplomatic Record of Forty Years, 1904–1945.* 2 vols. Edited by Walter Johnson. Boston: Houghton Mifflin, 1952.

Horton, George. *The Blight of Asia.* New York: Bobbs-Merrill Company, 1926.

Hull, Cordell. *The Memoirs of Cordell Hull.* 2 vols. New York: Macmillan Co., 1948.

Iatrides, John O., ed. *Ambassador MacVeagh Reports, 1933–1947.* Princeton, N.J.: Princeton Univ. Press, 1980.

Lansing, Robert. *The Peace Negotiations: A Personal Narrative.* Boston and New York: Houghton Mifflin Company, 1921.

Lovejoy, Esther Pohl. *Certain Samaritans.* New and revised ed. New York: The Macmillan Company, 1933.

Ludendorff, Erich Von. *Ludendorff's Own Story.* 2 vols. New York and London: Harper & Brothers Publishers, 1919.

Mackenzie, Compton. *First Athenian Memories.* London: Cassell & Co., 1931.

———. *Greek Memories.* London: Chatto & Windus, 1939.

Morgenthau, Henry. *Ambassador Morgenthau's Story.* Garden City, N.Y.: Doubleday, Page & Co., 1918.

———. *I Was Sent to Athens.* Garden City, N.Y.: Doubleday, Doran and Co., Inc., 1929.

Nicolson, Harold. *Curzon: The Last Phase, 1919–1925.* New York: Houghton Mifflin Company, 1934.

Selected Bibliography

_____. *Peacemaking, 1919*. London: Constable & Co., Ltd., 1945.

Papadakēs, Stavros Styl. *Synchronoe Amerikanoe Philellēnes: Anamnēseis misou aiona* [Contemporary American Philhellenes: Memories of Half a Century]. Athens: Pechlibanidēs and Company, 1967.

Pamphlets and Reports

American Red Cross. *Annual Report for the Year Ending June 30, 1918; 1920; 1922; 1923; and 1924*. Washington, D.C.: The American Red Cross, 1919, 1920, 1922, 1923, and 1924.

_____. *Final Report: Department of Civilian Relief*. Compiled by A. Winsor Weld. Athens: P. D. Sakellarios, 1919.

_____. *Relief Work among the Aegean Islands*. Compiled by A. Winsor Weld. Athens: P. D. Sakellarios, 1919.

_____. *Relief Work among the Villages of Mount Pangaeon*. Compiled by G. C. Barry. Athens: P. D. Sakellarios, 1919.

_____. *Relief Work in Eastern Macedonia*. Compiled by Edward Capps, Horace Oakly, and Henry B. Dewing. Athens: P. D. Sakellarios, 1919.

_____. *Survey of the Hospitals of Greece*. Compiled by Carl E. Black, M.D. Athens: P. D. Sakellarios, 1919.

_____. *The Typhus Epidemic in Eastern Macedonia*. Compiled by Samuel J. Walker. Athens: P. D. Sakellarios, 1919.

National Bank of Greece. *Report for the Year 1924 of the Governor of the National Bank of Greece*. Athens: "Hestia," 1925.

Near East Relief. *To ergon tēs amerikanikēs perithalpseos tēs eggys anatolēs en elladi: Septembrios, 1922–Dekembrios, 1924* [The Work of the American Near East Relief in Greece: September 1922–December 1924]. Athens: Phoenikos Press, 1925.

_____. *Collection of Pamphlets Containing Speeches, Appeals for Money, etc.* New York: The Near East Relief, [date not clear].

Ulen & Company, *The New Water Supply for Athens, Piraeus and Environs*. Athens: A. Pallis, 1929. An enlarged edition (forty-two pages), bearing the same title, was published in 1931.

Monographs and General Studies

In English and French

Alexander, G. M. *The Prelude to the Truman Doctrine: British Policy in Greece, 1944–1947*. Oxford: Clarendon Press, 1982.

Allen, Harold B. *Come over into Macedonia: The Story of A Ten-Year Adventure in Uplifting A War-Torn People*. New Brunswick: Rutgers Univ. Press, 1943.

Auty, Phyllis and Clogg, Richard, eds. *British Policy towards Wartime Yugoslavia and Greece*. New York: Harper & Row, Publishers, 1975.

Bardeau, John S. and Stevens, Georgiana, eds. *Bread from Stones: Fifty Years of Technical Assistance*. Englewood Cliffs, N.J.: Prentice Hall, Inc., 1966.

Barker, Elisabeth. *Churchill and Eden at War*. New York: St. Martin's Press, 1978.

Barros, James. *The Corfu Incident of 1923*. Princeton, N.J.: Princeton Univ. Press, 1965.

Bell, David J. V. *Power, Influence and Authority: An essay in Political Linguistics*. New York: Oxford Univ. Press, 1975.

Bierstadt, Edward Hale. *The Great Betrayal: A Survey of the Near East Problem*. New York: Robert M. McBride & Company, 1924.

Booras, H. J. *Hellenic Independence and America's Contribution to the Cause*. Rutland, Vt.: The Tuttle Company, 1934.

Brown, Mrs. Kenneth [also listed as Vaka, Demetra]. *Constantine: King and Traitor*. New York: John Lane Company, 1918.

_____. *In the Heart of German Intrigue*. Boston and New York: Houghton Mifflin Company, 1918.

Campbell, John and Sherrard, Philip. *Modern Greece*. New York: Frederick A. Praeger, Publishers, 1968.

Cline, Myrtle A. *American Attitude toward the Greek War of Independence*. Atlanta: Higgins McArthur Co., 1930.

Clogg, Richard. *A Short History of Modern Greece*. Cambridge and New York: Cambridge Univ. Press, 1979.

Couloumbis, Theodore A.; Petropulos, John A.; and Psomiades, Harry J. *Foreign Interference in Greek Politics: An Historical Perspective*. New York: Pella Publishing Company, 1976.

_____. *Greek Political Reaction to American and NATO Influences*. New Haven and London: Yale Univ. Press, 1966.

Cumming, Henry H. *Franco-British Rivalry in the Post-War Near East: The Decline of French Influence*. London: Oxford Univ. Press, 1938.

Dakin, Douglas. *The Unification of Greece, 1770–1923*. New York: St. Martin's Press, 1972.

Daniel, Robert L. *American Philanthropy in the Near East, 1820–1960*. Athens, Ohio: Ohio Univ. Press, 1970.

DeNovo, John A. *American Interest and Politics in the Middle East, 1900–1939*. Minneapolis: The Univ. of Minnesota Press, 1963.

Dobkin, Marjorie Housepian. *Smyrna 1922: The Destruction of a City*. 1966. Reprint. Kent, Ohio: Kent State Univ. Press, 1988.

Earle, Edward Mead. *Turkey, the Great Powers and the Bagdad Railway: A Study in Imperialism*. New York: Macmillan Company, 1923.

Eddy, Charles B. *Greece and the Greek Refugees*. London: George Allen and Unwin, Ltd., 1931.

Eulambio, M. S. *The National Bank of Greece: A History of the Financial and Economic Evolution of Greece*. Athens: S. C. Vlastos, 1924.

Selected Bibliography

Evans, Laurence. *United States Policy and the Partition of Turkey, 1914–1924*. Baltimore: The John Hopkins Press, 1965.

Feilchenfeld, Ernst, H. *Public Debts and State Succession*. New York: The Macmillan Company, 1931.

Field, James A. *America and the Mediterranean World, 1776–1882*. Princeton, N.J.: Princeton Univ. Press, 1969.

Forbes, N.; Toynbee, A. J.; Mittany, D.; and Horvath, D. G. *The Balkans: A History of Bulgaria, Serbia, Greece, Rumania, Turkey*. Oxford: The Claredon Press, 1915.

Frangoulis, A. F. [also cited as Phrangoules, A. F.]. *La Grèce et le crise modiale* [Greece and the World Crisis]. 2 vols. Paris: Librairie Félix Alcan, 1926–27.

Friedrich, Carl Joachim. *Man and His Government: An Emperical Theory of Politics*. New York: McGraw-Hill Book Publishing Company, Inc., 1963.

Fry, C. Luther; Ross, Frank A.; and Sibley, Elbridge. *The Near East and American Philanthropy*. New York: Columbia Univ. Press, 1929.

Gigg, George S. and Knowlton, Evelyn. *History of the Standard Oil Company (New Jersey): the Resurgent Years, 1911–1927*. Vol. 2. New York: Harper and Brothers, 1956.

Gidney, James B. *A Mandate for Armenia*. Kent, Ohio: Kent State Univ. Press, 1967.

Grabill, Joseph L. *Protestant Diplomacy and the Near East: Missionary Influence on American Policy, 1810–1927*. Minneapolis: Univ. of Minnesota Press, 1971.

Helmrcich, Paul C. *From Paris to Sèvres*. Columbus: Ohio State Univ. Press, 1974.

Hibben, Paxton. *Constantine I and the Greek People*. New York: The Century Co., 1920.

Hoover, Herbert. *An American Epic: Famine in Forty-Five Nations, 1914–1923*. Vol. 3. Chicago: Henry Regnery Company, 1961.

House, Colonel Edward Mandell and Seymour, Charles, eds. *What Really Happened in Paris in 1918–1919*. New York: Charles Scribner's Sons, 1921.

Howland, Charles Prentice. *Survey of American Foreign Relations, 1928–1931*. 4 vols. New Haven: Yale Univ. Press, 1928–31.

Howard, Harry N. *Turkey, the Straits and United States Policy*. Baltimore and London: The John Hopkins Univ. Press, 1974.

Hyde, Charles Cheney. *International Law: Chiefly As Interpreted and Applied by the United States*. 3 vols., 2nd revised edition. Boston: Little, Brown and Company, 1947.

Iatrides, John O., ed. *Greece in the 1940's: A Nation in Crisis*. Hanover and London: Univ. Press of New England, 1981.

————. *Revolt in Athens: The Communist "Second Round," 1944–1945*. Princeton, N.J.: Princeton Univ. Press, 1972.

Israel, L. Fred, ed. *Major Treaties of Modern History, 1648–1967*. 4 vols. New

York: Chelsea House Publishers in association with McGraw-Hill Book Co., 1967.

James, Robert Rhodes, ed. *Winston Churchill: His Complete Speeches, 1897–1963,* vol. 3. New York: Chelsea House Publishers, 1974.

Kaltchas, Nicholas. *Introduction to the Constitutional History of Modern Greece.* New York: AMS Press, 1965; reprint ed., New York: Columbia Univ. Press, 1940.

Kousoulas, D. George. *Modern Greece: Profile of a Nation.* New York: Charles Scribner's Sons, 1974.

Ladas, Stephen P. *The Exchange of Minorities: Bulgaria, Greece, and Turkey.* New York: The Macmillan Company, 1932.

Larrabee, Stephen. *Hellas Observed: The American Experience of Greece, 1775–1865.* New York: New York Univ. Press, 1957.

Latouriette, Kenneth Scott. *World Service: A History of the Foreign Work of the Young Men's Christian Associations of the United States and Canada.* New York: Association Press, 1957.

Lawson, John Cuthbert. *Tales of Aegean Intrigue.* London: Chatto & Windus, 1920.

Leon, George, B. *Greece and the Great Powers, 1914–1917.* Salonika: Institute for Balkan Studies, 1974.

Levandis, John A. *The Greek Foreign Debt and the Great Powers, 1821–1898.* New York: Columbia Univ. Press, 1944.

Lord, Louis E. *A History of the American School of Classical Studies at Athens, 1882–1942.* Cambridge, Mass.: Harvard Univ. Press, 1947.

Macartney, C. A. et. al., eds. *Survey of International Affairs, 1925.* 2 vols. London: Oxford Univ. Press, 1928.

Maniakes, C. N. *America and Greece.* Athens: Anestis Constantinidis, 1899.

Marcoglou, E. *The American Interest in the Cretan Revolution, 1866–1869.* Athens: National Centre of Social Research, 1971.

Mavrogordatos, George Th. *Stillborn Republic: Social Conditions and Party Strategies in Greece, 1922–1936.* Berkeley: Univ. of California Press, 1983.

Mears, Eliot Grinnell. *Greece Today: The Aftermath of the Refugee Impact.* Stanford, Calif.: Stanford Univ. Press, 1929.

Miller, William. *Greece.* New York: C. Scribner's Sons, 1928.

Samuel E. Morison. *Maritime History of Massachusetts, 1783–1860.* Boston: Houghton Mifflin Company, 1921.

Pallis, A. A. *Greece's Anatolian Venture—and After: A Survey of the Diplomatic and Political Aspects of the Greek Expedition to Asia Minor, 1915–1922.* London: Methuen & Co. Ltd., 1937.

Papacosma, S. Victor. *The Military in Greek Politics: The 1909 Coup d'état.* Kent, Ohio: Kent State Univ. Press, 1977.

———. "NATO and Greece." In *NATO and the Mediterranean,* 189–213.

Edited by Lawrence S. Kaplan, Robert W. Clawson and Raimondo Luraghi. Wilmington, Del.: Scholarly Resources, Inc., 1985.

Pentzopoulos, Dimitri. *The Balkan Exchange of Minorities and Its Impact upon Greece*. Paris: Mouton & Co., 1962.

Politis, Nicholas. *The Economic Situation in Greece*. Athens, n.p., 1923.

Psomiades, Harry J. *The Eastern Question: The Last Phase*. Salonika: Institute for Balkan Studies, 1968.

Puaux, René. *La mort de Smyrna* [The Death of Smyrna]. Paris: 19 Place de la Madeleine, 1922.

Richter, Julius. *A History of Protestant Missions in the Near East*. New York: Revell, 1910.

Robinson, David M. *America and Greece: A Traditional Policy*. New York: Anatolian Press, 1948.

Rodocanachi, André. *Les finances de la Grèce et l'Etablishment des refugies* [The Finances of Greece and the Establishment of the Refugees]. Paris: Dalloz, 1934.

Salmon, Brainerd P., ed. *Glimpses of Greece*. Washington, D.C.: Hellenic Information Bureau, 1928.

Saloutos, Theodore. *The Greeks in the United States*. Cambridge, Mass.: The Harvard Univ. Press, 1964.

––––––. *They Remember America: The Story of the Repatriated Greek-Americans*. Berkeley and Los Angeles: Univ. of California Press, 1956.

Satow, Ernest. *A Guide to Diplomatic Practice*. London: Longmans, Green and Co., 1958.

Schmitt, Bernadotte. *The Coming of the War*. 2 vols. New York: Howard Fertig, 1966.

Seymour, Charles, *American Neutrality: Essays on the Causes of American Intervention in the World War*. New Haven: Yale Univ. Press, 1935.

Smith, Michael Llewllyn. *Ionian Vision: Greece in Asia Minor, 1919–1922*. London: Allen Lane, Division of Penguin Books, Ltd., 1973.

Spanos, John D. *The American System of Government and Greece*. Athens: Hestia, 1931.

Stavrianos, Leften S. "The United States and Greece." In *Essays in History and International Relations in Honor of George Hubbard Blakeslee*, 37–59. Dwight E. Lee and George E. McReynolds, eds. Worcester, Mass.: Clark Univ. Publication, 1949.

Theodoulou, Christos. *Greece and the Entente: August 1, 1914–September 25, 1916*. Thessaloniki: Institute for Balkan Studies, 1971.

Thomson, Sir Basil. *The Allied Secret Services in Greece*. London: Hutchinson & Co., 1931.

Wittner, Lawrence S. *American Intervention in Greece, 1943–1949*. New York: Columbia Univ. Press, 1982.

Young, Eugene J. *Looking behind the Censorships.* Philadelphia and New York: J. B. Lippincott Company, 1938.

In Greek

Aigidēs, A. *Ellas choris tous prosphygas: istorikē, demosiomikē oekonomikē kai koenonikē meletē tou prosfygikou zētēmatos* [Greece Without the Refugees: An Historical, Legal, Economic, and Social Study]. Athens, I. L. Aleuropoulou, 1934.

Andreadou, Andreou M. *Erga* [Works]. 3 vols. Athens: The School of Law, Univ. of Athens, 1939.

Bentērē, Georgiou. *Ē ellas tou 1910–1920.* [Greece of 1910–1920]. 2nd edition. 2 vols. Athens: Ikaros, 1970.

Christopoulou, Georgiou Ch. *Paratērēseis epi tou symphonon tēs koenonias ton ethnon* [Observations Regarding Agreements of the League of Nations]. Athens: Aggelos A. Kleisoune, 1937.

Daphnēs, Gregorios, *Ē ellas metaxy dyo polemon, 1923–1940.* [Greece Between Two Wars, 1923–1940]. 2 vols. Athens: Ikaros, 1955.

Delibanē, Marias Negropontē. *Ē oekonomikē anaptyxis tēs boreiou ellados apo to 1912 eos sēmeron* [The Economic Development of Northern Greece from 1912 until Today]. Salonika and Athens: P. Sakoula, Bros., 1960.

Dēmētrakopoulou, Andreou, Z. *Ta chreographa: Theoria kai praxis* [Debts: Theory and Practice]. Athens, n.p., 1952.

Karablias, Ioannēs N. *To drama tēs smyrnēs* [The Drama of Smyrna]. Salonika: Triantaphylou and Co., 1924.

Katakouzēnou, Simonos D. *En instorikon diēgēma* [An Historical Tale]. Athens: T. Tzabella, 1926.

Kostopoulos, Stavros. *Ta diasymmachika chreē kai o rolos tēs amerikēs* [The Interallied Debts and the Role of the United States]. Athens: n.p., 1928.

Ktenabeas, S. *Ai ellēnikai kybernēseis, ai ethnikai syneleusis kai ta dēmopsēphismata apo tou 1821 mechri sēmeron* [The Greek Governments, the National Assemblies, and the Plebiscites from 1821 until Today]. Athens, n.p., 1947.

Mager, Kostas. *Istoria tou ellēnikou typou* [History of the Greek Press]. 3 vols. Athens: Ioannēs Macridēs, 1959.

Malainou, E. I. *Istoria ton xenicon epembaseon* [History of Foreign Interventions], Vol. 7. Athens: n.p., 1963.

Misaelidēs, Kostas. *Ē katastrophē kai oe teleutaies meres tēs smyrnēs* [The Destruction and the Last Days of Smyrna]. 2nd ed. Athens, 1923.

Notara, Michaēl. *Ē agrotikē apokatastasis ton prosphygon* [The Rural Settlement of the Refugees]. Athens: Chronika Press, 1934.

Papamichaēl, Gregoriou. *Ektheseis tēs episkopēseos tou ergou ton en elladi organoseon tēs "Christianikēs enoseos ton neanidon"* [Reports Concerning the

Selected Bibliography

Examination of the Y.W.C.A.'s Work in Greece]. Athens: "Phoenikos" Press, 1932.

Protonotarios, Athanasios B. *To prosphygikon problēma apo istorikēs, nomikēs kai kratikēs apopseos* [The Refugee Problem from an Historical, Legal and National Point of View]. Athens: Pyrsou, 1929.

Pyrsou, Georgiou. *Symbolē eis tēn istorian tēs trapezēs tēs ellados* [Contribution to the History of the Bank of Greece]. 2 vols. Athens: E. Benake, Publishers, 1946.

Rentē, Konstantinou T. *Ē exoterikē politikē tēs ellados meta tēn 1en noembriou* [The Foreign Policy of Greece after November 1st (1921)]. Athens: Ioannou Batsou, 1922.

Skouzē, Dēmētriou G., and Geronta, Dēmētriou, Al. *To chroniko tēs ydreuseos ton athēnon* [The Annals of Athens' Water Supply]. Athens, n.p., 1963.

Articles

"America's Shock to Greece." *Literary Digest* 62 (September 27, 1919):16–17.

Bixler, J. S. "For the Heathen." *Nation* 115 (September 13, 1922): 253–54.

Beelen, George D. "The Harding Administration and Mexico: Diplomacy by Economic Persuasion." *The Americas* 41 (October 1984):177–89.

Burns, A. T. "Philanthropy and Foreign Relations." *Annals of the American Academy of Political and Social Science* 108 (July 1923):74–77.

Buzanski, Peter. "The Interallied Investigation on the Greek Invasion of Smyrna." *The Historian* 25 (May 1963):325–43.

Caclamanos, D. "Greece: Her Friends and Foes." *The Contemporary Review* 159 (April 1941):361–70; (May 1941):497–506.

Chambers, Ralph H. "Greece Engaged on Huge Reclamation Project." *Civil Engineering* (New York) 3 (April 1933):217–21.

Chater, Melville. "History's Greatest Trek." *The National Geographic Magazine* 48 (November 1925):533–90.

Christie, W. P. "Athens to Relieve Its Thirst." *American City* 44 (January 1931):95–97.

"Churches Appeal for War Against the Turk." *Literary Digest* 75 (October 21, 1922):34.

Corporation of Foreign Bondholders. "Report: 1932." *Near East and India* 42 (April 27, 1933):347–48.

Delendas, N. "Pos prepei n' antimetopisthē to zētēma ton exoterikon chreon mas" [How the Problem of Our Foreign Commerical Debts Must Be Confronted]. *Ergasia* 2 (December 4, 1932):1527–28.

Dennis, Lawrence. "Revolution, Recognition and Intervention." *Foreign Affairs* 9 (January 1931):204–21.

Dertilēs, P. B. "Le problème de la dette publique des états Balkaniques: L'endettement de la Grèce." *Les Balkans* 6 (July–December 1934):562–98; *Les Balkans* 7 (January–July 1935):61–107; *Les Balkans* 7 (August–October 1935):233–49.

———. "Recent Economic Progress." *The Financial News* [Special issue on Greece], March 23, 1931, 12.

Diomede, A. N. "The Greek Currency." *The Banker* 5 (February 1928):267–68, 270, 272.

———. "Central Banking Policy." *The Financial News*, March 23, 1931, 9.

Domesticos, A. "Productive Works in Greece." *International Labour Review* 30 (November 1934):601–22.

Drossopoulos, John A. "Greece Faces the World Slump." *The Financial News*, March 23, 1931, 10.

———. "Industrial Development in Greece." *The Banker* 5 (February 1928): 287–90.

Dulles, Allen W. "The Protection of American Foreign Bondholders." *Foreign Affairs* 10 (April 1932):474–84.

———. "The Recognition of New States and Governments: Greece." *American Society of International Law: Proceedings* 18 (1924):98–107.

Dur, Phillip. "Jefferson Caffery." *Louisiana History* 15 (Winter 1974):19–23.

Earle, Edward Mead. "The Outlook of American Imperialism." *Annals of the American Academy of Political and Social Science* 108 (July 1923):104–07.

"Economic Revival of Greece: Development Aided by British Capital." *The Financial News*, March 23, 1931, 25.

Eulambio, M. S. "Greece After the War." *Bankers Magazine* 100 (June 1920):891–99.

Evelpidis, C. "Economic nationale et finances de la Grèce." *Les Balkans* 2 (January–February 1933):379–400.

"Evidence Show Greek Refugee Views Conflict." *The Red Cross Courier*, January 12, 1924, 1–2.

"Full Report of Athens American Committee's Greek Refugee Survey." *The Red Cross Courier*, January 19, 1924, 1, 8–9.

Galib, Colonel Rachid. "Smyrna during the Greek Occupation," *Current History* 18 (May 1923):318–19.

Garoufalē, Maria. "*Den mporoume na gyrisoume piso*" [We Cannot Turn Back]. *Eleutherotypia*, July 14, 1986, 18–19, 44.

Gausmann, R. W. "Operation of the Athens Water Supply." *American Water Works Association Journal* (New York) 27 (November 1935):1458–76.

———. "Pos elythē to zētēma tēs ydreuseos ton athēnon kai tou piraios" [How the Water Supply Problem of Athens and Piraeus Was Solved]. *Ergasia* 2 (November 20, 1932): 1458–59.

Gennadius, J. "The Truth about Constantine and Venizelos." *Current History* 16 (August 1922):510–12.

Selected Bibliography

Georgalas, A. G. "Pos elythē to zētēma tēs ydreuseos ton athēnon kai tou pi-raios" [How the Water Supply Problem of Athens and Piraeus Was Solved]. *Ergasia* 2 (December 4, 1932): 1525–26.

Graham, William. "Greek Public Finance." *The Banker* 5 (February 1928): 264–66.

"Greece and the Bond Holders." *Near East and India* 42 (August 10, 1933):647.

"Greece in Difficulties." *Near East and India* 42 (June 22, 1933): 507.

"Greek Crisis." *Near East and India* 41 (March 24, 1932):239.

"Greek External Debt Service." *Great Britain and the East* 44 (February 21, 1935):230.

"Greek External Debt Service." *Near East and India* 41 (September 15, 1932):754.

Hadjikyriakos, A. N. "Developing An Export Trade." *The Financial News*, March 23, 1931, 16.

Harlow, S. R. "Turk in the Near East: What Would Roosevelt Have Done about It?" *Outlook* 132 (October 25, 1922):325.

Hibben, Paxton. "Betrayal of Greece by Lloyd George." *Current History* 17 (January 1923):545–51.

"Hoover Plan and the Balkans." *Near East and India* 40 (July 16, 1931):59.

Housepian, Marjorie. "George Horton and Mark L. Bristol: Opposing Forces in U.S. Foreign Policy, 1919–1923." *Bulletin of the Centre for Asia Minor Studies* 4 (1983):131–58.

Howland, C. P. "Greece and Her Refugees." *Foreign Affairs* 4 (July 1926):613–23.

_____. "Greece and the Greeks." *Foreign Affairs* 4 (April 1926): 454–64.

Hughes, Charles Evans. "Recent Questions and Negotiations: Greece." *Foreign Affairs* 2 (No. 2, 1923):xix–xxi.

Jaquith, H. C. "America's Aid to One Million Near East Refugees." *Current History* 21 (December 1924):403–07.

_____. "Greece Saves Herself." *Nation* 124 (May 1927):552–53.

Kyriakides, N. G. "America and Hellenism." *Outlook* 125 (June 9, 1920): 284–85.

League of Nations. "League of Nations: Annual Report of the London Committee." *Great Britain and the East* 44 (June 20, 1935): 771–72.

Logan, John H. "The Recognition of Mexico," *American Society of International Law: Proceedings* 18 (1924):107–25.

Logothetis, A. M. "La crise économique grecque: Le reglement des dettes privees envers l'entrangers" *Les Balkans* 3 (December 1932):217–21.

Malakases, John Thomas. "American Diplomatic Relations with Greece during the Last Part of Wilson's Administration and the Beginning of Harding's: The First Active American Intervention in the Internal Affairs of Greece." *Dodone* [Journal of the Department of Philosophy, Univ. of Ioanninon, Greece] 5 (1976):47–74.

May, Arthur J. "Crete and the United States." *Journal of Modern History* 16 (December 1944):286–93.

McHugh, F. D. "Water Runs from Marathon to Athens." *Scientific American* (New York) 143 (July 1930):24–25.

Mears, E. G. "The Unique Position of Greek Trade and Emigrant Remittances." *Quarterly Journal of Economics* 37 (May 1923):535–40.

Michalakopoulos, Andreas. "Pos elythē to zētēma tēs ydreuseos ton athēnon kai tou piraios" [How the Water Supply Problem of Athens and Piraeus Was Solved]. *Ergasia* 2 (November 27, 1932):1490–91.

Morris, Leland B.; Edwin, A.; Lyon, B.; et al. "Greece Passing through a Period of Readjustment." *Commerce Reports*, April 21, 1930, 191–93.

Nansen, F. "Re-Making Greece." *Forum* 71 (January 1924):18–25.

Nicolopoulos, G. P. "Making the Foreigner Welcome: When Hospitality Pays." *The Financial News*, March 23, 1931:14–15.

"Our Flag in the Near East." *Literary Digest* 75 (October 14, 1922):11–15.

Pallis A. A. "The Financial and Economic Aspects of the Refugee Question in Greece." *The Banker* 5 (February 1928):274, 276, 278, 280.

Papadakis, S. S. "The Greek Treason Trials." *Current History* 17 (January 1923):672–73.

Papanastassiou, Alex. P. "Agriculture in Greece." *The Banker* 5 (February 1928):293–98.

Polyzoides, Adamantions T. "Need of An American Policy in the Near East." *Annals of the American Academy of Political and Social Science* 126 (July 1926):68–70.

_____. "What the Greeks Think of America." *Travel* 47 (October 1926): 20–23, 54.

_____. "Who Murdered the Statesmen of Greece?" *Nation* 115 (December 13, 1922):661–62.

Rapp, William Jordan. "The Colonizing of Half A Million Refugees." *Current History* 20 (June 1924):408–14.

_____. "New Greek Republic." *Current History* (May 1924):254–62.

Rhodes, Benjamin D. "Herbert Hoover and the War Debts." *Prologue: The Journal of the National Archives* 6 (Summer 1974):130–44.

Riggs, C. T. "New Life in Old Greece." *Missionary Review of the World* 46 (August 1923):607–10.

"Road Construction in Greece." *Near East and India* 33 (June 14, 1928):759; 35 (June 20, 1929):788; and 37 (May 8, 1930):523.

Roberts, Kenneth L. "They Sometimes Come Back." *The Saturday Evening Post*, September 10, 1921, 12–13, 53–54, 61.

Skinner, Robert P. "America Faces East." *Queen's Quarterly* 54 (Summer 1947):158–71.

"Smyrna Refugee Situation Solved by Assimilation." *The Red Cross Courier*, January 5, 1924, 1–2.

Selected Bibliography

Spear, Walter E. "Public Works in Modern Greece." *Boston Society of Civil Engineering Journal* 8 (June 1921):203–23.

———. "Water Supply and Other Sanitation in Greece." *Engineering News Record* 86 (April 28, 1921):708–15.

Stewart, I. "Government Protection of American Foreign Investments." *Annals of the American Academy of Political and Social Science* 162 (July 1932):206–14.

Stimson, Henry L. "The United States and the Other American Republics." *Foreign Affairs* 9 [Special Supplement, No. 3] (April 1931):i–xiv.

Tatanis, P. P. "Justifiable Executions." *Nation* 115 (December 13, 1922):662.

Tsamados, M. "Greek Defeat in Turkey: An Allied Disaster." *Current History* 18 (May 1923):218–22.

———. "Venizelos Vindicated." *Current History* 16 (June 1922):592–94.

Wescott, Allan. "The Struggle for the Mediterranean." *Our World*, February 1923, 11–17.

"What the Turkish Menace Means to America." *Literary Digest* 74 (September 30, 1922):5–7.

Winkler, Max. "The Investor and League Loans." *Foreign Policy* 4 [Special Supplement, No. 2] (June 1928):20–22.

Wright, C. "For the Heathen." *Nation* 115 (April 16, 1922):163–65.

Zoldari, P. G. "Opportunities for American Banking, Trade, and Enterprise in Greece." *Banker's Magazine* 94 (February 1917):147–53.

Newspapers

American and British

Christian Science Monitor, 1 January 1924–31 December 1929.
Daily Telegraph, 18 September 1922.
The New York Times, 1 January 1916–31 December 1940.
Times (London), 1 January 1917–31 December 1940.
Washington Star News, 20 August 1974.

Greek

Eleutheron Vēma, 1 January 1922–28 February 1935.
Eleutheros Logos, 17 June 1923–26 June 1925.
Enosēs tou Ellēnismou, 17 November 1923.
Kathēmerinē, 1 November 1920–30 September 1923.
Proïa, 1 November 1925–16 May 1927.

Index

Index

Index

U.S., 143-44; role in refugee loans, 150-52, 156-57, 195-96; abandons gold standard, 198; intervention policy (World War II), 203-8 passim; ceases aid, 209. *See also* Allies; British-American rivalry; Franco-British rivalry

Greek-Canadian loan agreement, 161, 163, 187, 189, 191-92

Greek civil war, 206-7

Greek Republic: promulgation of, 79, 104; recognized by U.S., 79, 105

Greek state, creation of, 5

Greek War of Independence, 1, 2

Grew, Joseph C., 151, 154, 155, 180-81

Grey, Sir Edward, 37

Guaranty Trust Company, 13, 162

Hall, Barton, 70, 174

Hall, R. O., 164-65, 188, 189

Hambros Bank, Ltd., 150, 162, 163, 175-76, 180, 183-84, 195

Harding, Warren G., 60, 87-88, 111, 116-17, 132, 139; administration of, 70, 191

Harrison, Leland, 59, 162

Haskell, William H., 133, 141, 144

Hays, Will, 117, 132

Helbert Wagg and Company, 170, 182

Hibben, Paxton, 25-27, 70-71, 87-88

Hill, A. Ross, 118

Hoover, Herbert, 12, 71, 182-83, 196

Horton, George, 111-12

House, Edward M., 37, 40

Howe, Samuel Gridley, 2

Hughes, Charles Evans, 65-66, 70, 72-73, 76, 87-89, 105, 137, 139-40, 142, 143, 144, 155-57, 161-63

Hull, Cordell, 204

Immigration to U.S., 3-4, 29, 201

Inter-Allied Financial Commission, 40, 41

Inter-Allied Military Commission, 41

International Financial Commission (IFC), 9, 35, 37, 39, 53, 146, 156, 160, 184, 191-92

Intervention in Greek affairs: of Great Powers, 5-6; of Allies, 16, 20-21; U.S. and British, 203

Italy: foreign policy conflicts, 9; land claims in Asia Minor, 9, 109; Corfu incident, 10, 94; opposes recognition of Constantine, 44; return of Constantine and, 52-54 passim, maritime aspirations of, 62; promotes instability in Greece, 81; mentioned, 6, 21, 69, 84, 85, 98, 111, 198

Jefferson, Thomas, 1, 49

Jefferson Doctrine, 49-50, 56

John Monks and Sons, 178, 182-83

Jonnart, C. C., 32-33, 57

Jusserand, Jules, 63

Karamanlis, Constantine, 211

Karapanos, Constantine, 102

Keeley, Robert V., 212

Kehl, John E., 22, 23

Kellogg, Frank B., 175, 183, 195

Kelly, Nicholas, 187

Kemal, 46, 51, 80, 153. *See also* Ataturk; Mustafa Kemal

Kemalists, 46, 79-80, 110-11

King Constantine and the Greek People, 26

Kondyles, George, 97, 98, 101

Lambros, Spyridon, 29-30

Land reclamation projects, 177-85; Salonika Plain, 178-81; Struma Valley, 170-71, 181-84

Lansing, Robert, 28-29, 31

Latin America: Greek politics and, 65

Laughlin, Irwin, 163, 173, 174

Lausanne, Treaty of, 6, 135, 136, 144

Lausanne Conference, 81, 86, 90-91, 92, 151, 153-54, 155

League of Nations: refugee settlement and, 133, 136, 138-42 passim, 147; U.S. policy and, 139, 143-45; refugee loans and, 150, 152-56 passim, 159-60, 193, 195; mentioned, 94, 128, 198

Legitimacy, doctrine of, 50

Leygues, George, 55

Index

Index

World War I, 15–22 passim; Greece enters, 32; Greek soldiers in, 38
World War II, 203

Xanthopoulos, Constantine D., 161–62

Yalta Declaration, 207
Y.M.C.A., 127–28
Young, Arthur N., 69, 93–94, 157
Yugoslavia, 10, 92, 207
Y.W.C.A., 128

Zaïmis, Alexander, 32, 172, 194